# The Shirtsleeve Invention

## The Story of a Man and an Idea

Gloria Beasley Lausten

*Gloria Beasley Lausten*

3/10/2011

**To order additional copies of this book, contact:**
Xlibris Corporation
1-888-795-4274
www.Xlibris.com
Orders@Xlibris.com
66331

# Contents

This book is dedicated to Robin, Amy and Bob Jr., who loved their dad as much as I did.

# INTRODUCTION

This is Bob's story that I have wanted to tell for a long time. He had a poor start and was not a good student, but when he reached the beginning of his career, he was led by an idea that had a life of its own. From then on, this idea guided him at each new step until it was brought to fruition by the invention of the thermal protection material for the space shuttle. He knew instinctively that the creativity he expressed came not from his brain, but from something outside himself. He heard those ideas, as all creative people do and worked hard to bring them to light.

In writing this story, I was helped immensely in that both he and his mother saved almost every piece of paper they ever wrote or received. And of course, it couldn't have been written without the members of the lab team who are still here and who gave me their thoughts on the workings of the lab and the company, the anecdotes and the hard times and good times they experienced together. I was also greatly helped by the contributions of a member of Lockheed management who told the other part of the story and an engineer who tested the material outside the lab and brought another perspective. We met together three times at get-togethers where the men reminisced, told jokes and gave me the valuable insight and information I needed for a fuller picture of the invention and of Bob.

The early '50s saw the beginning of interest in high-temperature ceramics so that history, too, became an important part of the story.

I realize this is mostly a technical book and perhaps the parts of Bob's personal life are not of much interest to those reading it for information about his work, but I wanted to honor the man apart from his life as an inventor. This is what he was as well, with flaws, fears, tears and triumphs.

I have tried to be a "fly on the wall" and dispassionate in this story and have not always succeeded. Our life together was normal, but with an underneath excitement of things happening and being discovered. It was a good life.

A good bit of the book comes from tapes we made together in 1994. He was a good storyteller and when asked, could keep people enthralled for hours with tales of adventures in the lab. These tapes are his voice, enjoying and remembering the past as he saw it from the distance of almost twenty years.

I hope, too, I have honored his loyal friends, his lab team, as he did. He knew and appreciated their valuable contributions that made the creative ideas doable.

**GBL**

# About The Man Who Was An Inventor

Robert Martin Beasley, as far as I know, never thought he would be an inventor, or that he would ever be a member of the scientific community. There were no signs of interest in chemistry kits in his childhood. His grades were poor. He even had a hard time learning to read. At a very early age, being raised by a young single mother, he had to take responsibility for himself and did a pretty good job of it. In letters his mother kept and in his nighttime reminiscences with me, I saw that even in his childhood, he had a positive sense of his own integrity.

I didn't know him until we met in college in our senior year. I saw him as different from the other young men I dated. I didn't know what it was but from then on I knew he could do anything and be successful at it. He wasn't so sure of this, but I was and I was never disappointed.

Marriage and everyday tameness helped me to see him as a young man who had faults and who sometimes needed my help. He was not perfect, but his imperfections were not deliberate. He was shy in social situations and did not have much small talk, but he was always at ease with his friends and always made new ones. He never hated anyone, though he could get angry when he saw injustice. When he was given a position of authority, he never spoke of anyone as working for him but as working with him.

He had a wicked grin and a kind and sometimes rather ribald sense of humor that kept me laughing all of our forty-six years together. There was a certain sophisticated air he sometimes showed that surprised and delighted me. He didn't suffer fools gladly and wasn't afraid to be brave. And sometimes, of course, he was insufferable.

He wanted to be a good golfer, but never broke 100. He loved flowers and thought of himself as a gardener. His love of music was big-band middlebrow. Sentimental songs could bring tears, but he could be deeply moved by classical music. He was a great dancer, but could never learn to dance a waltz or cha-cha, even with lessons. He had very good table manners, but when given a bowl of ice cream, he held his spoon in his fist and scooped it into his mouth like a two-year-old.

In pinning diapers, he was much neater than me and he was the one who tied perfect bows on the backs of his little girls' dresses. He trimmed their bangs with great precision. He had a running board game with his son and took him to ice hockey practice at 4:30 a.m. on Saturday mornings. He loved the mountains and the water and took us camping and boating.

When they were small, he read bedtime stories to his children and tucked them all in. He taught me how to fry eggs. Sometimes he'd even vacuum. He went to church with us on Sundays. We felt safe in his decisions. He was proud of my accomplishments.

In the later years when the illnesses came, he always met them with a kind of nonchalance that brought them down to manageable size. His last handicap he met with grace and without resentment.

He was always proud of his inventions but not of himself as the inventor. I always told him I would write this book. He liked that idea.

# Foreword

It has been almost thirty years since the space shuttle made its first voyage into space and came back safely. Until the tragic ends of two of the shuttles, the comings and goings of the others were no longer such big news, generating perhaps thirty seconds of interest on TV news and appearing on page four in newspapers.

But before the '70s there was great speculation about the whole concept of reusable space ships. Up until then anything that went out of the earth's atmosphere more or less burned up upon reentry. Our astronauts crammed into vehicles coated with many layers of asbestos-type material that would burn up, but not completely. The partial burning away of this material generated gases which also carried heat away from the spacecraft, shielding those inside from more than 2000 degrees F caused by the friction of reentry. This process is called "ablation." It was well tested and safe, but scary when you thought about it.

After the moon landings, NASA needed something new to encourage the government to keep funding it. The idea of a space tug that could take things into space, leave them there and come back intact had been talked about. Like most good ideas, this concept grew until it became a shuttle, flying like an airplane, in and out of space, having turnaround capabilities, able to fly again in a few weeks.

Even before this time, Robert Beasley had a conviction that there were materials better suited to protect space travelers than the old ablative concept. Pure silica was the key, he believed. He had been working with high-temperature inorganic materials for some time and was beginning to get a "feel" for what they could do.

The biggest problem confronting NASA was how to keep the proposed aluminum body of a shuttle and everything in it from burning up upon reentry and also be lightweight, reusable, durable, waterproof and able to pass innumerable tests not yet proposed. As the space shuttle race began, bids were put out for the engineering of the body, which included its thermal protection system.

When Bob was not quite three, something happened that he never forgot. His mother had left her husband in Alabama and moved to West Palm Beach. She rented a small cottage and got a job at an insurance company. She always said he was so good that she could sit him down anywhere and he wouldn't move. Perhaps she thought he would be safe if she locked him in a room while she went to work. It was a small room at the front of the cottage where she kept her clothes and her ironing board, a rocking chair and a few of his toys. She probably gave him a pillow and a blanket, some water and something to eat. Her place of work was nearby and perhaps she checked on him during the day. He spent hours at the window looking at a weed growing out of a crack in the concrete street outside. The weed was his friend.

Sometimes he cried.

One late afternoon, as shadows began to darken the corners of the already dingy room, he became aware of a presence in there with him. It was up on a place where his mother usually did things before she left him and it had turned red and now had a hot, ugly smell that burned his throat. He watched it turn from red to blue to white. What frightened him most was that it began to hiss and pop and shake. He was sure it was going to come down and get him. He tried to get away from it by hiding in a corner, shielding himself with his arms and closing his eyes. There was nothing else to do. Suddenly the door burst open and someone ran in saying bad words to the thing and threw it out.

It wasn't until sometime later that he found that the thing was his mother's iron left plugged into a socket. He never forgot the fear he felt. Only as this story was being written could it be seen that this incident from Bob's childhood was one of the reasons he wanted passionately to bring astronauts safely back from space. It must have formed a very small nucleus of the idea that carried him forward throughout his life.

# Part One The Man

## Chapter One

# Beginnings

On the day of the space shuttle *Columbia's* first return to earth, April 14, 1981, Bob and I planned to sit quietly in our family room alone and watch it on TV. Many people from Lockheed's Program Office and NASA, Ames and many others, had been invited to sit in the front row bleachers at Edwards Air Force Base in California where the shuttle was going to land. News commentators at the landing site interviewed Roy Rogers and the Star Trek crew among others. They even interviewed people who claimed credit for inventing the material for the thermal protection system, L-I900, even though Bob, himself, had invented it.

He hadn't been forgotten by the local media, however. I had seen to that. I had been watching Channel 5, a San Francisco television station and heard the anchor, Dave MacElhatton, announce a series about people in the area who contributed to the space effort. They hadn't called Bob, so I sent MacElhatton a note about him and among other things said how he had been ignored, or perhaps forgotten, by Lockheed since his retirement due to health problems. I said I was my husband's champion and that was why I wrote the note.

A few days later, MacElhatton called me and asked for a TV interview with Bob. Channel 5 had called Lockheed and their Program Office said, of course, he was the inventor of the tile material. The interview was such a success that it was repeated on every TV station in the area. Bill Hillman, the interviewer, asked Bob if he was worried about the shuttle's safe return and Bob said, "Absolutely not! As far as the plane is concerned, I don't know how to fly one. I still don't know how the hell it got off the ground." Bob had become a great sound bite. (Of course, he did know how it got off the ground.)

So, a few days before the reentry, Evelyn Richards, a reporter for *The Palo Alto Times Tribune,* called and insisted that she be with us as *Columbia* touched down. She was so insistent that we finally agreed.

She came about fifteen minutes early and sat up straight in a rocking chair, facing Bob rather than the TV. She accepted a cup of coffee but never touched it. There was a little constrained conversation. The TV commentators were getting hyper as it got closer to the time of the estimated touchdown. She took out her notebook and pen as unobtrusively as possible, hardly moving, just watching for reaction.

Bob was sitting in his favorite chair, biting his nails, something he hardly ever did, I chiding him a little, just to break the tension. Evelyn's presence was forgotten as the *Columbia* appeared as a small dot on the television screen.

It was different for Bob than for the others watching. His invention held the safe return of John Young and Robert Crippen, those heroes who willingly lent their lives on the promise that his tiles would bring them safely back to earth. Many, many people worked to perfect his invention, but he could not help feeling responsible for the outcome of this first trial.

The shuttle grew larger on the screen and soon it became apparent that it had come through the 2,400-degree heat from the friction of the earth's atmosphere intact. We watched with millions of others as the ungainly but beautiful bird glided down the runway and came to a stop. The protective tiles had fulfilled their promise. It was over.

A few moments later, Evelyn asked Bob how he felt and she quoted him in her article, "That's the end of so many years of heartache you can't imagine. All the heartaches, all the stress, it was worth it." She ended her article thus: "Only when the television cameras closed on the mosaic of the reusable tiles did Beasley relax. Just a few minutes later the telephone rang. The person on the other end must have watched the same amazing scene. 'Well, congratulations to you, too,' Beasley said."


When asked at his wedding what was the happiest day of his life, the beaming bridegroom said, "The day I got out of the navy." Since his wedding day was only half over and he had been in the navy for nearly four years, this was a very apt response. Bob had joined the navy in May 1944, the day before his eighteenth birthday, so that he wouldn't be drafted into the army. There was a big farewell party on May 13 and he expected to be sent far away the next day. To his disgust and with a big letdown, he was sent, close to home, to Florida's Jacksonville Naval Air Station. His boot camp letters to his mother indicated an early love/hate relationship with the service and he chose never to rise above the rank of seaman, second class.

Perhaps the hardest thing for him then was never being able to be alone. On shipboard he slept in a bunk with his nose five inches below the one above him. When he was stationed on the aircraft carrier, the Siboney, his favorite time was when he was on night watch, on the aft deck, watching the phosphorus glow in the deep, quiet wake of the ship, listening to his thoughts.

For about ten months he had been given the opportunity to attend the Naval Academy Preparatory School (NAPS) in Bainbridge, Maryland. He never was quite sure why he was sent there. His grades in high school were mostly "Ds," and he showed very few signs of leadership ability up to then. It wasn't something he asked for, but it was some kind of an honor. He always said he was chosen because he was one of the few men on base who read real paperbacks rather than comic books. He liked Mickey Spillane and Westerns.

It was not easy for him at NAPS; the barracks were cold and leaky in the bleak Maryland winter (compared to Florida where he grew up), but he made a lot of friends; good buddies he kept for many years. His grades were less than average, the worst ones in physics, which he didn't like. Whether he would become an officer or not was taken out of his hands right before Christmas that year. On the train ride home for holiday leave, he became very ill and was taken to the hospital at the Jacksonville Naval Air Base. He had contracted scarlet fever. To bring down the rash and fever, he was given penicillin, a new miracle drug, but he didn't get better. Finally, they realized he was allergic to it. It was over six weeks before he was well enough to go back and take his final exams. He knew he would flunk out and to assuage his bad feelings about this, he decided to deliberately fail the history test,

his best subject and just do his best with the others. He really didn't
want to be a naval officer anyhow, not really caring for the ones he had
known. He was immediately sent back to regular duty as gunner on the
Sibone. The war was almost over.

After his duty as gunner on board ship ended, he was assigned to
a navy base in Philadelphia. At Thanksgiving that year, the men were
given leave. Bob and some of his buddies were going in to town to rent
a hotel room and go out and "raise hell." Bob had a secret plan, though
and on Thanksgiving Day, he left the others getting over their hangovers
and went by himself to the dining room of one of the big hotels
downtown. He wanted something special and elegant for Thanksgiving
Dinner. He must have looked handsome in his navy blues, young
and vulnerable. He said they outdid themselves serving him, waiters
hovering around him to make sure he had all he wanted. The maître d'
even showed him what utensils to use from the array of forks, spoons
and knives spread out on either side of his plate. It was a seven-or
eight-course meal and expensive, but he was never presented with a bill.
Afterward he went back to where his buddies were. They all wanted to
know where he had been, but he just smiled and never told them.

At the Fourth of July celebration that year, the navy band was to
march in the city's parade. Bob loved to march; he loved the cadence
and he really wanted to march with the band. Somehow, a buddy got
him a flute, which he held to his lips and pretended to blow. But he
was never able to march with the band after that.

He was discharged in November 1948 with medals for both good
conduct and sharp shooting and a chance for a college education. His
mother thought he should stay in the navy so it could take care of him
for the rest of his life, but he had other plans.

His two best buddies from Robert E. Lee High School in
Jacksonville, Tommy Booth and Herman Brooks (the three Bs) had
already been discharged from the army and were enrolled under the GI
Bill in the business school at John B. Stetson University in DeLand,
Florida, about a hundred miles or so south of Jacksonville and fifteen
miles inland from Daytona Beach. They were renting an apartment on
the second floor of an old, white, clapboard house downtown, close to
campus and they had room for him. Though he had thought at one time

of a career in business, a navy buddy had told him that chemists made good money and that was what he wanted to do most of all. His great uncle Jim had given him a book about inventors when he was eleven and he liked their stories.

It didn't seem to daunt him that he had got poor-to-failing grades in all his Science classes in school and in most of his other classes. He had spent most of his senior year at Lee writing his own excuses "from his mother" for missing classes and raising rather innocent hell with beer, cigarettes and late-night parties at the beach. All the young men of his age knew they would be drafted and then sent out to be killed. One Sunday, when they were seventeen, Tommy, Herman and Bob went down to the local Baptist Church and got baptized, but they still felt fatalistic about their futures.

Now, a more mature thinker and ready to get on with his life, Robert Martin Beasley enrolled at Stetson as a chemistry major. He had already decided to go straight through to get his degree because he was afraid he wouldn't go back if he stopped.

Stetson was an ideal campus for returning GIs. Elizabeth Hall, the mellow red brick administration building with its signature white cupola was a symbol of serene academia. It was a wonderful respite for those who were making the transition from the rigors and traumas of the recent past to finding their way to new lives.

DeLand was and is a small southern college town, quiet, catering to northern retirees who liked the ambience of its cultural activities. John B. Stetson, of Stetson hat fame, had visited DeLand and decided to make it his winter home. The DeLand Academy, founded by Henry DeLand, had already been established in 1884 and Stetson offered to endow it generously if it would change its name to his. It prospered and was called by some, the Athens of the south (along with several other universities).

Quiet DeLand changed drastically in 1946 when the enrollment at Stetson grew from six hundred to over eighteen hundred students, eight hundred of whom were returning servicemen.

It was a tradition that every freshman should wear a rat cap at all times. It was made of green felt with a little bill. It was unbecoming on the girls and looked silly on the men. Upperclassmen were supposed to somehow punish those caught not wearing one on campus. But the returning GIs refused to wear them.

There wasn't much the administration could do to monitor the men. They provided housing at the disbanded air force base in the officers quarters (the BOQ) a few miles out of town and included meals and a bus trip to and back from campus. A few rather run-down frat houses provided some rooms and rooming houses and apartments proliferated all over town. There were no sorority houses.

The women were kept under very close watch. There was a nightly curfew vigorously kept. Stetson was then partially endowed by the Florida Southern Baptist Convention, which decreed there would be no liquor on campus and no dancing, which they thought would raise immoral passions if allowed. However, women (girls) could smoke.

There wasn't much to do on campus for social recreation. Fraternities and sororities and other organizations held swimming parties at nearby DeLeon Springs where Ponce was supposed to have discovered the Fountain of Youth. The springs were very chilly, so it was more pleasant to lie or sit on a blanket on the lawn, working on a tan, playing cards, or just listening to the radio playing "Slow Boat to China" or "Her Bathing Suit Never Got Wet and She Was an Admiral's Daughter."

Organizations were allowed to hold dances off campus at the defunct air base in one of the hangars. The girls wore strapless evening gowns with corsages strapped to their wrists and the men rented black tuxedos or white dinner jackets. Music students provided great big-band sounds. Each dance ended with a romantic ballad: "I'll See You in My Dreams" (hold you in my dreams) or "Good night Sweetheart" (till we meet tomorrow), songs men of a previous generation sang to their sweethearts. Not everyone was that innocent, except naïve young girls who believed the words, which were, for the most part, true.

Most of the upperclassmen who lived in town or on campus chose to eat downtown at Georgie Boy's or Morris's, instead of at the Commons where the food was bland and plentiful. They were the favorite hangouts for inexpensive coffee dates. There were two movie houses in town: the Athens, with first-run offerings and the Dreka, better known as the Armpit, that showed Oaters and Saturday morning serials. The Slop Shop, a hangout in the middle of the campus was always crowded between classes. You could pick up your mail, buy cigarettes, drink Cokes, sit squeezed in at one of the small tables and talk in loud voices, not even trying to listen to the jukebox playing "I heard a crash on the highway but I didn't hear nobody pray" or *Mule Train.*

Homecoming was always a big weekend, with a parade, barbecues, visiting alumni, a play at the Stover Little Theater, a football game and a big-name dance band out at the base.

The favorite trysting spot was at the library where you could study or pretend to study and then go out back and find a bench in the Forest of Arden, a parklike setting densely filled with tall, moss-hung pine trees, which filtered out the light from the widely placed light poles. It was a great place for smooching with your true love, either there, or on the steps of the Art Building across from Stetson Hall, one of the women's dorms.

The sororities were allowed to have beach parties at Daytona in the spring provided they were heavily chaperoned. They always drew the guys like Florida fruit flies.

The one in 1950 was when Bob first noticed me because he thought I had good-looking legs.

A favorite place for the guys after they took the girls back to the dorm was a Road House on the way to Canandagua, the Three Sisters—better known as the Six Tits. Inside, the large two-room interior had a boozy, smoke-draped atmosphere, rather like a modern day pirate's den. Everyone sat on benches at long, green-painted tables, wet with beer dripping from foaming pitchers. The ubiquitous jukebox, usually playing Les Paul and Mary Ford's "I'm Lookin' Over a Four Leaf Clover" or "Good Night, Irene," could hardly be heard over the raucous conversations of young men let loose from impending domesticity. There were fights, usually squashed before they caused any harm. There was a small dance floor, seldom used, because campus women weren't allowed to go there. Sometimes the girls bribed the guys to sneak them in. Their presence was hardly noticed by the others, but their boyfriends kept close watch, anyhow.

Bob didn't have time or money for much dating, but he, Herman and Tommy sometimes went back to Jacksonville on weekends to party with old friends. However, he didn't neglect to have a good time whenever he could and he had a hollow leg, meaning he could drink a good bit of beer before it showed. He had started smoking when he was fourteen. Sometimes he smoked cigars, big, long ones.

He especially enjoyed jitterbugging to Big Band Swing records. When he was much younger, he wanted to take tap dance lessons and be like Fred Astaire, but lessons cost too much and he was afraid everyone would think he was a sissy. One of his mother's friends taught him the Fox Trot when he was about eleven. He said he would never forget the feel of her corset when he put his arm around her waist.

One time, during a spring break at Stetson, the three Bs decided they would go to New Orleans to see the sights. They went in the Model A with a convertible top and a rumble seat they had bought together. Driving straight through and arriving after dark, they ended up in a cheap motel and soon fell into deep sleep. Sometime before dawn, they awoke in terror. A train was bearing down on them, its headlights flashing through the uncurtained window, horns blasting, the heavy clanking of wheels vibrating the whole room. They were petrified and couldn't move. But the train passed by without hitting them and its sound and fury faded into the distance. When daylight came, they saw that the train tracks were about six feet from their room. Of all the sights they saw in New Orleans that was the one they said they remembered most.

But for the most part, college was a serious time for everyone beginning to experience what would be the rest of their lives.

Bob talked about some of his college experiences on a tape made in August 1994:

*Excerpt from 1994 tape*

I think I had some very good chemistry teachers. The head of the Department—Dr. Conn—was a very good teacher, though strict, very strict. And the second teacher in the Department was Dr. Vaughn, who had worked at DuPont. He was also a good teacher. There were other teachers, for other subjects, generally retired people who had taught elsewhere and so, there were very good teachers at Stetson.

Dr. Conn was a rather heavy-set, husky, shorter man, who had short-cropped black hair. He really looked sort of tough, like a bulldog and he wanted to act that way. He kept the young students on their toes. An example was in Organic Chemistry class where he just loved to get you to the blackboard for what seemed to be hours and he'd just spiel out a name and you were supposed to write it down on the blackboard. He would just review over and over again . . . that's the way he did it.

He would stomp around the lab and everyone was a bit in awe and afraid of him. Except one time I happened to walk by his office after he had raised Cain with somebody in class and he was in there giggling, so after that I think I knew what he was really like. I remember one time in class I was given a test-tube with an "unknown" in it. There was a substance in there and I was supposed to find out what it was. Well actually, there *wasn't* an unknown in it, it was just water. Dr. Conn liked to joke.

I remember an embarrassing thing happened to me in Quantitative Analysis. Dr. Conn gave me a test-tube with an unknown in it and I was supposed to find out what it was. Now, in conducting these analyses you'd have to use what is called a burette, which is an over six-feet-long tube that's calibrated and has a petcock at one end so you can let out water or solution a drop at a time. To start off, you need to wash the burette out and since I'm short, I really couldn't see over the burette very well, so I stuck it through my legs so I could reach the end. I was pouring water in and waiting till the water would get to the top, but I didn't realize I had the petcock open at the other end and it was running onto the floor. At that moment the door flew open and two men, Dr. Conn and a visitor he was trying to impress, came in and what they saw was an idiot standing there with a long tube sticking out between his legs and a large puddle of water on the floor behind him. *(sounds of giggling)*

The day that I graduated he told me, "Hey, I'd like to see you after the ceremony." And so, I went to his office. He gave me an inlaid plaque that he had made, which I still have, as a present to remember him by." (It was the insignia of the Chemical Society, Gamma Sigma Epsilon and Bob was its president that last year.)

I think you can get a picture of Dr. Conn. He loved the Honorary Chemistry Society . . . he loved the initiation. I remember the night I was initiated, I had to go to the lab and it wasn't lit very well . . . there was a tremendous roar, I don't know what they were using, but there was a roar of things, of doing things. And I went in and there was a pot boiling . . . just boiling, it seemed . . . metal. Dr. Conn insisted that I stick my hand into this boiling pot of shiny, liquid metal. I don't know whether I did or not . . . well . . . I know I did . . . it was cold because it was liquid mercury and looked exactly as though it was a pot of boiling liquid metal.

Bob loved to read, nothing highbrow, mostly detective stories or historical fiction. He was a deliberately slow reader because he liked to read descriptions and savor the writer's use of words. He even enjoyed reading his history textbooks.

He saved his theme papers from English 101 and 102. Some show an appreciation for current problems going on in the late '40s (similar to the ones we have now), atomic energy, the race problem and a write-up of a forum he attended on the Marshall Plan. Some were more mundane. He had as many As and Bs as he did Cs on those papers.

There was one paper for which he got an A. Perhaps he was serious about it. It was written in his best handwriting, spelling and punctuation perfect except for a missing question mark at the end of the last sentence. If he was serious, it might have been under the influence of a few beers. They always put him in a sentimental mood.

## Aurora

Of all the beauty in the world there is none so majestic as the dawning of a new day. The rising light of morning heralds the day by gradually piercing the darkness of night. The glimmering light is an artist's inspiration as it sends forth its radiant colors to play and flow over the roiling cloud formations. Lurid red, blue and all the colors that nature can blend are hued together to present the prelude of a new and glorious day. The sun, that fiery gift to the universe is in an eclipse; but wait, now it slowly rises, casting a magnificent specter as its illumination splashes, dashes, glitters and struts over the sparkling dew left by the night. Is the dawn's beauty only to be seen? No, there is music which none of the greatest composers have been able to capture. With the first appearance of daylight, the music is low and glowing as the light, but as the dawning becomes more intensified, so does the music become brighter and louder until at last it is piercing the stillness in a joyful manner as the light is piercing the cold darkness. Could Aurora, the Roman Goddess of Dawn, have possibly been beautiful enough to warrant her to be compared with the splendor of the dawn.

Bob was possibly serious about this essay because he loved dawns and sunsets and was interested in mythology.

His mother, who was quite generous, liked to buy things she thought the recipients should have and she also liked to clip information out of the paper and underline the parts she wanted to have read and send them to those she thought needed the advice. One day Bob got a package from her containing two pairs of pants she had gotten on sale. One was tomato red and the other a cross between grass green and algae. Along with these was a newspaper fashion tip for men that recommended wearing a tie around the waist instead of a belt. Bob thanked her for them but decided that he would be thought too "cunning" if he ever wore them, especially if he wore them with a tie for a belt.

This was an inspiration for another theme paper, which only merited a B, perhaps because it had a lot of mistakes and cross-outs and was rather wrinkled.

## In Style

When I was buying my clothes to wear in college, I bought a green shirt and a red tie. It is hard to describe the particular green of the shirt for it seems to get greener each day. The best way I can describe it is to say that it is about five shades greener than envy and two shades lighter than jealousy.

You may wonder why I bought it. That is easy to answer. The clothing salesman hypnotized me and then proceeded to tell me how this particular shade of green matched my complexion, how collegiate I would look when I wore it and how all the best dressed college men were wearing shirts of this type. How could I resist when he told me all these wonderful things! He even had me in such a trance that I even agreed to introduce a "new look" for men by wearing the red tie around my waist in place of a belt.

I wore my green shirt and red tie on Christmas Eve. Everyone complimented me on my taste in selecting clothes. Even my best friend told me I should either be in a sideshow or in Robin Hood's band. I thanked everyone and told them I was merely celebrating Christmas by wearing the traditional colors of red and green. After receiving so many compliments, I went home and dreamed about green dragons, which were spitting red flames at me. I imagine the reader has guessed by now that this night was the last time I have ever worn my green shirt and red tie in public.

If you have a color-blind friend who needs a beautiful shirt and tie, send him around. I will treat him right.

His grades were average and he had to work hard to catch up on what he had not learned in high school. He loved his history and government classes, did well in speech and English and was even able to tutor some of his friends in math and statistics. He might have had a partial photographic memory because he taught himself the typewriter keyboard and was able to type flawless letters whenever he had the chance. He worked hard and conscientiously and apparently some of his professors noticed this.

Tommy and Herman belonged to a newly established local fraternity—Sigma Omega—and they nominated Bob for membership. Meetings were held at the BOQ. He was upstairs the night of the nomination, could hear everything that went on in the meeting down below and heard himself being blackballed. The local became a Chapter of Lambda Chi Alpha the next year and in his senior year, Bob was elected their High Alpha, the president. He took his office seriously and was instrumental in helping to buy a large old residence not too far from campus for their Chapter House. He worked with Lambda Chi alumna in town who led him through his part of the process.

In the spring of 1950, my last quarter at Stetson, I noticed Bob walking on the other side of the street holding hands with one of my sorority's cute blonde pledges and for no concrete reason I could ever figure out, I knew he was the "One." Though he had dark hair, brown eyes and a soft southern accent, he wasn't tall and not really handsome. I didn't even know how I knew his name. But there he was, my future. Fortunately, the cute blonde, who was also a great dancer, found other boyfriends. So a few of my friends arranged that Bob and I meet, at last, face-to-face. It was almost like high school. He had been told that I thought he was "nice." So, when he saw me leaving a sorority apartment Open House (by design), he caught up with me, asked if he could walk me back to the dorm and I said "yes." Through the years, whenever he was feeling sentimental, he would look softly at me with his brown eyes and ask in loving tones, "Little girl, will you walk along with me?" And I would always answer rather shyly, "Yes."

He still had another quarter to go until his graduation in December—had an uncertain future ahead of him and had not even thought of settling down. It took him only a month, though, to realize he wanted to marry me and finish the rest of our lives together. It seemed as though we had always known each other.

All his life, Bob had yearned for a stable, conventional home: his own room, a mother and father who loved each other and maybe have some brothers and sisters.

Instead, his mother left his father when he was about two. His mother, Lou DeFoor had been seventeen when he was born and his father, Robert Wilson Beasley, eighteen. He never remembered his father, but knew they had met in his mother's hometown, Morrow, Georgia and they lived in his mother's boarding house in Birmingham, Alabama. When Bob was almost three, Lou decided she didn't want to live with Robert anymore and moved to West Palm Beach to be near her cousin, Bill Redelsheimer and his new bride, Dot. From then on, they lived with other people, relatives or in rooming houses until he reached his teens.

Summers were spent visiting his grandfather, Marlin DeFoor and his second wife, "Aunt" Emma, and other relatives in Morrow, his other grandmother, Naomi Chapman in Hazelhurst, Georgia, or with Dot and Bill Redelsheimer and their son Billy and later, daughter Patty, in Miami.

His great aunt Ida, who lived in an apartment in Jacksonville, was the island of solidity in his life. His mother always went back to Aunt Ida when she was broke or had an argument with someone or just needed a new place to stay. Lou's mother had died when she was seven and her brother Ed, two. Their father left them with his parents and Lou had always felt he had abandoned them. The two children were not wanted by the sixty-eight-year-old grandmother, Maryanne Huie DeFoor. Their grandfather, Martin DeFoor, a respected Baptist preacher, was too busy caring for his two parishes to bother with what was a woman's duty. It was a very unhappy childhood and Lou never got over it.

Lou loved her baby, but as he grew older, he became sort of an appendage. She never forgot him but expected him to take care of himself at a very early age.

He never remembered that he ever had lunch to take to school. One of his favorite treats was the little half pint of milk and a graham cracker all the children got after morning recess.

He learned early on to keep all his possessions neatly in a pile and to not cause anyone any extra trouble when he was visiting. But he was an enthusiastic, fun-loving, inquisitively typical little boy. There is a snapshot taken when he was about four or five. It shows a group of tall young men in white shirts and straw hats. Sticking his body out between the legs of the young men was a skinny, darkly tanned little boy dressed in bib overalls and no shirt, mugging for the camera. This was Bob.

His grandmother Chapman called him "dear little Bob" and Uncle Bill said he was bright. His letters to his mother in the summers were usually cheerful and full of his activities, but many ended with how much he loved her and missed her and wanted to be with her.

He usually enjoyed his summers because his cousins Bill and Marvin Redelsheimer were often visiting, too, at Grandma Chapman's boarding house in Hazelhurst, Georgia. Bob started traveling by himself when he was six and was responsible for a heavy trunk with most of his possessions in it. He learned how to read the train timetables and make his own reservations.

His letters to his mother were also filled with enthusiasms of things he wanted to build or explanations of how things worked or the outlines of books he was reading.

In 1932, Robert, Bob's father, came to Jacksonville so that he and Lou could get a divorce. If he wanted to see Bob then, Bob never knew, because Lou had arranged it so that they would not meet. He never did find out anything about his father. Lou would never discuss him, so he decided early on he would just be proud to be a Beasley whether he had a father or not.

He was always a latchkey kid and after school, he'd usually play outside a friend's house until it got dark and he knew when it was time to go home.

In 1933, Lou moved to Washington, D.C. where she got a government job as a secretary in the Chief Counsel's Office, which was at that time called the "Bureau of Internal Revenue." She left Bob behind with her father for a year so that she could get settled. During that time, Otto Wittschen, a lawyer who helped arrange the divorce from Robert, followed her there and they were married. He had temporarily left his practice and was working for the FBI.

The summer of that year Bob burned his feet badly by walking barefoot in lime and was bedridden for some time. The scars remained all his life.

His grandfather took care of him as best he could and Lou sent money from time to time to help out. The two lived in an office in a large building in downtown Birmingham, which fortunately had a full bathroom. Times were hard then in the middle of the depression.

When the next school year started, Bob was sent up to Washington and at last he had a semblance of a real family and a father. Otto was older than Lou and had been married before. He took a great interest in Bob and seemed to realize that his stepson had potential for getting ahead in life. Bob said, later of Otto, that he had taught him three things: good manners, how to study and how to wash off the ring from around the bathtub. His summer letters home referred to Otto as "Dad." The only problem was that Otto was an alcoholic, a binge drinker and Lou finally left him after they moved back to Jacksonville.

Washington, D.C. was a fascinating place, almost a small town in those days and Bob thoroughly enjoyed everything about the city. He rode his bicycle all over, swam in the basement swimming pool at the Mayflower Hotel for a small fee and explored the winding paths at Rock Creek Park not too far from their apartment. He and his mother watched Roosevelt's inaugural parade in the rain.

His rather passionate nature began to emerge evidenced by a letter he wrote to a young lady in his class written in green ink. He was about eleven.

October 7, 1937

Washington, D.C.

Dear Darling,

I'm so sorry that I said what I did yesterday I didn't mean it, you are the swates girl I know of. I love you so much that I cant put it in words, I hope you love me, but I guess you love Dicky but I don't know. I will love you always sweatart. Are you going to the show Saterday If yiou are will you go with me.

Hears wishing you luck honey.

Youre Truly

PS Heares 4 or 5 kisses

   BB


Evidently Darling never got that letter. His mother kept it in an envelope addressed and sent to his grandfather, also written in green ink.

Granddad must have been much amused by this letter sent to him by his grandson. And Darling must have been very confused being addressed as granddad!

That incident is probably why Bob used to quote, "Do right and fear no man. Don't write and fear no woman."

Bob had a hard time with his spelling even in his early years in college, but he learned all the chemical names easily.

He never referred to that time in his life except to say that when he got bigger, he could defend his mother when Otto became abusive. During that very traumatizing time, he coped the best way he knew how by getting the best grades he had ever gotten in school, As, B+s and Bs. Perhaps, deep down, he hoped this would please Otto so much that he would want to change and continue to be his dad.

There were several stabilizing influences in his life besides Aunt Ida, grandparents and the Redelsheimer family. He became a member of Boy Scout Troop 10 in Jacksonville. Its laws and duties he endeavored to keep and he loved working on earning his badges.

Troop 10 had an excellent scout master, the father of one of the boys. "Pop" Meacham took them camping on weekends at the Boy Scout camp in the scrub at Orange Park and let them work out their problems themselves, looking up occasionally from his book to see if their loud noises meant anything serious. Bob became patrol leader when he was twelve and the troop won an award for the most improved troop in the Greater Jacksonville Area Boy Scouts. His greatest desire at that time was to become an Eagle Scout, but Lou moved to the other side of town when she left Otto and he couldn't get back to meetings.

He also enjoyed going to the Christian Science Sunday School on Sundays, several blocks from the apartment in Washington and in downtown Jacksonville, where he gained a deep understanding of God as his spiritual Father/Mother who was always there to take care of him. He never forgot what he learned and at times this was a great help and comfort to him.

He always had some kind of way to earn money. Aunt Ida had him bicycle all over town to pay her bills, for which he earned fifteen cents apiece. He pumped the bicycle standing up in hopes this would lengthen his legs. He had a paper route, sold *The Saturday Evening Post* from door to door and worked for a mean butcher who later became his friend. When he was sixteen, he worked after school in J. C. Penney's men's department. He also was a member of Casa Nobilium at Robert E. Lee High School.

After his discharge from the navy, his mother met him at the train station with a strange man. Lou had married Marcus Larkin Tyrone a month or so before but had not yet told Bob. Mark was a tall, rather pear-shaped, bald-headed man, looking older than his forty years. He had a round, innocent face and a trusting nature. This was his first marriage and he didn't mind that Lou made most of the plans for their future. The two men had a mutual dislike at first, Bob still in shock, but gradually they learned to love and appreciate each other.

Later, Mark and Lou built a house in a new subdivision outside Jacksonville and Bob had his first room he could truly call his own. He painted it forest green with white trim. He would only be able to enjoy it for a little while before he would be graduating from college and be off on his own.

That spring, Bob gave me his fraternity pin. It was not really his pin. He had bought it secondhand from Herman, who had graduated. Tommy was now working for his father who sold used cars and Herman had a good job at the Barnett National Bank in Jacksonville.

After my graduation, I went back to my parents' home in Eustis, about thirty miles from DeLand. During that summer, I went over to Stetson on weekends and stayed in the dorm with one of my friends, or Bob would catch a ride to Eustis. We wrote to each other almost every day. Phone calls were too expensive for frequent use.

On one of our double dates at Stetson that summer, we decided to get married after graduation as soon as he got a job.

Letters were important for us both. Bob could express his feelings much better on paper. I saved all he had sent me and tied them in a pink ribbon.

In the meantime, he was very busy, not only working hard at his studies, but with the commitment involved in being the High Alpha of the fraternity. He could hardly wait for graduation. The new frat house was now open, complete with housemother/cook and he had had to set up new rules, some of which were not popular, such as having to pay mandatory rent.

Once in awhile, he would write to me about his fears and cares for the future.

### *Part of a letter, September 29, 1950*

I am very, very tired of school and am ready to go to work for a while. I will be glad when the quarter is over so that I will know a little better just which way I am headed in this old world. I am a person who must always be working towards a definite goal or else I am definitely lost. I always like to set my goals higher than I can reach so that when or if I fall short, I will have gone higher than if I had only set my goal within my reach.

At present, for the first time, I don't have a definite goal or know just which way I am going or know what I want ultimately and to say the least, I am rather lost. I do know what I want ultimately, but I can't see or seem to begin to see just which paths I should take through life. The only thing I can do is trust in God for He has always led me in the right way and blessed me with what some people might call "wonderful luck" but what I call God looking out for me and blessing me. I try not to worry for I feel all is with Him, my destiny, service, or whatever you call it, that I was placed on earth to do and He will show me the right way as He has already done in the past. But as I said, I feel sort of lost at present.

I will be looking forward to your letters and also seeing you at this and future weekends. I love you so.

Goodnight, darling,

Bob

Dr. Vaughn, who had taken an interest in Bob, suggested that he go back to school for a higher degree rather than go to work right away, but Bob thought that was something he could do in the future after having some work experience and earning a decent income. He knew now that he didn't want to set his sights on just getting rich, but was worried about providing for me and the family we hoped to have.

The only jobs there seemed to be for chemists in Florida then, where we both wanted to stay, were at orange juice processing plants testing for sweetness. Bob did not want to settle for that and evidently Dr. Vaughn didn't want him to, either. He suggested that Bob write for applications at chemical companies around the country.

### Part of a letter sent to his mother, November 27, 1950

Dear Mother,

I went to see Dr. Vaughn today and we had a long talk. He said that I should send a letter asking for an application blank for these companies and that I will hear from them very soon. Then he is going to write recommendations to them.

He thinks I may end up at the DuPont Hydrogen Bomb project. At least that is a thought. He said that I would have to start at the bottom but that in about 5 years I will (maybe) be making between $5,000 and $7,000 a year and after that there isn't a limit.

I certainly had a good time over the holidays and Gloria said she did, too. Gloria really does like you and Mark.

Love,

Bob

He asked his mother to type up the requests for applications for him. She was, by that time, secretary to the agent-in-charge of the IRS at the Jacksonville Regional Office. However, of the five applications sent, two companies answered "No Thanks" and two said they would keep his application on file but had no openings. DuPont answered but not until late that winter.

Part of the problem for returning GIs looking for jobs was that employers were afraid that after hiring and training these men, they would be redrafted and sent to Korea. There was a pretty well-founded rumor that the draft would be reinstated and regardless of previous service, older men like Bob would be called up first.

Bob wasn't sure what his status was, after almost four years in the navy and was worried along with everyone else. Those who had not finished their enlistment time, because of the end of the war, were already being called back. It was so sad to see friends giving up their futures for this second ill-thought-of war.

One weekend evening late that summer, Bob and the few guys at the frat house who were in summer school decided to have an impromptu cookout at the beach with their dates. There were five or six couples, including Bob and me. We piled into several cars for the trip to Daytona and found an ideal, secluded spot down the beach by some sand dunes.

There was still enough sunlight to find driftwood for the bonfire. The tide was going out and the ocean was calm. The hard white sand had a sheen of afterglow from the setting sun behind us. Some of the couples walked to the edge of the water to look out at the horizon. A full moon would be rising soon.

Usually beach parties were noisy with horseplay, banter and thrown balls, but this one wasn't. It was more like a farewell party. When it was almost dark, someone lit the fire and we got out the hot dogs and potato chips, the beer and cold drinks in the washtub filled with ice. We sat close together enjoying the fire-blackened hotdogs and melting marshmallows strung on opened wire coat hangers. Now there was quiet laughter about things that no longer seemed so serious. The light of the fire was too bright for us to see the moon and stars and moving planets, but we could see each other through it as though in a remembered dream. Bob and I sat close, his arm around me. Gradually we all talked less and less, listening instead to the hush of the waves, all of us feeling a kind of timeless kinship with each other.

Then it was time to leave if the girls were to get back before curfew. We packed up everything, but a little breeze blew some embers into some dry beach grass behind us and fire spread quickly toward the dunes, heavy with more grass and bracken. There were beach cottages up on the bluff and the fire was moving quickly in that direction. Bob immediately had some of the men start a backfire and the rest threw sand on new fires wherever they started. The backfire stopped the spread of the flames and the fire was soon put out. In the distance, we could hear the sound of sirens coming toward us but we didn't have time to wait.

We girls knew we were given this wonderful opportunity to see our men as true and brave heroes doing intelligently and quickly what had to be done. The mood going back to Stetson on the narrow road was one of pure romance, an adventure that turned out successfully and honorably. The men got us back in time for a quick kiss and a whisper of love before we had to say goodnight.

Thinking back on it, Bob thought of it as a farewell to something we would never have again, all of us together, in harmony and brotherhood, but also as a good portent for the future—adversity overcome with intelligence, fearlessness and ability.

Bob was twenty-four and eager to begin his new life with me. I was in Eustis, working for an interior decorator and it was hard for us to be apart. We had decided to set the date for our wedding as soon as Bob graduated and found a job.

Money continued to be a problem for Bob. The government gave each ex-serviceman getting an education under the GI Bill $75 a month for personal expenses. Lou helped out by sending him an extra $25. His schedule was too burdened for a part-time job and they were hard to find in DeLand, anyhow. On Christmas holiday breaks, he had a seasonal job at the U.S. Post Office downtown unloading huge amounts of mail from boxcars pulling up at a railroad siding. It was a back-bending job, but the pay was pretty good, with overtime. That last Christmas, after graduation, he saved enough to buy his first car. Tommy's father gave him a good deal on a dusty blue, four-door, prewar Chevy sedan. It looked like a box compared to the postwar models, but the engine was good and it cost nine hundred dollars for a monthly payment of $57 a month.

Graduation Day was December 15, 1950. By that date the next year, Bob would get a job, get married, move a thousand miles away to another job and have his first child.

Looking over the scene in Birmingham, 1927

Bob and friends, Jacksonville, 1931

Billy, Marvin and Bob, at Grandma Chapman's, 1938

Boy Scout Troop 10, Jacksonville, Florida, 1939

Brand new Navy Blues, 1944

NAPS, Bainbridge, Maryland, 1944

Going on to a new life, February 10, 1951

Elizabeth Hall, Administrative Building,
Stetson University, Deland, Florida

Herman and Tommy in New Orleans, 1949

# Chapter Two

# Niagara Chemical Company

There were a few chemical companies in Jacksonville, most with main headquarters up "north." Bob had some nebulous choices. If he were hired by one of them, the possibility would be that he would have to leave Florida. Or he could take off a few years and then go back to school for a higher degree as Dr. Vaughn suggested.

*Letter to Gloria from Jacksonville, January 15, 1951*

Darling,

I spent the day uptown today and went by several Chemical Companies and an Employment Agency. I found out today just what happens to an application after I fill it out. This happened at one of the plants. The secretary took a red pencil and drew large circles around "single," "college" and "draft status." It seems that my draft status is holding me back and not my qualifications. I have decided that I must get out of the cold immediately and give up my hopes of a good job. In other words, I am going to have to take the first decent job offer I get or I may be in the Army before I realize what happened. It is most discouraging to find out that I am not even considered seriously after they find out my age and marital status.

I went to see the man at Cook Co. and he is only in the process of putting up the plant here. There are only going to be about 3 employees from the old company elsewhere and the rest will be new. The plant will not be too large, but the company is. If he will make me an offer that I think we can live on, I think I may take it for it seems to me to be a real opportunity with this setup here. It may not be much of a start, but it will put me in the industry, allow us to get married and give me a chance to get some experience. Honey, I am getting worried about the draft and almost ready to take anything.

Times ahead look very bad to me. We may have to postpone a honeymoon until later and keep some money in reserve. We are going to have to save everything we can and proceed cautiously. We may have a hard time at first and may have to live rather closely. Let me know how you feel about things.

Darling, the threat of my being drafted gets worse each day, for each day brings the legislation closer. I am beginning to feel that we had better start now and not later. We had better enjoy what we can today for tomorrow we may not be able to. It seems we had better live for today until there is a future in this old world for a young married couple. I think we should see about setting a date and go on and be married, for the way things look I may not be able to stall a job off for three or so weeks. I have the job now at Railway Mail and feel and hope it will last until I can make the change to whatever and wherever it will be.

Do you want to go ahead and get married having faith in the future (a job) and try to live on what I am making now? If you do and we live on my present salary we will have to live very, very close and will have only each other. I don't think you would have any trouble getting a job here. In fact, you would have better chances than I do. Let me know, Darling. This will truly be building together.

If I do get drafted then we will have had some time together. If you would rather wait and see what the future holds, well let me know. We may not have the very best apartment but maybe we can make it home and will be happy. You said you would go to Arabia—well, here we go.

I do know we have nothing to worry about for we will make it alright. God will look after us and guide us through these

times safely. He has always guided me right before and now is
no time for Him to stop.

Love,

Bob

### Excerpt from a letter written the next day

I am going to take off from work today and go out to a
Chemical company for an interview. The other day, Sunday,
Virginia saw me waiting on a bus when I got off from work
and evidently she told her sister who works at this company
that I had graduated for she called me today and said her sister
had called from work and said that some of the officials from
the main office from N.Y. wanted to see me. Evidently she had
mentioned me to them. She works for Niagara Chemical Co. I
think they make insecticides.

I don't know what it will net me but I never pass up an
opportunity.

### From a letter written the next day, January 17, 1951

Honey, the interview I had may turn out to be a good
job. I'll know Monday. The starting pay will be $275 with
about a $25 raise every six months and next year I would
get a bonus thereafter which could range between $300 and
$1000.

This is based on the profits of the company and the men in
supervisory work. I think I would work here in Jax for a month
or two and then in New York State for about three and then
maybe take over the plant in Pompano Beach. It is a small
plant down there but it could be a wonderful testing ground
for something even bigger and better in the future. It seems
as though their man down there has not been in the service

before and is expected to get his taste of it any day now. It is an organization full of young men. The man here is only twenty-nine.

It sounds good. I would be in an essential industry and if I didn't want to stay on with them in a few years I would have gotten valuable experience and maybe have changed my draft status.

Hold on to your hat; keep your fingers crossed for we may get married yet. On this score, I'm ready anyhow, I think! Honey, if I do get an offer, I will have to take it and this will cut out our honeymoon, but it looks like that will have to come regardless of which way I turn. Are you willing? Would you be satisfied? I wish that you were up here so that we could talk over things, especially as they happen and not in a letter in which I never can think to put down just the things I mean to say.

This was a stressful time for Bob. When could we get married? After being sure of the job at Niagara, he couldn't ask them to let him start later than they wanted him. And where would we live? The wedding itself left him in a sweat. He suggested a small home wedding, perhaps at my grandparents' large home in the country.

Fortunately, I didn't want a big wedding and agreed about the honeymoon and Mom and I had everything figured out, except for the date.

### *From a letter written January 18, 1951*

I have been so upset trying to work the wedding in when the man at Cook said I may have to go to Kansas City and the man at Niagara said that I may have to go to Buffalo and I don't know if I would. This is certainly upsetting to me. I am going to have to take either offer if extended and I don't know when they are going to require me to go to work.

Darling, let's go on and plan for Feb 10 and get this thing over with. I'll get us an efficiency apartment here to live in. It will probably not be very much for I am not sure of my income and can't get anything nice until I am. We can look for another place together. We will have to make out the best we can until I have a dependable income.

The job from Niagara was offered and accepted and it seemed like the right decision, at least for a start.

### Part of a letter, January 31, 1951

Well, tomorrow I give Niagara a try. I'm anxious to see just what the work will be like. I've made up my mind that I'm going to like it, for I plan to work with them for a while and give them a good chance to show just what they have to offer me.

### Part of a letter, February 1, 1951

So far I like the company, but as yet really haven't done any work. I have bad news for you today for I think they are going on the fourth shift (they run three ordinarily) around the 17th of the month. I will be foreman on this shift and will have the oddest hours you have ever heard of. I will work 5 days a week—one of the days, Sunday, will be from 8AM to 5PM and then two of the days I'll work from 12 AM to 8 AM and then the other two days I'll work from 4 PM to 12 AM. I'll have Friday and Saturday off. They are hard and odd, but we will have to manage without thinking about how unpleasant they are, OK?

I wish they could wait until March before beginning, but why should they hold up production for us, huh?

### *Part of a letter, February 4, 1951*

Dearest Gloria,

It was a really nice to talk to you last night. Five more days and I'll see you again after what seems centuries. Six more and we will be married. The days have been creeping by at a snail's pace since you were up here New Years. I'll be so glad when all of this waiting is over.

Honey, so far—two days, the job has been fine. I haven't been with them long enough to really do any work, know what is in store for me, or to form an opinion. I'll be glad when I know more about their plans for me in this organization.

Wedding plans were made as simple as possible, to the satisfaction of every one. It would be in Eustis at my parents' house. The small wedding was to be conducted by my uncle Walter who was a retired Lutheran minister. Afterward, friends from Stetson, Jacksonville and Eustis were invited to the reception.

After the ceremony, I was touched when we turned around and I saw that the only tears shed were those of my grandfather, Harry and my new father-in-law.

Our new home in Jacksonville Beach was a one-bedroom furnished apartment in a block of buildings a few streets in from the ocean. The furniture was motel-style Danish Modern, placed on a brown tile floor. Two unmatching wedding present lamps lent some early marriage ambience to the room. The focal point was a very large black space heater next to a square walk-in closet. The bathroom was big enough for one and the metal furniture in the bedroom squeaked whenever it was touched. The kitchen was a slit, also big enough for one. The redeeming feature was a small balcony made of concrete. It wasn't big enough for a chair, but one could stand on it and see the ocean between the buildings across the street. Bob had wanted to find a place in town, but what he could afford and what was available didn't coincide. Anyway, we both liked the ocean and could hear it at night when everything was quiet.


Other young couples lived there too; most of them were naval air force trainees from Jacksonville Naval Air Base. Only too frequently, the wives were widowed when their husbands were killed learning how to fly. Otherwise, it was a fun place to be, temporarily.

Bob liked his job well enough and was made supervisor of the new swing shift, which he said was fine, but really way down the line as far as the company was concerned. His job description included being directly responsible for production, quality control, warehousing, receiving, shipping and maintenance. The men under him didn't seem to mind that this "kid" was their boss and he never thought of himself as one. He never liked to think of being anyone's boss.

The swing shift was hard. On some days he would have about four hours sleep before he had to go back to work. And he smelled of sulfur, the main ingredient in the insecticides they were making and long showers didn't help.

We adopted our first cat, a little gray kitten with white paws. She had come up to Bob, mewing, in the parking lot at work and he brought her home. Her name was Jezebel. Her digestive system needed an overhaul from the crickets and grasshoppers she had eaten and the vet's bill was a whopping $17. Now we were a family.

Bob thought it would be nice for me to take a month or two to get settled into married life before getting a job. Lou was on the lookout for one for me and found what looked perfect for a former art student without too many skills. It was at an art store in town to work as a salesperson. It sounded good to me too, even though I would have to take two long bus rides to get there. However, "fate" stepped in.

One morning, sometime in early April, as I was cleaning out the coffee pot, I felt nauseous and threw up and continued to do so almost continually for the next three months. When I wasn't throwing up I was sleeping. During that time I often said that Bob must truly love me to put up with all of it.

We were going to have a baby sometime in the middle of December. Holding a job under the circumstances of early pregnancy, for me, was not doable. However, surprised as we were (we had planned on waiting two years before starting a family), we were happy about it. Money would be tight, but we didn't mind the thought of being poor for a while longer.

DuPont finally followed up on the application Bob had sent them way back in November and had him fly up to their headquarters in Delaware, but they decided they didn't want him. Bob was beginning to realize he should look actively for a job in his chosen field of Chemistry if he wanted to do something with it and before he forgot everything he had learned. The promise of management training and a promotion to plant manager in Pompano Beach had sounded good, but there were no guarantees. And even in paradise, a job like that could become boring. There would be no scope for him to learn new things, even if there were opportunities to improve his golf game.

One day as he was getting some test tubes out of a box, he noticed the address label. It said, "Corning Glass Works, Corning, New York." He had never heard of the company, even though it was famous for its Pyrex cooking ware. Lou typed up a nice letter asking for an application and one came back soon after.

Corning Glass Works had been established in 1868 when it had been moved to Corning via the Erie Canal from Brooklyn, New York, its original location. Some of their earlier products were still produced in the '50s, such as railroad signal ware, thermometer tubing and pharmaceutical glassware. Thomas Edison asked Corning to produce the first incandescent bulb blanks in 1879. It was a good company with a good reputation.

About two weeks after he sent the application back to Corning, he got this letter:

CORNING GLASS WORKS
Corning, New York
In reply refer to:
E. S. Stebbings

July 27, 1951
Mr. Robert Beasley
208 North 10th Avenue
Jacksonville Beach, Florida

Dear Mr. Beasley:

We are in receipt of your application of July 19th and
wish to advise that we have an opening in our Research and
Development Laboratory. This opening carries a weekly salary
of $461.75 a month for a 37½ hour week. However, most of
staff is working 40 hours a week so that your weekly take-home
pay would be a little greater. Please advise if you are interested
in this position and when you could report to work.

Final employment is contingent upon a satisfactory physical
examination at our plant hospital.


Very truly yours,

E. S. Stebbings

To be offered a job like that, sight unseen, was highly unusual.
Needless to say, it was unexpected. Bob took very little time deciding
whether or not to take the offer. He found out a little more about the
Glass Works and its good reputation. And someone told Lou that the
country around Corning was "gorgeous."

To Bob it was another one of those times when good things just
happened to him.

He wrote back and accepted. He asked to be given two weeks to
give notice to Niagara. They wanted him to report to work on August
27, 1951.

Jezebel found a new home with my parents in Eustis. On the way
up to Corning, we stayed overnight in Maryland to visit my family
there. Bob got to meet most of his new relatives at a shore picnic at my
aunt Ann's house on the Magothy River.

# Chapter Three

# Corning Glass Works

Early Saturday evening on August 25, we came into Corning. So far nothing had looked gorgeous. In fact, it was depressing. One little coffee shop was still open and we had something to eat. We hadn't seen any motels on the outskirts and it looked like there were none in town. The waitress in the coffee shop said there were some cabins for rent in the woods on the road to Horseheads. They had a vacancy, but there were no restaurants anywhere close by for breakfast the next morning. All we could do was go to sleep in the lumpy bed and at least be thankful for that.

Perhaps because we were naïve about what companies did for new employees, we hadn't asked for help about moving. And we weren't offered any, either.

The next morning, Sunday, both of us realized we were really on our own in a new world, so after breakfast at the same coffee shop, we decided to look for a church. There was a little Christian Science Church in town in an old renovated house and we decided to go there for comfort, if for nothing else. The order of service was simple and comforting and the hymns uplifting.

It turned out to be another one of those good things that happened to us. There were other young couples there, too and small children and warm and friendly older people and even a vice president from the Glass Works. The soloist, who was also the wife of the high school football coach, rented rooms and one would be vacant on Monday night and we could move into it if we liked. There was even an invitation to a Labor Day party at someone's beach house on Lake Keuka (one of the Finger Lakes) the next week.

Monday, the twenty-seventh, Bob thought he should leave early and find out where he was to report to work. Neither of us had any breakfast. I said I'd just stay in bed and sleep until he got back.

This was the first time I had ever seen Bob unsure of himself, but I knew why. He would be going into a job where he would have to prove himself and he wasn't sure he even knew enough to get by. That afternoon he got back to the cabin feeling much better. He had found the main gate downtown, passed his physical and all was well. He thought he would like the Glass Works.

He also found out why he had been hired sight unseen. Later it was written up in Stetson's Alumni Magazine, *The Pro Veritate* in the summer of 1981:

What happened next might be called providential. In Corning's New York office, a Stetson graduate who had also studied under Dr. Conn discovered Bob's application. Ray Voss, '41, thought that Stetson would be a good place to look for the additional manpower Corning then needed. He called Dr. Conn and enquired about Beasley.

"I knew Dr. Conn to be a good evaluator of people, so when he gave Bob a good evaluation, I had confidence in suggesting Bob for the position. We were good friends and colleagues for close to ten years," Voss recently recalled.

That evening, we moved into a pleasant room upstairs in the Jacoby's house. After asking around, we found there were several apartment complexes, one about quarter of a mile from the Glass Works and one a few miles out of town.

The one—and two-story, town-like buildings had been built very cheaply during the Second World War and were inexpensive to rent. We chose the one close to work. It was aptly named Crystal Gardens because it was laid on a foundation of a large run of melted glass cullet that had had too many flaws to be used. We rented a small, one-bedroom apartment, about the same size as the one we had just left, but instead of a distant beach view, we could look across the busy, wide main street to a filling station and a New York State Armory. But it was a home and we were grateful for it. And it was affordable. Bob had taken a cut in salary to come to Corning and things would be very close. We wouldn't be able to afford a phone right away or a delivered newspaper.

We figured out that if I felt the baby coming, I could run across the street and phone Bob from the filling station. And he saw a lot of discarded newspapers at work and could bring one home at night. He figured out that we would be able to start a savings account in about six months.

Bob was settling in well at work, too and knew it was exactly the right place for him to be. Glass Chemistry was a new field and he was right in the middle of it. But the town was another thing. Very few newcomers really liked living in Corning. It was only fifteen miles from Watkins Glen, reputed to have the least sunshine than any other place in the country. It seemed to be that way in Corning, too. The town lay in a narrow valley surrounded by hills formed aeons ago by glaciers. The one behind Crystal Gardens was called Rattlesnake Hill. The sun cleared the hills long after sunrise and let itself back down at an early hour in the evening. In the winter, there were snow flurries quite often but rarely enough to cover the ground.

There were pleasant towns outside the valley: Horseheads, Painted Post, Big Flats, Bath, Bolivar (named after Simon Bolivar and pronounced Bollaver) and the big city to the south, Elmira. Cornell University, Binghamton and Rochester were easy to get to. The countryside around Corning and the other small towns were still bucolic in the '50s. It made me think of an older era of hollyhocks, white picket fences and pictures on calendars of little girls in sunbonnets holding baskets of kittens.

The Chemung River was one of the divisions that cut the town in half. Along the south side of the river, there was a small baseball stadium and an empty field. Corning had a Hot Stove League team. A concrete bridge spanned the river and was part of the main street, Centerway, which led to the Glass Works' main gate and the downtown. In the past, the shallow, rocky stream sometimes rose and flooded the town and the Army Corps of Engineers, concreted its natural banks with dikes. Across the river from Crystal Gardens and on one of the higher hills were the large homes of the important people at Corning. At the top, the Houghton family, owners of Corning Glass Works, had their mansion. On the street below lived the vice presidents and so on down to the valley floor. We lived all the way across the river. Most of those houses down there were painted dull colors.

At one time, way back, when Corning was a logging community, the railroad laid tracks secretly through the middle of the town after midnight to thwart the objections of the townspeople who were against it. In 1951, people trying to get from one side of town to the other still had to wait, sometimes as long as a half hour for freight cars to trundle through and sometimes even longer when the train would stop inexplicably with its last cars covering the crossing. Though it had been many years since the engines let off soot and ashes, owners still painted their tall, clapboarded homes gray or brown to hide the dirt. There was another section of town, Southside, with older houses, too, but which was a little homier.

But it wasn't all bad. Very nice people lived there, some newcomers like us and those whose families had lived there for quite a few generations. Almost everyone was connected in some way with the Glass Works. There was a little section of new homes not too far from Crystal Gardens in a little park. The downtown had some nice stores. There was a very nice Tudor-style library and Bob was very happy to see the Fox Movie Theater. The small Frederick Carder Museum, a forerunner of Steuben Glass, the expensive, hand-blown glass the Glass Works produced, was located on the main street. Around 1954, Woolworth's opened a store and was a huge success.

At the end of the bridge, as it came into the downtown area, was the Glass Works Main Gate. At that time, it was the main entrance to everything; manufacturing, business offices and even the research labs.

Traffic circled around an old clock tower, an old landmark that is still there. A touch of class across from the Main Gate was the Baron Steuben Hotel, the only restaurant that used white linen tablecloths and napkins. This is where most of the visiting VIPs stayed.

One great redeeming feature in town, just a few blocks from Crystal Gardens, was the new Corning Glass Center built in 1951 to celebrate its centennial year. An early brochure said it was dedicated to the art, science and history of glassmaking. Part of the large building held the Glass Museum with its grand collection of ancient and modern glass. The objects were arranged chronologically with the earliest about thirty-five hundred years old. In another section, Corning's household products were featured and visitors could push buttons on a screen to indicate which new designs of kitchenware they liked best. Everyone liked the special studio for Steuben Glass. Talented glass blowers and etchers sat behind large windows and did their magic in front of an audience. It was an outgrowth of an earlier company and named after Steuben County where it was first produced.

There was also the Performing Arts Center. The Cleveland Symphony Orchestra performed there regularly. We purchased season tickets and were gaining some sophistication in music appreciation. We never forgot the deep joy of hearing Andres Segovia play his classical guitar.

Bob was finding his way around the lab, making friends and beginning to learn about glass and ceramics. He said it was like going to graduate school. Dr. John Sheldon was a mentor to him.

### *Excerpt from 1994 tape*

The first man I was assigned to was Dr. Sheldon. I arrived and was sent to his office, which was just like Fibber McGee's closet. You could hardly open the door with all the stuff on the floor, on the benches and the tables and the desk and wherever. And so, I went in and Dr. Sheldon had this guy, Harold Travis, his gofer to take me around. I guess he wanted me out of his hair, so for about a week, I followed this fellow around with nothing to do. I stayed right behind him and I followed. That was it.

Dr. Sheldon, in the afternoon, would like to come out of his office and look through my microscope. He had a background in them; I think he had taught how to use them in school. But anyway, he would look through my microscope and show me different things and how to use it. And though I had not been trained in this field at all, it was from that time with Dr. Sheldon that I learned a great deal of information. I appreciate the time he spent with me. But it was a hard time for Gloria, though, because she would have to wait dinner for me. He would always show up just about quitting time and he wouldn't mind talking late.

Sheldon was going to be involved in what they thought would be a good idea . . . to make aperture masks for color television . . . out of a photosensitive glass that Dr. Stookey had invented. They set up a lab, if you want to call it that, to investigate photosensitive glass. And the thing that I did first . . . I guess since I was a chemist . . . I was the only one to conduct the work of etching the photosensitive glass. So, I etched the glass, the aperture mask, with hydrofluoric acid.

When I first started out . . . television . . . black and white television came out of World War II with radar bulbs, round radar bulbs. And after the World War they had this ability to make round bulbs. They were black and white bulbs and just about then, when I was there, they were beginning to think about color television. It was to be with a much larger bulb and you had to put a shadow mask inside of it. And then later, you put on the face mask—the face part of the bulb. I knew that the photosensitive shadow mask that I was working on would have to be completely registered to fit around the new, larger bulbs, if we used them. And so I sagged one, to have the absolute contour to match the inside of the face mask. It would have the phosphorous dots put on it.

And they were quite excited because they were wondering how they could do it at about the same time I was out in the back room making it. Evidently, they were in a meeting and when they became aware that, that man, I already had it, they became quite excited.

The interesting thing is that we had a pilot plant run and as sometimes happens when you have a pilot plant run, things don't go exactly right. The photosensitive glass, all of a sudden, was so photosensitive that you felt like you couldn't smoke in the same room with it, because it was so sensitive to heat. And so, the pilot run was really brought to a skidding stop because of the failure of the melt of glass. The large melt of glass would ultimately become what is now Pyroceram. In other words, it didn't need any photosensitivity to it, it just needed heat. And so, Stookey used that material to make Pyroceram.

### *Letter to Mark and Lou, August 12, 1953*

Dear Folks,

I guess you know by now that Color TV will be out by the end of the year unless one of the industries raises an objection. The sets will be too expensive and changes rapid after they come out—so when your set is a few years older from now, then you can get a color set.

I am working hard. You know we are setting up a new Pilot Plant run of our aperture masks—about $1,000 per period to begin with (sometime in the future). Management allotted $500,000 for a run, but it already looks like a million will be more like it. Anyway, they are building a tank to melt our glass and are going to light it August 27th—then the fun begins! This is really a big step, my first project going into Pilot Plant and someday probably to production. The Glass Works is banking everything on the "sagged mask" (of course they can make flat ones) and I was the first one to sag an aperture mask. It makes me feel good to not only know that I have contributed something, but to put my fingerprint on it and show what it is.

The first RCA tubes will not have glass aperture masks—instead, they will have metal masks—but the glass will come—especially since we can sag them and that is impossible to do with metal. The sagged mask was not my idea since Corning is not originating ideas, but is working in conjunction with the different companies. I merely heard that someday in the future better tubes could be made if an aperture mask could be curved to the same curvature as the face of the TV panel. So last February, I started work on my own to see if a mask could not simply be "sagged" (by heating) to this shape. I'll never forget my first attempt (a success), for I put the sagged mask on my desk and stepped out of my office for a moment. When I came back, I saw Dr. Munier running down the hall with it and everyone has been running ever since.

The mask was flown up to CBS Hytron immediately and they were so excited that they pounded on the desk wanting to go into production right then and there, for this made them feel that they had something that day which they only hoped might be obtained sometime in the distant future. RCA will use their flat mask to begin with, because they are ready to get it approved and to start producing it.

Corning is putting a lot of money up—saying that a sagged mask will find its place in industry. Of course we know it may not be used at all, but at least I have the satisfaction knowing I contributed a small amount to the development of color TV. I just thought I would tell you about the "sagged mask" for I don't recall mentioning it before. It's funny how things work out. I sagged the first mask just as interest in a flat glass aperture plate died completely (possibly to be resumed in a few years, but until then there would be no interest). And ever since the first sagged mask there has been more interest and push on our product than ever before. Management doesn't sink a million dollars into something for nothing.

Tonight I went to a dinner at the club held for all involved in color TV and they (management representatives) told us that between the colored bulb (Corning will be the sole producer except what they let out to avoid anti-trust) and the sagged aperture mask, we had presented them with a blank check for its future. It makes us feel good, to say the least.

The weather has been cool and pleasant. I believe the only complaint I have in the world now is that my St. Louis

Cardinals are a miserable 4th in the pennant race. We are healthy, solvent and happy. Gloria is beginning to like Corning and I am, too.

I'm sorry I haven't written very much, but so many times after work, I don't like sitting down at night. I hope to do better as time goes on and there is less pressure at work. Please don't let that stop you from writing whenever possible.

Love,

Bob

Bob benefited greatly in knowing Dr. Donald Stookey, one of the best-known and inventive glass scientists in the world. His inventions covered not only unbreakable dinnerware, but Fotoform, a photosensitive glass on which photographs could be reproduced, going all the way through giving a 3D effect. (The glass was used on the façade of the United Nations Building in New York.) Among many other breakthroughs, he invented very special laboratory ware, Vycor that could stand very high heat.

Dr. Fred Bickford was his first lab boss at Corning. Bob respected him very much as a hands-on, hard working scientist who didn't mind getting his hands dirty. In some ways, he emulated Bickford's style when he had his own lab, enjoying working out how to get the job at hand done and letting those who worked with him enjoy it along with him. It was a perfect environment for a new, eager-to-learn junior scientist.

The Glass Works library was a great source of information for him. He spent many hours taking notes from various periodicals and books on the many different aspects of glass and ceramics. He explored and consumed enough information to allow him to feel he could contribute something to the research department. And he was always ready to listen to someone who knew more than he did.

He was also making good friends, Ray Voss, Forrest Peters, John Dunne, Bill Kroeck, Harold Stetson, Mary Splann and Tom Vasilos, Joe Dunbeck, Joe Sullivan, among others. It didn't seem to matter at Corning then, whether one had a higher degree or not, as it did later, at

Lockheed. Dr. William Armistead was a fair and respected director of research.

### Excerpt from 1994 tape

Well, experience, it all seems to point to something eventually and when I was working on the photosensitive glass, I became aware of many things. For an example, I became aware of an air leak in the furnace. Because we were not getting uniformity of the development, I traced it to an air leak in the furnace. And also, even a fingerprint . . . when you were etching something in hydrofluoric acid . . . why a fingerprint would get fired in . . . the sodium from a fingerprint could get fired into the glass . . . and make its composition different. It would etch differently. Later on, that became interesting. And, also, sodium, what it would do to glass, became of interest.

Now, what else did I work on? I think it was Dr. Dalton who had a concept for a new controlled ceramic. Ceramics are refractory particles. For example, luminescence ceramics are particles of aluminum—aluminum oxide all cemented together with a glass phase. And even pottery is that, more or less. And Dalton thought we could make a control . . . the dielectric property of an alumina ceramic, if we were to take the aluminum oxide powder and mix it with a powder of a very specially melted glass phase. It worked beautifully, but it was not used. As a matter of fact, today I think that they have a product called Glassics that's glass and ceramics.

But in this, I had the opportunity to get in on melting the glass composition, which is a very, very protected thing, a secret thing at Corning: the composition of the actual glasses. They don't melt compositions, they melt numbers. They melt five parts of number six and one part of number five and so on and that's the way they make it up, to keep it secret. But I was lucky in that I got to be in the very tight fraternity of glass chemists at Corning.

I was able to melt glasses and study the influence of their composition on the dielectric properties. And in doing this, I not only found various things that they already knew about the influence on the composition . . . on the dielectric properties . . . but I found out that some of their very best electrical glasses . . . that had electrical properties, were influenced by different ingredients, for an example, sodium. And I made a study by varying and decreasing the amount of sodium in the components of these compositions and the study of their influence on the dielectric property. And I found that this, in some instances, no matter how pure you could make it, you could still detect its influence. And that had an influence all the way into my silica work.

# Interdepartmental Communication
**From W. H. Armistead, Director of Research at Corning**
To: Mr. R. M. Beasley

cc: Mr. J. P. Dunn
Mr. W. H. Kroeck
Mr. H. Stetson
Dr. T. Vasilos
Mr. R. O. Voss
October 19, 1956

Thank you for your fine Summary of the Alumina Electrical Ceramic Research Program. This work has been very well done and it has brought forcibly to our attention the very great importance of alkali impurity on high temperature electrical properties of glass.

It is unfortunate that the glass composition men have, in a sense, let the ceramic group "down" by not supplying you with better glasses needed to formulate better electrical ceramics. I feel personally responsible for this state of affairs, for not having pushed a vigorous glass composition development program to get you the "extra good glass" so obviously needed. Partly, this is due to our lack of high temperature, high frequency measuring equipment which is needed for such a development. This equipment is now on order and should be received soon.

It may be that the "alkali-free" awareness created by the electrical ceramic research program will in time lead to the development of that "extra good" glass. Then we can evaluate our prospects in alumina electrical ceramics.

William H. Armistead

A year or two later, Dr. Edward Condon was hired at Corning as a director of research.

### *Excerpt from 1994 tape*

Dr. Condon was a very nice man. And would you believe it? He looked almost like Dr. Conn. He had been head of the Bureau of Standards in Washington, D.C. And along came the McCarthy Witch Hunt. Dr. Condon had earlier been on the faculty at The University of California, Berkeley. And as a faculty member at Berkeley he had many friends and evidently, among the people that came to his house, some weren't friends, but people who had just attended things there and one of the people was one McCarthy was drumming against. Remember, McCarthy would ruin people's lives by saying, 'Well, maybe they are not guilty, but they are a weak link to Communism,' and he drummed up so much about this past connection that Condon had with these people, though he had never done anything, he was called a weak link in the United States government. And so, with the furor that was raised, Dr. Condon had to leave the Government even though what he had was not a critical job. It was just the head of the Bureau of Standards and that was not a security risk job at all. And after that, Corning hired him.

I met him as a Director of Research. Dr. Sheldon had transferred by this time out of the laboratory and became one of the chief scientists of the Electrical Division. And he was interested in the ceramic glass—the alumina oxide which would have high, very good electrical properties.

It was set up that I would bring a sample out to the Bureau of Standards in Boulder, Colorado and also to Gladding McBean in California, out here on the Peninsula for tests. So a trip was set up for Dr. Sheldon and me to fly across the country with Dr. Condon who was going to introduce us at the Bureau of Standards and go on there to Berkeley and I was going on to L.A.

This was Bob's first business trip for Corning.

### Excerpt from 1994 tape

Corning always thought that their men on the road were an advertisement for the company . . . so they didn't have their people go to the local greasy spoon to eat, or travel on planes sitting in the tail in third class. We sat in First Class. So, on my first business trip, we arrived at the Brown Palace Hotel in Denver. And the surprising thing was that Dr. Sheldon and I were booked to share the same room and I have never done this before or since. Well, that night as we were going to bed, I asked if I should open a window. I think it was early spring. And here was this room, this huge room. I know the windows were about twelve feet high if not higher, just the largest room I had been in, since I lived in something like a cracker box. And I remember his comment, that we could live in that room for a month, even if it were hermetically sealed and never run out of air. So the window stayed closed.

One time, at a special luncheon for the department, for some reason, he never knew why, Bob was seated next to Dr. Condon who was at the head of the table. Dr. Condon was served first and though everyone started to eat when they were served, Dr. Condon waited until Bob was served, the last one. Bob was one of the least important people there. Indeed, Dr. Condon was a very nice man. In 1968, Dr. Condon left Corning to become the head of the Scientific Study of Unidentified Flying Objects at the University of Colorado, for the USAF.

It wasn't too far to the due date for the baby to be born that Bob found we were able to afford a phone. The two sets of parents would have gladly helped out with finances, but we wanted to make it on our own. We were poor but actually enjoying the challenge. There were a lot of Spam casseroles and doctored dishes of hot dogs and beans and homemade Christmas presents.

On December 15, 1951, on her due date, during a snow storm, Robin Marie Beasley was born, looking just like her father. He tried not to show his concern when I started early labor. Right after we found I was pregnant, while we were still in Florida, we went to the movies. It was a film in which Sophia Loren gave very graphic birth in a field. It frightened Bob so much that we had to leave. He thought it was terrible to scare people like that. He was cool enough, though, before we went to the hospital, to carefully shave and dress.

He had asked around at work how much the hospital charged for delivering babies. Since I was pregnant before he started working at Corning, we were not eligible for hospital insurance. He diligently saved enough to cover the fee and when he came to the hospital to bring Robin and me home, he said he swaggered up to the checkout desk with a roll of cash in his pocket only to find the fees had been raised. He said it was like letting the air out of a balloon. But he was allowed to take his family home and be billed the next month.

Now we were a real family—not just newlyweds. Bob enjoyed getting Robin ready for bed every night, in a crib crammed into our bedroom, but convenient for late-night feedings.

When summer came that year, he was given one week of vacation. There wasn't any money to go anywhere, but "fate" stepped in again. Around the lab someone started a weekly baseball pool at fifty cents a head for predicting baseball scores. Bob seldom bet on anything because he usually lost, but this time he won fifty dollars—just enough to get us down to Maryland to visit Aunt Ann and Uncle John. A phone call assured us we were welcome. It was usually open house anyway at the Beall's home on the Magothy, a tidewater river off the Chesapeake Bay. On the strength of those fifty dollars, we could afford enough gas for a round trip, buy our share of groceries and take everyone out to dinner at Buschmann's Restaurant down the road.

Every year after that, while we were in Corning, for our two-week vacation we drove down to Florida to visit the parents in Jacksonville and Eustis. Bob had a chance to play golf and I said that for me, at least it was a change. The highlight of these vacations were seeing family, going to the beach and making a quick stop at Stetson.


After several years and several raises, we thought it was time for Robin to have a new brother or sister. That meant a larger place to live. Across the parking lot was a row of two-story, two-bedroom apartments, complete with basements and still affordable. They faced a little weedy front yard instead of the busy main street and one of them became vacant. Its previous tenants were famous for their little boy, about three, who one day sat with his legs dangling over the sill of his upstairs bedroom window and said in a loud, deep voice like his father's, "What the hell is going on down there?"

### Letter to Mark and Lou, August 1953


We are very pleased and happy in our new apartment, for there is adequate room for the time being anyway. The heating system, which we have had occasion to use in the mornings, is very good and I am looking forward to a nice toasty winter without any cold rooms and corners. Even though to rent is high ($74.00 a month) we don't feel pressured to buy a home like we used to do when we were so cramped. I've been busy painting and fixing up since we've been here. My present project is to paint the basement and build shelves.

Money was less tight and we could afford meals out once in a while and hire babysitters. Life was good. Aunt Ida, who worked in the fabric department of Cohen Brothers in Jacksonville, sent us some slipcover material to cover our mismatched sofa and chair. We were still in our old apartment when we decided to make the slipcovers ourselves. We rented a sewing machine and Bob, after work, pulled down the shades, lit a big fat cigar to affirm his manhood (he said) and pinned and cut out the fabric for me to sew. It turned out quite well. He had worked it out already in his head before he started. That was the way he tackled all his work.

Amy Lou Beasley, after waiting a couple of weeks after her due date, was born, during a rainstorm, shortly after midnight on June 11, 1954. She looked like herself. Bob loved having two little daughters.

Work at Corning continued to be interesting. The lab continued to expand and at one time, Corning rented an empty building downtown in which Bob and Forrest Peters carried out experiments using, among other things, a ball mill, which polished and rounded pieces of glass and ceramics. The two really enjoyed the freedom of that little building.

Bob usually walked to work. It was about a quarter of a mile away and usually enjoyable except in the winter when early morning snow flurries blew horizontally across the bridge. It was the first time he wore a felt hat. He said it kept his head twenty degrees warmer. The old Chevy was traded in for a used, two-door Chevy hardtop.

We acquired another family member. Manly was a marmalade cat, a present from our egg man. Bob named him Manly after Stan "the Man" Musial of the St. Louis Cardinals, his favorite baseball team.

Bob's favorite Saturday activity in the summer was to lie prone in a comfortable position, turn on the radio and listen to whatever baseball game that was being played. It was very soporific for him.

The background noise and the voices of the commentators usually put him to sleep.

He also liked to listen with Robin, who was just a little over two, to Big John and Sparky, a children's program. He especially liked the theme song, "The Teddy Bears' Picnic" (if you go down to the woods today, you're in for a big surprise).

We also bought our first TV, a secondhand black and white nineteen inch portable Zenith. A little old lady, who only watched it on Sunday afternoons after church, sold it to us. Now we could watch the Mickey Mouse Club, Ed Sullivan and Dinah Shore singing about seeing the USA in a Chevrolet. It turned out to be a good buy and still worked when we gave it away ten years later. Unfortunately, Manly died about a year later and Bob buried him on the plot of ground we had just bought.

Bob had continued to get raises and a good bit of it was put in a savings account. A small housing development had been started out of town on the way to Elmira called Hickling Heights. Several friends were building homes there. We found a lot we liked, a quarter acre with a hedgerow of trees along one side. A well was dug and when we had more money apart from savings, we planned to build our own home. We had a catalogue of prebuilt homes in kits. We loved the one called the Iris and wanted one just like it.

In June of 1956, Bob was sent to MIT for a two-week summer session on "Theories and Practices of Ceramic Forming." The children and I were able to go along and we stayed with family friends in an apartment in an old, large brownstone on Commonwealth Avenue in Boston. And in June of 1957, he was selected to attend a Gordon Research Conference at New Hampton, New Hampshire and I was able to go with him.

The Gordon Conferences were (and still are) held for the purpose of providing a place for presentation and discussion of new ideas in biology, chemistry and education in an informal setting. Only active persons in their field were accepted. For Bob, it was an exciting exchange of ideas and an opportunity to meet others who, like him, were able to look at all six sides of a problem and then open it up to see what was inside. Discussions started on Sunday evening and continued with morning and evening sessions through Thursday. He considered it a privilege to be there.

The theme of the one Bob attended was "Metals at High Temperatures." Seventeen people (out of fifty-eight attendees) gave papers during the first section and Bob was asked to conduct the discussion of observations and conversations at the end of the session.

In his report on the conference back at Corning, he showed there was special interest in the higher temperature ranges that missiles encountered during reentry and in composite structures for guided missiles. Higher temperatures to metallurgists were between 1000 degrees F and 2000 degrees F. He also noted much interest in Dr. Stookey's Pyroceram. DuPont, especially, was interested in Pyroceram pipe and tubing. He closed his report saying, "I believe that this is a real opening for Corning Glass Works in the missile field. However, proper test data will be needed."

His career was going well; he was associated with many respected scientists and was receiving raises as well as promotions. He was learning about the depth of glass and ceramic research, new things just beginning to come to light.

### Reports: September 1951 to June 1957

### Process and Product Development September 1951-July 1954

This work involved developing practical processes for materials in the laboratory curiosity stage and then engineering them into useful products. Because of the unique properties of these new materials, they were usually parts to be used in components for the electronics field. Some examples of these parts are aperture masks proposed for color TV (actually worked on practically every system proposed for color TV—RCA, CBS, DuMont, Lawrence, etc., storage tubes, characton tubes, potentiometers, printed circuits, etc.).

I have helped plan, set up and equip four new laboratories and a large-scale plant operation.

## Development of Technical Ceramics July 1954-June 1957

These high alumina ceramics were designed (dielectric properties) to be used in high frequency electrical applications such as magnetron windows, klystrons, miniature tubes, etc. Responsible for composition work, developing practical processing procedures, fabrication techniques, firing, testing and evaluation. Supervised six people in these activities.

This project was later changed to the present permanent Ceramic Research Department of which I am now a member. This work also enabled Corning to obtain classified government contracts on ceramics.

Recent memo to me from Director of Research: "Thank you for your fine '*Summary of the Alumina Electrical Ceramic Research Program.*' This work has been well done and has brought forcibly to our attention the very great importance of alkali impurity on the high temperature electrical properties of glass."

Presently investigating the factors that influence the mechanical and thermal behavior of polycrystalline materials at temperatures near their melting point; our long-range aim is to develop high strength, high temperature materials.

He was also honored by being asked to work in Dr. Stookey's lab. It was a hard decision to turn it down. It was never offered formally, so he could do so without seeming to be unappreciative. Had he stayed, working under Dr. Stookey, he would have had little opportunity to work on new ideas that kept coming to him that were not related to Dr. Stookey's work. It was about this time he knew he would have to leave Corning.

Bob's feelings about a move were strengthened by a confidential talk with a recently retired Corning vice president whom he respected and admired. He told Bob that he probably had gone as far as he could go on his own at Corning, even though he and his work were respected. It was nearly a year before the next right step showed up.

### *Excerpt from 1994 tape*

After about six and a half years, I don't know, I look back and I felt I just wasn't getting anywhere. There were no particularly interesting things to work on and I had filtered down to working on just the same old thing all the time. And so I decided it was time to leave. I even thought that maybe I would change my career and study business and be able to change to something else.

We sent out applications everywhere and I did see one little ad in the American Ceramic Society Bulletin for a company I never heard of called Horizons Incorporated, located in Cleveland, Ohio. I sent them an application and they asked me to come over on a weekend. It ended up that I got the job.

Our first home in Corning, on the right, 1950

Forrest Peters, Dr. Fred Bickford, Pierre Landron, Bob,
in the Research and Development Lab, Corning, 1954

Our first slipcover!, 1952

# Chapter Four

# Horizons Incorporated

## Horizons Incorporated

2905 East 79th Street

Cleveland, 4, Ohio

October 11, 1957

**Mr. Robert M. Beasley**

20 Fulton Street

Corning, New York

Dear Mr. Beasley,

We enjoyed your visit with us on October 4, 1957 and all of us were favorably impressed with you. We believe there is a real opportunity for professional growth in our organization at this time. The Ceramics Department is only starting its real growth, which presents the unusual situation of virtual ground-floor opportunity.

I have been authorized to offer you a position at Horizons as Projects Supervisor at a starting salary of $800 per month. Horizons would reimburse you for the cost of moving up to the sum of $500 against applicable invoices. This offer remains open to you for one month after the date of this letter.

Because your visit here was so short, you may desire to visit us again to become better acquainted with us and with the Cleveland community. Should you have that feeling, we would be happy to arrange with you another visit.

I think it would be mutually beneficial to have you join our organization and we are looking forward to hearing from you soon.

Yours sincerely,

C. G. Harman

### Horizons Incorporated

Head, Ceramics Department

Cleveland, at that time, was not considered a very desirable place to live. But it was a big city and both Bob and I had lived near big cities and liked them. And Cleveland had a good baseball team (Cleveland Indians and Catfish Hunter), a university, Western Reserve and a world-renowned art museum. And Cleveland itself was surrounded by very livable communities. With the help of an agent, we looked at several rentals, but none of them seemed right.

The job was accepted. Corning said it was sad to see Bob leave and we were given several nice farewell parties and a Steuben glass bowl to remember everyone by.

We found an apartment in Shaker Heights about six miles from Horizons. It was downstairs in a double house and even had a fireplace I hoped to have. The house seemed like a Tudor mansion compared to what we had in Corning, even though we only lived in the downstairs half of it. Even the movers thought so as they brought in the rather meager amount of furniture from Corning. Bob would be traveling a lot and having the neighbors upstairs gave me a sense of having someone close when he was gone.

Shaker Heights, originally a real Shaker community was a town of beautiful homes, built in the early twenties as a restricted community, but no longer had that stigma. The style of architecture ran to Tudor, Georgian, Federal and some, just plain palatial. The streets were tree lined and even the less expensive areas of two-family homes were charming. If there had been a running stream through it, the town would have resembled the paintings of Thomas Kinkade

Work at Horizons was going to be interesting and his coworkers easy to work with. They became instant friends. Neighbors were friendly, too and our new landlord, Anton Kelvin, introduced us to a friend who helped us to buy our first refrigerator and stove and some furniture to fill up the empty spaces. Our upstairs neighbors, the Derys, became family. One of their daughters babysat for us. Alex Dery was a part-time artist and he invited me to join his art group. It was good to be able to hone my art skills a little.

Money wasn't as scarce either and we often went to Shaker Square after church on Sunday for brunch at Stouffers and sometimes to the Cleveland Art Museum or for drives in the lovely Ohio countryside.

### *Excerpt from 1994 tape*

Looking back, I'm rather stunned that I made this move but things worked for the best. The thing that stuns me is that Horizons was a company that had no products. The only thing that it did . . . it did research for government and industry, so its one product was its brains. But the thing that stuns me when I look back in my mind's eye, I realized that I left Corning—a hundred year old company of rather large size and fairly well-known—and I went to one in Cleveland, down in the very, poorest of poor sections of Cleveland.

It had been a laundry . . . they had taken it and divided it up a little bit with an office or two and then just a vast area which then they could put some benches in and call it a lab. And, so I left what seemed to be security for this change, but it was the best move I ever made and I know I was led to do it.

Horizon's work was research for government and industry. That was their only product. And so, as such, it meant that I had many varied tasks. I remember one problem a rubber glove manufacturer had. They used beautiful, ceramic-glazed forms in the shape of a hand, which they would then dip into latex. And they had a problem that there would be little imperfections on the latex gloves. It was very eerie to be in the place where they dried the gloves—thousands of pale hands hanging down from the ceiling. And it developed, after looking at it, I found the problem really was the glaze on the forms had little bubbles in it, which, if they popped, they made a depression for the latex to grab hold of and be deformed. And so, from that, I worked on correcting the formulation for the glaze, which wasn't their glaze, but it was a glaze that they had bought. So, I worked out that . . . both a way to repair it and also how to fix the problem the manufacturer of the form had in the first place—how they could change their glaze to not have bubbles.

Another problem was that a brick manufacturer, all of a sudden, couldn't make bricks anymore. The carriers would come out of the kilns . . . instead of bricks, they would be piles of sand and he didn't know what happened. I investigated that and found out, "Well, your grandfather may have built this factory and this business on top of a nice clay deposit for bricks, but in the generation past—you now only have sand; you've used up all the clay." Now, forty years later, I don't know what the owner did about it, but at least the problem was identified.

There was another problem I worked on. There was a plating manufacturer who worked around the clock. He had these great, large vats of liquids—solutions in which they hung down their racks of materials to be plated on. And all of a sudden, their quality control just went out of whack. Their yields were practically nothing, particularly for one shift. Of course, it got dispersed so they could hardly tell which shift, but there was this problem. And so we investigated and couldn't find that there was anything wrong with the process at all. Nothing was wrong. And yet, the problem persisted. So, eventually we put up a camera without people knowing it, over the tanks. And we found out that really late in the wee hours of the morning, on that shift, not always, but sometimes, one of the men would have to urinate; and so it was his habit to urinate in the tank. And of course, that just destroyed all the chemistry in the tank and ruined all the plating for that shift and for numbers of shifts after that until the tank was refilled. And so that was the problem. I guess the employee left the company and they were alert to the problem from then on.

Another problem I worked on . . . someone wanted bricks glazed . . . and I worked on a glaze for bricks and another glaze for Hall ceramics and Hall pottery, which I didn't know anything about.

And it came from that, I was trying to develop things—ideas that I could sell. And one of the things that came to me was they wanted to make a radome shape. And I thought about doing it by winding filaments, so I unraveled glass fiber from a glass cloth and wound it around something, I don't remember what and saturated it with Ludox, which was a source of colloidal silica from the DuPont Company. I was organically winding glass fibers and inorganically bonding them with silica, but there was no way to sell it.

But there was another job that came along. Someone had a product called Inlay Crete. Back east in the old, old, buildings there were lots of buildings that were put up with cement floors. And the cement floors over the many years developed cracks in them and crumpled and whatever. And so this company had a product they called Inlay Crete. It was to inlay a new material over the top of concrete to resurface it. They had a product and had done well, I guess, with it. But, all of a sudden they had a problem that their Inlay Crete in itself, made cracks. And so I started mixing up cement. I got a cement mixer, which I knew nothing about, mixing up cement and making blocks and working on it. And while I worked and made these blocks coated with Inlay Crete, I found out that really the problem was . . . and this delighted the manufacturer . . . the problem was that people when they mixed up their Inlay Crete didn't really follow the directions exactly and they varied their water content. If they put in too much water it would crack. And if they didn't use too much water it wouldn't crack.

And so, the thing that delighted them . . . I found out the thing to do was to use less water, really reduce the amount of water that you would mix with your Inlay Crete. And to do that, I used a surfactant . . . a wetting agent. And that really solved the problem. And the company was delighted because they thought, 'Oh, now we have a new product. We're going to sell wet water.' Whether they did or not, I don't know.

It seems as though I had become a science detective, with all I did at Horizons and at Corning with the fingerprints on the photosensitive glass, plus the melted photosensitive glass that could not be utilized or even smoked around because it was heat sensitive. And so it just seemed that there was one problem after another and I really ended up just being a detective.

Bob and Dr. Harman worked well together. Dr. Harman was also rather short and round with a shock of dark hair and a bulldog stance like Dr. Conn and Dr. Condon. Together they wrote a paper, "Possibilities of Inorganic Bonded Molding Materials," and in November 1959, Bob presented it to a conference given by The Steel Founders' Society of America. A letter was sent to Bob by its Technical and Research Director:

Dear Mr. Beasley:

The Technical and Operating Committee of Steel Founders' Society and I wish to express our grateful appreciation for the important part which you played in the success of our Fourteenth Annual Technical and Operation Conference. Your paper, *"Possibilities of Inorganic Bonding Materials,"* was of great interest to the audience. Your presentation of the paper was excellent and I have heard many complimentary remarks on it.

There were approximately 300 to 350 men at your session. This should indicate to you the interest they had in your paper and your remarks. I also want to thank you for the excellent way in which you cooperated to make our Beer and Discussion session such an interesting one.

Personally, I want to thank you for the excellent job you did in preparing and presenting the paper. I hope it was an interesting experience for you and that we can call on you again in the years to come. I assure you that your efforts were very much appreciated.

Congratulations on the exceptionally fine job!

Sincerely yours,

Charles Briggs

Technical and Research Director

Bob was good at giving talks about his work and could do so in interesting, low-key ways. While he was shy in social situations, he could hold his own when it came to talking about his scientific interests. He continued to attend symposiums and conferences related to the work at Horizons. He was away often and though he was always glad to be home, he enjoyed being away, too, if it wasn't too long a time. Though he loved his home and family, it was fun after a day's work in some town, to go out to dinner with his cohorts and not even have to think about domestic issues for a little while. Fortunately, few domestic issues came up.

Articles written in the small, in-house publication, "*Unfolding Horizons,*" shows the increasing interest in ceramic fibers in the manufacturing community and therefore in Horizon's Ceramics Laboratory. These articles show how fast high-temperature ceramics research and development were growing in just a few years. Bob was in the right place at the right time.

## Unfolding Horizons March-April 1958 Vol. 2, No. 2

### A New Era for Ceramics

An industrial revolution, triggered by new bold scientific developments rather than artisan's skill, is taking place today in one of the world's oldest industries, the ceramic industry.

Limitations once imposed by the clay-like materials have been overcome by the properties of entirely new classes of ceramics. Many of them are doing a far better job than the materials they replace and some of these startling new products do a job no other material can do.

Magnetic ceramics, more properly called ferrites, have emerged from the laboratory curiosities of the mid '40s to the radio receiver antenna rods, TV deflection yoke cores, microwave components and memory cores of today.

Besides vital and expanding applications in all types of electronic and communications equipment, both military and civilian, ferrites have branched out into such related fields as toys and door latches.

Ceramic or ferrite permanent magnets are so new that their possibilities have scarcely been touched. Their light weight and their employment of all non-strategic materials (rather than cobalt and nickel used in metal magnets) are added factors in their favor.

Although the magnetic properties of ferrites have allowed some reduction in size of magnetic components, no story of miniaturization is more dramatic than that of ceramic capacitors and printed circuits. Developed in World War II, barium titanate and titanium oxide electronic components have allowed important size reductions in everything from proximity fuses to portable radios and TVs.

The unique electrical properties of these materials are as important as the size reductions they permit. Some ceramic compositions have been developed with dielectric constants as high as 10,000-20,000 for special applications permitting entirely new design and circuitry.

One of the more recent developments which promises to expand the design possibilities of ceramics still further is metalizing. Metal coating can be tightly bonded to a ceramic shape, which, in turn, allows that shape to be brazed, welded, soldered, or otherwise fastened to metal parts. These metalized

coatings have made possible ceramic-to-metal seals in
vacuum tubes. They've also made possible a wide range of
ceramic-to-metal assemblies where the abrasion resistance
of ceramic materials in certain spots can improve an overall
structure.

As startling as some of these developments have been, they
seem only the forerunner of far more widespread application
of these new ceramic materials. Evidence indicates they may
be the forerunner of still more new classes of materials such
as fiber-reinforced ceramics which will help the industrial
revolution in ceramics roll forward with even greater force.


## Unfolding Horizons March-April, 1959 Vol. 3 No. 1

(Under the heading of: Research in the Year Ahead)

### Trends in New Products

### Materials to Resist Excessively High Temperatures

In the art of modern weaponry and specifically in the
building of missiles there have been recurring slow-ups and
even complete stoppages of progress due to lack of materials
of construction which are capable of tolerating terrifically high
temperatures developed in the burning of propulsive fuels.

To solve these problems a great deal of attention has been
devoted to scientific building of materials which are not known
to appear in nature. These materials are produced by a process
of synthesis involving a combination of previously known
materials or elements in very precise ways.

Similarly, even though certain organic fibers of considerable
importance (generally known as asbestos) are available in
nature, these high temperature problems require a fibrous
material of much higher melting point to provide the means of
fabricating structures of low bulk density for thermal insulation
purposes. Such fibers also have the potential incorporation into
metal and ceramic structures to achieve, at least in part, the

familiar reinforcing action typified by the use of steel bars and wire in concrete aggregates.

Presently, scientists and technologists have succeeded only in producing fairly short lengths of these interesting inorganic fibers. However, it is clear that ways and means will be found to produce these in almost endless lengths to be used in the weaving of fabrics of phenomenal strength and temperature resistance. Reference has been made to ceramic structures incorporating fibers. It is interesting to note, in this connection, that through these means plus other developments, it appears that ceramic structures and materials are well on their way to replacing metals and metallic alloys as basic materials of construction. In those areas where high temperatures are advantageous, such as propulsion of missiles and other vehicles, it is obvious that metals, with the possible exclusion of titanium, tungsten and similar high melting point metals of which there are but a few, will be replaced with ceramics. In addition to greater resistance to temperatures shown by the ceramics over metals, they have the greater advantage that generally they are much lighter and will provide the all-important weight saving advantages so vital in modern weaponry. While it is always hazardous to predict what future scientific developments will yield; it now appears rather certain that the age of metals, so far as new applications are concerned, may be coming to an end and we may be coming to a new age of ceramics; new because a prehistoric age of ceramics preceded the age of metals.

## Unfolding Horizons June-July, 1959 Vol. 3, No. 2

### New Ceramic Fibers Resist Elevated Temperatures

In what is described as a "major scientific breakthrough" in the search for materials which may be successfully used at extremely elevated temperatures, is the announcement of the development of unique ceramic fibers by scientists at Horizons Incorporated.

Horizon's President, K. M. Bartlett states that these fibers are expected ultimately to be used in temperatures up to 4500 degrees F.

Until these fibers were first produced, existing materials were available for continuous service up to only 2000 degrees F with 3000 degrees F as the top limit for certain fibers under very short duration pulse conditions.

The new ceramic fibers are immediately useful as insulation material in both loose and mat form. Other applications, such as fibers for plastic laminates, for paper and cloth and possibly nuclear fuel elements, are obviously indicated, but as yet, are not under active development by Horizons.

In terms of vital importance of its expected applications, by far, the most impressive feature of the new material is in its insulation properties. For example, a three-quarters inch thick batting of zirconia fiber has protected an aluminum sheet from melting, in an oxygen acetylene flame, though the temperature of the flame is capable of boiling aluminum.

In addition, since the bulk density of the fibers is low—about three pounds per cubic foot—the material is expected to find extensive use as lightweight insulation in rocket, jet and nuclear applications as well as high temperature reactors and process equipment of all types. And another important feature is the material's thermal shock resistance which is outstanding. Technical details of both the new material and the process used to produce it are equally revealing.

The process encompasses a variety of ceramic materials including most of the refractory oxides and represents a departure from conventional methods of forming glassy filaments and single crystal whiskers. The fibers are polycrystalline in structure and being non-vitreous, can be repeatedly recycled to temperatures near the melting point without softening or embrittlement.

In the case of zirconia fibers (most development work to date has been concentrated on zirconia), the useful temperature limit is about 4500 degrees F, thoria oxide and berylia should go even higher.

Fibers are relatively short, ranging from fractions of an inch to about three inches in length; random cross-sections range from approximately one to ten microns.

In presently attained strength and flexibility, the fibers compare size for size, with untreated soft glass and are therefore recommended for use where bulk mass or a mat will serve.

Horizon's scientists are optimistic about increasing fiber length to a point where it can be spun and woven or used as reinforcing in structural ceramic shapes (which is possible even today, in some degree).

While work has been concentrated on zirconia, work has also been carried out on fibers of other materials including alumina, silica and mixed oxides.

It is expected that almost any oxide will fall into the pattern, including those of chromium, hafnium and uranium.

Bob worked on developing the zirconia fibers.

## Cleveland Plain Dealer, March 11, 1960

Development of a ceramic fiber to strengthen plastics and metals was disclosed today at Horizons, Inc. Hitherto, virtually all fibers used in plastics was glass.

The use of fibers in metals represents a major scientific breakthrough, says John Cameron, sales director at the plant at 2905 E. 79th Street. However, this phase in ceramic fiber development is still experimental.

Production of ceramic fibers for the plastics industry is already underway. An East Coast firm has been licensed to produce the fibers.

Cameron anticipates that the Army and Navy will be the first customers for a ceramic-plastic composition. They have already shown an interest.

Of immediate need is a composition capable of withstanding the tremendous friction missiles and rockets must endure.

"Ceramic fibers offer far greater resistance to erosion than glass fibers now used in rocket nozzles and cones" Cameron said. "The erosion occurs as a cone reenters the earth's atmosphere at 24,000 mph a clip."

"Early tests on metal-ceramic-fiber fusion indicate a threefold increase in metal strength" Dr. Eugene Wainer, Director of Research said. "Flight requirements of the space age require lengthy and rapid heating cycles as well as radiation and erosion problems."

"No single material today overcomes all these obstacles," he said. "Horizons has combined nickel chrome alloy with ceramic fibers."

## Unfolding Horizons April-May, 1960 Vol. 4, No. 1

### Research: A $12 Billion Business

Research and development work, the scientific search for new products and sometimes even new industries, is one of the most rapidly growing businesses in the nation.

The question, "Who puts up the money?" is getting a different answer today than it did ten years ago. During the early 1950s, the federal government supplied only about 40% of all R & D funds, through research on government projects and through grants to industry. Today, the tide has turned; industry supplies only 40%, while the federal government picks up the tab for the rest.

By the end of the 1960s, the picture is expected to change. Industry will spend a lion's share, while government reverts to its old position. This represents the best guesses of industry experts, although drastic changes in economic conditions could easily alter these percentages.

The correctness of these estimates will be governed by an economic growth rate slightly in excess of the rate over the past five years and partially on a continued belief by corporate executives that solid investments in research are a certain way to continue corporate success.

Early in 1959, after John Cameron was named director of sales for Horizons, the company was ready not only to solve technical problems for other companies, but to go further into developing its own products for the new age of high temperature ceramics. More articles appeared in the *Cleveland Press* business pages about Horizon's new ceramic fibers and a very comprehensive article was published in *The Wall Street Journal* on June 15, 1960, on its front page.

## Scientists Develop New Fiber, Say it's as Hard as Sapphires

### Cleveland Firm Foresees Use in Space Vehicles, Skins, Nose Cones for Missiles

By George Melloan, Staff Reporter

CLEVELAND—A few years ago, a British movie spun a story of an amazing white suit that was indestructible until it finally disintegrated into a heap of powder.

A Cleveland research firm, Horizons, Inc. has developed shiny fibers strikingly similar to those that might have produced the fictional white suit. A suit made of them might be almost indestructible, officials claim. They say the suit's wearer could have his back stroked with the white flame of an acetylene torch and hardly feel a tickle.

The fibers approximate the physical properties of one of nature's hardest substances, sapphires. They are inorganic, meaning they

derive from rocks and ores. Most fibers are made of organic
or once living materials, a category which includes coal and
oil. Until recently, glass fiber, derived from sand, has held the
spotlight among inorganic fibers. Now, not only is glass fiber
enjoying a boom, it is getting some new and startling cousins.

## Protecting Space Passengers

One use for Horizon's fiber may be to help form coverings
for space vehicles to protect the vehicles and their passengers
from the intense heat caused by air friction when they reenter
the atmosphere. Other possibilities: a textile skin for 2000
miles per hour and faster aircraft that would withstand the
tremendous rigors of such speeds; or space parachutes that
wouldn't burn up from reentry friction. Although Horizons
sees little demand for indestructible white suits, it believes
fire-fighting suits would be an application. Presently, such suits
are made from another inorganic fiber: asbestos.

Horizons is making a start by negotiating a licensing
agreement with an eastern chemical firm which expects to
produce the fibers that will to help reinforce plastic nose cones
for missiles.

Horizon's fibers are creating a quiet stir among scientists who
are conducting a search for new space materials. "It sounds
almost too good to be true," says a materials specialist for a large
research organization which is trying to get samples for testing.

"If it will do what they say it will do, it is very exciting,"
says a military researcher in Washington.

Horizon's claims one of its fibers will withstand a pull of
3 million pounds per square inch and temperatures of 3750
degrees F, which is 25% higher than the temperature which
turns steel to white liquid. By varying the basic material used,
the temperature limit can be pushed up to 4750 degrees F.
Although this cuts the fiber's strength to 300,000 to 400,000

psi, that is considerably stronger than the limits of present fibers. Glass fiber, for instance, will go no higher than 200,000 psi and that's far higher than any organic fiber.

Horizons' basic discovery is a means of producing fibers from extremely hard heat-resistant materials found in the earth. These are called metallic oxides which are crystalline combinations of metal and oxygen. Perhaps the best known and one which Horizons finds to have great strength, is aluminum oxide. Also called alumina, it is one of the hardest substances known outside of the diamond. In one form, it is a material of which sapphires, rubies and several other precious stones are composed. Aluminum oxide is also known to the layman as the gritty abrasive used in grinding wheels and high grade sandpaper.

Except to say that the process is relatively simple, Horizons isn't telling how it produces the fibers. However, John Cameron, Horizons Sales Manager, estimates that the aluminum oxide fiber could be sold commercially for $10 to $12 a pound, which is about the cost of high temperature glass fibers.

J. E. Burke, manager of ceramic studies at General Electric Co.'s research laboratories in Schenectady, N.Y. says he doesn't know how Horizons produced its fiber, but although he is aware that work at Horizons was developing along the same lines of study at G.E. He says the usual process of producing fibers from metallic oxides begins with vaporizing the oxides at an extremely high temperature in a hydrogen atmosphere. The oxides are then condensed out of the hydrogen atmosphere and form fibers, or "whiskers" as they are deposited.

Mr. Burke isn't quite sure where the best practical applications for oxide fibers lie, but he confirms the possibility of achieving tremendous strength and heat resistance and describes the development of oxide fibers as a major scientific achievement. The fibers have been in the laboratory for some time. The principle deterrent to practical use has been the tendency of surface flaws to develop either while they are being formed or afterward, thus weakening them. Horizons claims to have licked this problem.

Until a year or so ago, commercial applications of inorganic fibers were restricted to glass fibers, which were first introduced in 1931 and asbestos. Fibrous glass, nonetheless, is gaining new ground in a new variety of uses. Its supporters believe that the future looks even better than it did a few years ago when its use as a reinforcing agent made possible plastic boats and automobile and truck bodies. Sales last year were just short of $300,000,000, nearly double the figure in 1954. Producers are spending $9 million to boost output capacity to overcome shortage of the material, which is used in such varied products as draperies, golf clubs and electrical insulation.

As demand grows, glass producers are pressing research. According to James Slayter, vice president for research and development at Owens Corning Fiberglass Corp. in Toledo, active studies are being made of a variety of inorganic fibers. "We're in a great industry and it has only started to grow." Mr. Slayter declares Owens-Corning is the largest provider of glass fibers.

General Electric, about 18 months ago came up with a heat resistant fiber made of quartz. It resists heat up to 1800 degrees F for long periods and up to 3000 degrees F for a short time, the company claims. Almost all of G.E.'s output of this fiber is going into military applications.


Bob was enjoying the detective jobs he was given at Horizons during the first year or so and was getting excited about working on perfecting ceramic fibers and initiating a good many of the breakthroughs they had. He enjoyed working with Dean Fisher who was a mechanically minded, practical worker. The two became fast friends.

Shortly after the New Year in 1959, we found we were expecting another baby. Though in the enthusiasm of very early marriage we had decided four children would be nice, in reality having two seemed just right and Bob loved having two daughters. I blamed the surprise on the electric blanket my parents gave us for Christmas, but Bob claimed he thought it was something else. Our son, Robert Martin Beasley Jr. was born on September 24, 1959, just before dinner. His doctor said he was perfect.

We also acquired a new cat, Petty, a female calico who immediately knew in her mind that she was a true family member and decided early to add some kittens to it. Petty had three babies and was a very good mother. She was also a promiscuous cat and had two more sets of kittens before we were able to have her spayed.

With the new baby taking up residence in the girls' bedroom, we thought it was time to buy our first house. A little white colonial was for sale by its owner down the street and the price was right. An offer was made and accepted, with the understanding that we couldn't move in until the old owners' new house was finished. That was all right, since the owners would be paying us rent for the house in the meantime. It was a wait of about three months until moving day.

### *Letter to Mark and Lou*

Hotel Vermont

Burlington, VT.

March 22, 1960

Dear Folks,

Having a wonderful time—wish you were here. We are going to a skiing lodge tomorrow afternoon.

Actually, I'm here on business. G. E. is making a monster—a 30 mm cannon for the Air Force called the Vulcan. It is really fantastic, fires 6,000 shots a minute. It can't be appreciated without seeing it in operation. Makes you feel like you are going to be killed just watching it. It is beautifully designed and all ready to go *except* that they have one basic fault that makes it unacceptable. Our sales manager and I came here after they called for help, quick.

Well, we have been successful (after pulling a certain amount of hocus-pocus) even beyond our expectations. Just pulled it right out of the hat, so to speak.

It was so nice talking to you Sunday. I have been planning to call you, too. We have all been doing just fine. Bobby's rash looks better and it really doesn't bother him.

We are really ready to get into the house and for once, live by ourselves. I'm a little fed up living with other people and am ready to buy even if we were to move out and lose a little money after a short while. At any rate, we will probably be around a while for I feel that I should at least see how the fibers are going to go and at what rate. Besides things are not so bad at work now—not a bed of roses, but OK.

Still haven't found those GD (gosh darn) garbage can lids. Plenty of snow is on the ground even though someone said it is spring.

Guess that your tax work will be coming to an end. Hope it has been a good year. I think that it is nice that people come back each year. Lets you know that you have been performing a good service.

I'll write again soon. Hope your trip to NYC works out.

Love,

Bob

But things weren't really going well.


### *Excerpt from 1994 tape*


Horizons was a very small organization and it was headed by a man who was Director of Research, Eugene Wainer. He called himself the Father of Barium Titrate. Well, that may be. I never knew of anything else he did and I never knew about him doing that. But really, as I learned from the workers who had been there a long time, Horizons had had another organization in Princeton, New Jersey and Horizons was set up by a man and Wainer, who had been at Princeton with him.

Well, that man died and now Wainer was the new President and the Princeton operation had shut down before I got there. And so, really, when I got to Horizons, in Cleveland, it was on such a downhill slide . . . filtering away . . . that really hardly any work ever came in. So, it wasn't very good.

At the time, I was doing my scientific tasks and a Ph.D. in charge of the Metallurgy Department which didn't have much work, either, would come over and watch me. His name was Maurice Steinberg, but everybody called him Mo, then. I believe he was impressed because I would take on everything.


Morris Steinberg, who received his Ph.D. in Metallurgy at MIT, joined Horizons in 1948 as their first director of science and also a director of the company. The company was two years old. He left Horizons in 1958 to join Lockheed, realizing his future at Horizons would be limited. At Lockheed, he was made Director of the Materials, Propulsion and Ordinance Department in 1959 and put a number of groups together in Palo Alto, Sunnyvale and at a Test base in Santa Cruz. Several people besides Bob and Dean Fisher came out from Horizons under his aegis.


### *Excerpt from 1994 tape*


Steinberg left to go to Lockheed in California. The Physics Department had a couple of people rattling around like BBs in a boxcar. There really wasn't anybody but Dean Fisher in Metallurgy after Steinberg left. My boss in the Ceramics Department had left, so it was really in shambles. All of the departments were closing. And so, I was trying desperately to study . . . to get out of the field of Science entirely. To do anything, because I wasn't going anywhere that I could see.

By this time, Bob had become so unhappy with what was going on in his professional life that he decided to see if he could change professions. He had always had a liking for business and had taken a few business courses at Stetson. He enrolled at Western Reserve (now Case Western Reserve) in their night school to get his prerequisites for a master's in business. He might not have been entirely ready to give up being a chemist/ceramist, but taking the classes gave him direction to go in an entirely new field and that helped lessen his depression. He also knew he could easily get a job at other chemical companies in the area if he wanted to.

One large reason for his unhappiness at Horizons was its director. Dr. Wainer liked to dabble in psychology and it became evident that he was often pitting one man against the other, to see what would happen. At first, it was very covert, but everybody was unhappy and sometimes suspicious of the other people they worked with. Still, Bob's thoughts were on exciting things happening in ceramics.

### *Excerpt from 1994 tape*

I had become friends with Dean Fisher who had worked for Mo Steinberg. He had written to Mo that he was unhappy and Mo hired him on the spot to go to Lockheed in Palo Alto. Dean and I corresponded and he knew my situation. I mentioned, if you see anything out there, let me know, because it's getting bad here. I guess he mentioned to Steinberg that I was certainly available and so, Steinberg set up for an interview for me, so I came out.

The interview, in May 1959, was a very impressive one. Bob was taken all over the beautiful places in Santa Clara valley, including Skyline Drive that overlooked the lower part of San Francisco Bay and the eastern foothills of the Sierras in the background. He was given a tour of the Lockheed facility at Palo Alto, met a few important people and was taken to dinner at the Palo Alto Country Club. He came back very impressed but still not sure, yet, what he should do. We had just moved into our house three months earlier and he had gotten almost all his business school prerequisites but he still had some ideas about improvements on some of his ideas for ceramics he had been thinking about. He and one of his favorite people, Herb Johns, wanted to try a few experiments. Bob approached Wainer with these ideas, but instead of giving Bob and Herb the go-ahead, Wainer gave the project and ideas to someone else to work on.

This gave Bob the reason he needed for leaving.


July 5, 1960

Dr. E. Wainer

cc: K. Bartlett


R. M. Beasley

Ceramics Department

I would like to submit my resignation as of the last of this month, July, 1960. My stay here at Horizons has been both interesting and illuminating. I would not have missed it for the world and do regret that it must end here.

R. M. Beasley


Before he left Horizons, Dr. Harman wrote this letter of recommendation, just in case Bob needed it:


August 31, 1959


To Whom It May Concern:


This is to certify that Robert M. Beasley has worked under my direction as a Research Project Supervisor. He has been so engaged since December, 1957 to date. I have found Mr. Beasley to be conscientious, energetic, imaginative and competent. He has proven his ability to conduct research projects with originality.

I can recommend Mr. Beasley highly for a research worker in fields where he has had experience.

Yours sincerely,

Cameron G. Harman

## Horizons Incorporated

Head, Ceramics Department


While at Horizons, Bob and Herb Johns received two patents: *Inorganic Fibers and the Preparation Thereof, 3,110,545* and *Inorganic Fibers and Method of Preparation, 3,082,899.* A few years later, Horizons was out of business.

Bob had loved what he had seen of California, especially the weather. He had always battled depression in colder, gray climates. California was another sunshine state, like Florida. And at Lockheed, he hoped to continue work on the ideas just beginning to come to light for him. So, when he received the job offer from Lockheed, he accepted.


**LOCKHEED AIRCRAFT CORPORATION** Missiles and Space Division, Sunnyvale, California

June 8, 1960

Mr. Robert M. Beasley

3626 Rolliston Road

Shaker Heights, Ohio


Dear Mr. Beasley,

We are pleased to acknowledge your acceptance of a position with the Missiles and Space Division.

You are scheduled to report at 7:30 a.m. on August 22, 1960. Please bring your Social Security Card, birth certificate or naturalization papers and if applicable, military discharge papers. Our office is located at 962 El Camino Real, Sunnyvale, California. If you did not have a physical examination by your local physician, also bring your Lockheed medical chart with the first page completed.

We look forward to your association with Lockheed. If we may be of further assistance, please let us know.

Very truly yours,

R. C. Birdsall

Employment Manager

Lockheed Corporation had gotten its start back in 1912, founded by the Lockheed brothers, Allan and Malcom. It changed its name several times, went into bankruptcy during the great depression and was finally bought and brought back by the Gross brothers, Courtland and Robert. The headquarters were established in Burbank and the company went on to be one of the main airplane companies in the country. It was especially famous for its "Skunk Works," named for the smells from a plastics factory nearby. Kelly Johnson and his crew, among other developments, made the U2 spy plane and the Blackbird. It was a secret organization and often did its wonders with limited time and resources.

In 1954, the new Missiles Systems Division was formed at Burbank and two years later, land was purchased for a new plant in Sunnyvale and acreage leased in Palo Alto for its headquarters. By the end of 1956, Lockheed was in the missile business. The division was renamed Lockheed Missiles and Space Company in 1961. It was considered a good company to work for.

We had been in the new house in Shaker Heights only three months and were just beginning to get settled in. We would have to sell it. Though the seller's market had suddenly dropped, we hoped someone would come along and like it as much as we did. But the market was bad and there were no takers. The realtor suggested that it be rented and that seemed the best thing to do under the circumstances. One of the men at Horizons offered to help as an agent with any maintenance problems that came up with the renters. In a few weeks, a doctor and his family moved in and the house continued to be rented until it was sold about ten years later.

Lockheed was paying for the move, including a place to stay until we found a house in the area that met our needs.

Bob decided this was a wonderful opportunity for us to see the country and make the trip west into a real vacation. We bought our first new car, a small Valiant station wagon, for the trip. We would go down the east coast from Maryland to Florida to say good-bye to relatives, go through the Florida panhandle, on the southern route, with detours to see the Grand Canyon, Bryce Canyon, Flagstaff and other attractions along the way. Bob especially wanted to see "Indian Country," where he had imagined, as a young boy, he was there, on his horse, racing the train as it took him to Georgia or Miami.

Packing would be left to the movers, but with all the paraphernalia needed for two young girls and a baby, plus clothes and picnic food—those things would crowd all the space we thought we would have, so we bought a luggage rack and located an old gray canvas tarp Bob had acquired during his navy days to cover it all up.

But there remained a big problem. Petty had gotten out of the house right after she had weaned her last litter, found an admirer and had her third set of kittens four weeks before we were to leave. The SPCA said they would have to separate the unweaned kittens from their mother and probably have to destroy them. That was not an option for us. All our friends owned large dogs. No one wanted a mother cat and four kittens, no matter how charming. The only recourse was to take them along and hope for the best. So to what we already packed, we added a bushel basket for the babies and mother, a cat pan, cat food and a leash.

There was a little going-away party with the neighbors. Almost everything was packed under the tarp, which loomed almost as high as the car itself.

We had planned to get an early start the next morning, but when Bob went out to the driveway, he saw that someone had written on the side of the car, in red poster paint, "California or Bust." It did look like a covered wagon. It took almost an hour before Bob could get the paint off. And still the words showed palely through the beige enamel of the car.

Finally we were ready, about eleven o'clock—kittens in a basket in the back, the girls in the second seat, the baby's diaper changed. But Petty had gotten out of the house and we couldn't find her. She had become skittish with all the activity and even needing to feed her babies didn't lure her back. Eventually, she was found in the backyard hiding under a patch of lilies of the valley and was carried, squirming and yowling all the way to the car.

The car had already turned hot in the August heat, but Bob had to roll up all the windows to about two inches to prevent Petty from squirming out. She stood on his left shoulder, alternately moaning or thrusting her nose into the small opening. Behind him, Amy was blowing on a kazoo and Robin was bouncing up and down. The baby needed another change. We drove down the main street to get onto the highway. The light was red. An old, high-bodied truck pulled up beside us and the driver, a woman, looked down interestedly at the scene and started to smile. Bob smiled balefully back at her. She started to laugh. Bob lowered the window another half inch and yelled out that that was nothing—we also had a basket of kittens in the backseat. The light turned green and as we pulled away, Bob could see the woman in the rearview mirror, still at the light, uproariously laughing and banging her hands on the steering wheel. After that, it seemed funny to us, too.

The trip down to Florida wasn't bad, except for running into a tropical storm at Virginia Beach and Petty trying to run away at every rest stop. We decided to go through DeLand and take a turn around Stetson. Two miles out of town, Petty got over her constipation in a tremendous way. She obviously felt better after that, but for the thirty miles to my parents' house, the rest of the passengers did not. My parents offered to take Petty and the kittens out of pity for everyone, including Petty.

On the way to California, Bob did all the driving and I did everything else. About halfway through the trip, Bob decided, before we got to our next motel, we would all have a minute or two of screaming and yelling. It was surprisingly relaxing.

Bob enjoyed driving and during the quiet times on the way, he thought deeply about new ideas that kept coming to him, processes and experiments he wanted to do.

The last stop before Palo Alto was in Bakersfield. We had just seen the desert spectacle of Las Vegas at night spread out before us and dusty Bakersfield, though it was in California, was a sad letdown.

The next day, driving up old 101 (before it was a freeway) things still looked dusty. There were no green vistas, only curtains of haze. As we drew nearer to Palo Alto, sound barriers along the highway cut off any signs of habitation.

We found the Flamingo Motor Lodge, on El Camino Real, in Palo Alto, where the company had reserved rooms for us. It was just what we needed, a small suite with a little kitchen and a big swimming pool not too far away. Set back from the street in a small grove of redwoods, it did seem to feel a little bit like how we had imagined California, but it didn't seem real yet.

Our home in Shaker Heights, Ohio, 1958

# Part Two

# The Idea

# Chapter Five

# Lockheed

In February 2000, August 2004 and July 2005, I invited those of Bob's coworkers who still lived nearby to come to my home in Sunnyvale, enjoy a meal of Armadillo Willy's ribs and talk about what happened to them and Bob thirty years ago when they, among other things, worked together to perfect the invention known at first as LI-1500.

Amy set up an omnidirectional microphone and the men reminisced, asked and answered questions and enjoyed being together again. Robin transcribed the tapes for me and Bob Jr. helped me remember dates I had forgotten.

These discussions became an invaluable tool for writing this book. There wouldn't have been the invention or the book without these men.

**GBL**

Bob was to present himself at Lockheed for his physical on August 22, 1960, at 8:00 a.m. He passed the exam and was given the employee number, 605597. His title was Senior Scientist and he was thirty-four years old. An orientation meeting with his new boss, Dr. Harvey Crosby, head of the Chemistry and Plastics Department, was scheduled for 1:30 p.m. on September 1, 1960, in Building 52-35 in the Palo Alto facility. Bob felt comfortable with his new boss right away. After some "getting to know you" conversation, Harvey told Bob that Lockheed had lost the contract for which he had been hired and asked him, "What are you going to do now?" Bob recalled later to me that he answered, "Hell, I don't even know the way to the men's room. How do I know what I'm going to do?" He felt quite shaken. But he did find the men's room and when he got on the elevator to leave, a sweet young thing made a pass at him. By the time he got back to the children and me at the Flamingo, he felt better and decided he would hurry up and invent something so he wouldn't be fired.

One of the first things he did when we got to Palo Alto was to go to a stationery store and buy a logbook in which to write down the ideas he had been mulling over on the trip and later, the new experiments he would make in the little lab in the garage of our new rented house.

We were fortunate to find an inexpensive place to rent on the south side of Palo Alto, close to work and with a grammar school in the next block. This Eichler-designed house was one of the first ones ever built, in the late 1940s and of an innovative, modern layout. It looked small and it was small with a living room/dining room combination, redwood board and plywood walls, stained from a flood several years before and a pass-through to a slit of a kitchen, reminding us of the one we had had at the beach. There was one bathroom and the laundry space was outside the kitchen door under an overhang. But the back of the house had ceiling-high windows that looked out on a small lawn and an overspreading apricot tree. And it had three bedrooms and the rent was right. We were only going to live there until we could afford to buy something a little larger. Also it had a big plus; there was a little room built into the side of the garage, with shelves and electrical outlets. Bob was able to set up a very rudimentary lab there and work on his new ideas, recording everything in his new logbook.

The movers had decided to stop off in Texas to visit family, but finally got to 1026 Amarillo Street and unloaded everything from the attractive home in Shaker Heights to this little one on a side street, two blocks from the freeway and a drive-in theater. The men had done a good job packing and we were amused to discover they had even brought the old garbage cans still filled with garbage.

Several years later the landlord offered to sell us the house at its appraised value. The house payments would be lower than the present rent, so we bought it. Now we owned two houses.

As we had at Corning and later, in Shaker Heights, we decided to go to church our first Sunday in town and immediately made lifelong friends.

### Excerpt from 1994 tape

Well, I desperately started trying to get a job. I now worked for a company, but I found out that this company, as far as I was concerned, worked for somebody outside. So, if I was looking for work, I had to get it from outside. And while we had passed right by Sunnyvale, I didn't know that Lockheed had a large factory in there. I didn't know that they were even in Burbank which is their main office. And, where I was in Palo Alto—that was a very small laboratory division. And so, what I really did was try to start inventing or thinking of something that I could interest somebody in that would have enough support to give me money . . . a charge number. That's all I needed, a charge number. Or else I would be out in a week. The chemistry lab was a support organization and you were supposed to have problems presented to you by the programs within the company.

The Palo Alto Lab was the show place of Lockheed Missiles and Space Company. Most of the company's Ph.D.'s and VPs had offices there. It borrowed some of its ambience from Stanford University nearby and one could look out of its windows and see gently rolling hills with cattle and horses grazing under the shadows of wide-spreading oak trees. Here most of the research of the company was carried out by individuals and small groups and they were well-funded. It had an easy-going atmosphere, rather like a well-run club. Most of the money earned by research came from the Palo Alto Lab. If you had an idea you wished to pursue, you had the opportunity to explore it there. The Sunnyvale Plant, on the other hand, was in the flatlands and was composed of boxlike buildings ranging over a large area, a typical industrial landscape and it was all business.

Palo Alto was/is a university town full of older, quaint Spanish-style homes and cottages, larger newer homes and beautiful, well-landscaped mansions. Stanford Shopping Center and a new style mall, Town and Country Village were enticing places to shop. San Francisco was less than an hour away. And there was Stanford University with its football team. We went faithfully, all of the family, during football season to all the home games, sitting up high under the flagpoles and cheering for the home team.

The town had grown larger in the past few years to the other side of Oregon Avenue (kind of like the middle class other side of the tracks) and this is where many Eichler homes and their imitations were built. The Fishers lived in Santa Clara, a nearby town and Dean and Pauline and their sons and our family visited with each other often and celebrated our first Thanksgiving in California together. Bob showed Dean some of his experiments in the little garage room.

Harvey Crosby's lab in Palo Alto was working in areas of organic and inorganic materials, laminating plastics to be used on missile nose cones and other projects.

Dean was also working for Harvey Crosby. That was a big plus for Bob. Dean was a man who didn't mind trying different things, but also had a sense of practicality that more than made up for a lack of a college education. His comment about some of the Ph.D.'s he knew was that they were educated beyond their intelligence. Bob enjoyed watching him turn his bifocal glasses upside down when he was working on anything overhead. Bob also worked with three other men who became his good friends, Les Shoff, Doug Izu and later, Harry Nakano.

Harvey probably didn't know what to do with Bob, so he gave him a little room with a small winding machine and then left him alone. Les worked next to this place and began to wonder what that clicking noise was that came through the wall. His curiosity was piqued, so he opened the door and found Bob tap dancing to the rhythm of the winding machine. That one thing made them instant friends.

Harvey Crosby was easygoing. The group from his lab went out to lunch together a lot and occasionally had parties like the one in 1961 when the group and their spouses all went up to San Francisco to celebrate the vernal equinox.

Bob meant it when he told me he would have to hurry up and invent something. He ordered small samples of materials from various suppliers and in his little room in the garage, he mulled over his ideas writing them down in his logbook—the new ideas that eventually led to the thermal protection system that would keep people and things safe in space.

### *Excerpt from 1994 tape*

The first reentry systems, or the first heat shields . . . I don't know if you would call them reentry systems because I don't know that they exited, was with the V2 rocket in World War II . . . from Peenemünde, Germany. And they really only stayed within the earth's atmosphere. I don't really know if they got up that high. They were lobbed over so to speak. So really, they stayed down and the heating was not a problem. Their main purpose was to protect the warhead until it got to its destination and it blew up. I believe that was probably glass phenolic, where its only purpose was really to resist and protect the warhead . . . resist the friction of the atmosphere. And if there was some thermal protection, it would only be because of its thickness.

And of course, the way it works, is it charred. It made a very, very, hard char, like a very hard charcoal brick. And the glass . . . and later reprosil which is essentially silica—the glass in the heavy heating on the outmost exit nearest the surface—the hottest area—would melt and contribute to the anti-erosiveness . . . and the firmness and the hardness of the structure. And the unused part, of course, would be what would insulate the warhead. That was from Peenemünde—the technology that largely was taken over and brought over with the V2 rockets and was used in the Mercury and Gemini programs. And successfully, but what happened, is that they really weren't worried so much about coming back home, they were worried about surviving the earth's atmosphere during the flight and exiting. And the vehicles themselves were parachuted away.

The Apollo was even that way. Now, I don't know whether the heat shield on the Apollo was reprosil or nylon phenolic. The instance of nylon phenolic was not as abrasion resistant as the glass phenolic or reprosil phenolic, but what it did when it made a char, the nylon portion vaporized . . . turned to vapor. And that then, as it percolated up through the char, was supposed to be transpiration cooling . . . was supposed to take away some of the heat that way. But these were the main heat shields, reprosil glass phenolic and then the transpiration cooling for the nylon phenolic or the organic fiber phenolic. By and large, that then was really the technology of reentry systems, thermal protections, TPS, for thermal protection systems.

And it had always been that way and it probably always would have stayed that way because there was very much the thought, "if it ain't broke, don't fix it." And don't worry about any perfecting or improving of it. We know that it works and we don't dare change it. And so, there was just a closed mind to even a whisper that, "Gee, maybe you could make it a little better."

So, I began to think of it and I thought, that really, rather than send these things up and HOPE they would perform the way you wished; in other words, hope that a char—a strong char—would occur by burning and that the material inside might decompose and cause transpiration cooling, hoping it would work well enough. Or in the other instance, hoping that instead of decomposing, it would melt and help resist the char. And if it were thick enough, overly thick, then the unused portion could be used as an insulator. I began to try to promote . . . hey, why don't you design on the ground, when you have absolute control over it, the actual condition of the material that you wish it to be? And that was the product that became Lockheat, named by Leo Schapiro. And it was resented by the people who were with the "If it ain't broke, don't fix it" group.

A new lab 52-30 was set up by Morrie Steinberg for experimental work on this new concept. Though he later went to corporate headquarters in Los Angeles as a vice president, Steinberg remained interested in Bob and his ideas and promoted them where he could.

Dr. Leo Schapiro was put in charge of the lab. Leo was a consulting scientist and senior member of the Materials Science Laboratory at Lockheed in 1961. His doctorate in metallurgy was from the University of Wisconsin. Besides the lab, he was also manager of Ocean Systems at the Palo Alto facility.

In early 1962, Bob sent a report to Leo discussing the current Lockheed development program including structural, thermal, impregnation methods and material qualifications.

Of the thermal properties experiments being conducted in the lab, he wrote, "the work along these lines of evaluating the effectiveness of various materials and methods of utilizing them as thermal blocking structures, it is becoming apparent from our past work that the most efficient structures will be 'built' of varied components utilized in a manner within the structure to yield an optimum performance as defined by an application. To approach the maximum utilization of the desirable properties of each building component, it is essential that their characteristics be known both individually and in its combinations."

The next paragraph described how he liked to conduct the work at hand. "While the 'kitchen sink' approach to research favored by some investigators may be used on occasion to determine the potential shifting emphasis or direction, the underlying theme of our activity will be a progression or 'building block' type of investigation. This may be a slow method initially, but I believe it will be fully justified in the long run by yielding a sounder understanding of the contribution and function of each component in the final design of useable structures.

"The present activity is as broad a coverage of materials as can be expected within the limits of our equipment and a four-and-a-half-man effort. Many varied systems are being carried out concurrently. Mr. Fisher has volunteered to work on a temporary basis on the afternoon shift in an effort to overcome some of the equipment limitations. I feel that a primary reliance on the 'kitchen sink' method of investigation is an attempt to further accelerate the effort that will lead to over-design and an accompanying weight penalty and little advancement in the knowledge of materials."

In May 1964, a spiral-bound publication was printed by the company:

### Thermal Protection Concepts for Lifting Ferry Vehicles

And the foreword reads:

The concepts and materials presented in this document represent the contributions of many individuals. The Lockheat concept was originated and developed by R. M. Beasley. C. F. Merlet and W. E. Shannon have integrated the total LMSC activity on the Lockheat concept and identified a variety of potential applications. Dr. L. Schapiro has been responsible for process development activity associated with the material. K. M. Kratsch has contributed to the synthesis of improved material formulations through thermodynamic analyses and in conjunction with T. J. Keliher performed the thermal analysis described herein. The activity has been sponsored by the Lockheed Missiles and Space Company Independent Development Program.

D. M. Tellep, manager of Launch and Entry Thermodynamics

The core group of men, who were there in the lab at the beginning, stayed much the same all through the development of the material: Harry Nakano, Chuck Dewey, Bill Ravenelle, Al Pechman, Pat

McCormick, Dean Fisher, Les Shoff, Doug Izu and supported by Joyce Livingston Wathen, who was the lab secretary.

Harry Nakano said he joined the group by accident because he was carpooling with Dean Fisher to Palo Alto from Sunnyvale. His charge numbers weren't coming in and he was worried about losing his job. Dean told Harry he may as well join the new group. That is the way the lab personnel grew, one person recommending another or another just fitting in, or someone needing a job and who could add something to the group. Some came and some left, but it was a good nucleus group and the lab gained the reputation of being a good place to work.

Pat McCormick was interviewed by Doug and Bob in 1961 and was invited to join the lab. As he described it later at the get-together in my home, "We had a lab right across from the office and there was a winding machine that intrigued me, that end of it. So I got tied up in filament winding. Even after work was done on the LI material, I stayed with that end of development and other contracts on the other side. But then, after the tiles came, I did a little high-temperature marking and that kind of research and then Harry and I would play around with the electric end of it and all that kind of thing.

"When I first started working with Harry, he said, 'Do you have any qualms about working with high heat?' and I said I had great respect for it and he said well, that was fine. It was a closed area at that time and a kind of close-knit group that made different things."

Harry said of Pat, "Pat was a great doer. You know, we all talk about things we should do, but Pat would make it into an object. He made programs successful because he catalogued everything." Pat also went back to college and finished his degree, doing it the hard way, attending night sessions. His fellow lab partners were very proud of him for his accomplishment.

Because of his good disposition and willingness to try anything, Bob nicknamed Pat, "Sweetie."

## *Excerpt from 1994 tape*

There was a proposal to the Air Force Materials and Avionics Laboratory at Wright-Patterson Air Force Base in Ohio and I made a write-up which I could hand out as I went around and talked here and there and everywhere about trying to make a designed reentry system material—designed entirely and optimized only for the demands of the application and not one that you sent up that was overly thick and very heavy and that you hoped it would decompose in the way that you wanted it to. They weren't interested.

Lockheat was never used. But it is that thought that was the early lead-in to the LI material, the designed materials that I later did for the Shuttle. Because, when they finally got to it, the Shuttle had a returning body that was big, not just a tiny capsule. And they had to be very sensitive to weight. And it was this weight standpoint that allowed me an entry point into the TPS work at Lockheed.

Bob and Doug gave presentations at two symposiums in 1964 and in early 1965 on Lockheat's properties and possibilities, but there were still no takers. The official-looking brochure they had printed as a handout was titled:

### *Filamentary Composites*

INTRODUCTION

A continuing program of development is in progress at LMSC to provide new technology for advanced thermal protection systems, radomes and nozzles. This work, which began in 1960, has resulted in the production of fully integrated multipurpose units, capable of performing several of the following functions in combination: structural-load bearing, heat rejection, insulation, transmission of electromagnetic radiation and when required, the functions of shielding from meteoroids.

The unique structures of these multipurpose units is designated by the term "Lockheat," the name given to the product deriving its chemical and physical makeup from a consideration of the mission it will perform. The choice of materials and the materials' relative proportions in a particular Lockheat structure depend upon the requirement of the structure to function at the temperatures, pressures and for the duration of exposure imposed by the mission. Additionally, the material makeup will be influenced by the requirements for load carrying and for transparency to electromagnetic radiation advanced systems required materials which, in addition to being thermally resistant and protective, must contribute to structural strength and under certain conditions, provide cooling through the process of ablation and/or sublimation. Lockheat structures can meet these requirements by reason of their unique internal construction, which is an erosion-resistant, inorganically bonded, refractory-fiber network of controlled porosity. This structure is the framework on which various thermal protection systems can be built. The various combinations of systems are described by their functions as 'coolant,' 'coolant-insulation' and 'insulation.'

Lockheed never went ahead with any plans to develop or promote Lockheat any further. The company had a policy of not funding anything that did not already have a customer. However, when sending out promotional material later about Lockheed's early research in thermal protection systems, Lockheat was always mentioned as a forerunner, but by 1966 Lockheat was "toast."

Around this time, Bob and Bobby joined Indian Guides. A friend at work told Bob what a good activity it was for a father/son relationship. They joined a group just forming and the two chose their "Indian" names—Bigfoot and Littlefoot. They bought official moccasin kits, but never finished making them. The fathers bonded very quickly, but the boys did not. Half of the boys were already good friends and the others just stood around and watched them play. The dads sent the boys outside, usually. One time, when they were meeting at our house, some of the boys threw stones at a neighbor's garage door and the very irate owner stormed over and demanded a new paint job. The next Saturday, three of the fathers, to make amends, gave the neighbor's garage door a new coat of paint. The group broke up not too long after that.

We started taking advantage of the nearness of San Francisco's night life. We liked to go up on the train and spend the weekend. We enjoyed the theater, window shopping at Gumps and eating in whatever famous restaurants we could afford. For a few years we belonged to the Commonwealth Club and attended those events we were interested in. Our favorite place to go was the dinner show at the Venetian Room at the Fairmont Hotel. That was the venue for most of our favorite singers. Bob said we'd better see them soon because everyone was getting a little long in the tooth. Tony Bennett, the Mills Brothers, Mel Tormé, Vic Damone and Ella Fitzgerald were among our favorites. Bob was a good tipper, but he just didn't like giving the maitre d' a big wad of cash when the room was small enough for anyone to see the stage from any table. The maitre d' must have finally remembered us from previous visits because once he actually smiled at us and took us to a table very close to the stage. When Vic Damone came out, he saw my beaming face and nodded a hello to me. He became my favorite singer. One time, Bob went to the men's room just before the entertainment started and met Ella Fitzgerald in the lobby as he was coming back. She very graciously said hello to him. From then on, she was his favorite singer.

Bob liked Frank Sinatra's style and his voice. He liked his appearance of insouciance. Bob would have liked to appear insouciant, too. So one time we flew to Las Vegas, where Frank was going to play at the Sands. He, too, was getting a little long in the tooth.

We didn't gamble, but just wanted to enjoy the decadence of the place. That afternoon, we went up to the roof on the top floor of our hotel by the large swimming pool to do some lounging and perhaps take a little nap. However, a mariachi band was playing there and soon we were surrounded by quite a few fashionably dressed, bejeweled women and even more fashionably dressed noisy children. The waiters catered to them almost exclusively.

We watched all of it, trying not to stare, not that we were noticed by anyone. Afterward we wondered if we had been surrounded by the distaff side of a mafia-type family.

That night, we finally were able to get seats for Frank's show. We were so far back that he appeared to be about an inch tall. He was not in voice and told so many "in" jokes with his surrounding coterie, that it was all a big disappointment. But it was worth it. We had seen "Ol' Blue Eyes" even if we were too far away to see actual eyes.

Throughout the years, Bob wasn't one to worry about his health, but he did have some challenges besides his heart condition, including a bleeding ulcer, high blood pressure, prostate problems, psoriasis, ear trouble from a broken ear drum and later, glaucoma. He never let them become part of what or who he was, however, but just dealt with them as best as he could. The psoriasis was the hardest to deal with because he was very fastidious and the psoriasis was always there. Every means was used to get rid of it, including steroid creams and pills. It became less aggressive after he retired. Most of these problems started after he came to Lockheed.

### *Excerpt from 1994 tape*

Very early when the thoughts for Apollo were just beginning to form, Lockheed thought that NASA would be asking for a radome that would go on top of the command module. It would be very unusual in its requirements because it would have high, intense heating for a short time if there were an abort. And the rocket, which was above the radome would be used to pull the Apollo away from the launch vehicle. In the event that that might happen, that would require one type of thermal protection. The other would be a more prolonged, low-intensity heating which would occur as the Apollo returned to earth and the friction of air on it would raise the temperature slightly. And that would require a very good insulator to protect it for a long period time.

So there were two thermal considerations in addition to the considerations of the electrical properties so it would be transparent to the electromagnetic radiations. There are what's called "sandwich" radomes, meaning laminations of different types of material which can be transparent and there's an instance where one surface of material can be dense and another material be a different density and they'd be transparent if the other material had the arithmetic mean and dielectric constant between it and the outer material and air. In other words, there'd be three things: air, the outer material and then the insulating material.

Well, Lockheed thought there was going to be a request for a proposal for this. So, I was able to get bid and proposal money to build and demonstrate the capability of making such an item. And I did—it was called the Apollo Radome.

I selected for it a filament-wound exterior of silica fibers and that's significant for later on, because the silica fibers, the only domestic silica fibers that I'm aware of, were from G.E. So, these were from G.E. and I intended to bond them with colloidal silica—Ludox, made by DuPont.

These two materials would have the identical dielectric constant. The filament-wound structure would still exhibit some porosity after winding and bonding. And that porosity would be filled with a methyl methacrylate—an organic—which also had the same dielectric constant as the other two materials.

Therefore I had a material that had the same dielectric constant throughout. The inner material, of course, was again, a cast staple filament made by Johns Manville . . . a silica fiber. Luckily at this time, what I got happened to be pure, purer than usual, I was to find out and bonded by silica. I believe that it just happened to work out to get the right dielectric constant of the mixture . . . of that composite of binder and random fibers. I happened to arrive at a density of roughly fifteen pounds per cubic foot. This fifteen pounds per cubic foot structure represented a very good inorganic insulator. And it was cast and bonded, as I said and machined to fit inside the already wound and formed inorganic bonded filament outer structure, which happened to have an organic in its content also—methyl methacrylate. They were bonded together to form the sandwich radome. The materials were made and tested and worked absolutely perfectly.

Unfortunately, a proposal was never requested and none given. Because by then the Apollo program . . . the formulation of its thoughts had been drawn together to where they realized they were not going to have a radome on the apex of the command module.

Nevertheless the long and short of it is, one was made and tested. It was perfect in the way it performed, but it was put aside. To me, there was significance because the materials involved and the way I had put them together, formed a background for what was to come. The low loss, low dielectric constant characteristics of silica had been ideal for the Apollo Radome. The same material—silica—when amorphous, could exhibit ideal properties also for a thermal environment. As long as they stayed amorphous, that is, they exhibited nominal density and an extremely low thermal expansion and when the fibers formed there would be very, very low conductivity—being a fiber almost opaque to radiation. So this did form a basis to build upon thermal environments.

Bob and Doug wrote up a paper (written mostly by Doug) on the work on the *Apollo* program ending.

Acknowledgments: The authors would like to acknowledge the work of James A. Elam for the electrical design; G. W. Allen, E. D. Fisher and R. D. LeBleu for contributions to materials development and fabrication; and R. E. Griffith and W. M. Steffen for fabrication and manufacturing aid.

Note: Since this work, the communication system on the *Apollo* Command Module has been redesigned and radome relocated. This radome configuration is no longer planned for use.

Bob began to be noticed at Lockheed. He wasn't shy about promoting his ideas even if no one cared to hear about them, except his lab partners. They all were a team, but more like family. There were no feuds or cliques, no secrets from each other. There was loyalty to Bob and Doug and to each other. Enthusiasm was high even in the dark days when there were trying problems to be overcome. Most of them had caught the idea, Bob's vision and felt privileged to be working with it.

Pat McCormick put it this way, "Everyone got along very well. It was a closed area at the time and a kind of a close-knit group that made different things. After the material was developed for the tiles, Bob had an idea: let's try to make a manifold, you know, put it inside a manifold and see if we can capture some odds and ends that are gong out into the atmosphere. So I made a bunch of pieces and then we ran them in a truck—one of those Lockheed trucks for a thousand miles or so. I don't remember how many miles there were on the truck, but you know, there was something different all the time. But that is what research is about."

Joyce Livingston Wathen was great at her job, which could not have been easy. She worked for both Leo and for Bob and Doug and stayed with the lab when Bob became manager in 1974. She made certain that Bob had special salt-free meals when he flew on business trips and was good at keeping up with all the loose ends that kept things running smoothly. After Joyce retired, other secretaries joined the group, integrated with the Program Department and Fran Ta'a worked more closely with the lab group.

Bob often said that without Doug Izu's help, the tiles would not have been developed. He knew and appreciated that Doug had all the attributes he didn't have. In fact, Doug was Bob's alter ego. They trusted each other completely. In the office they shared, Bob's desk was piled with papers; only he knew where to find and Doug's was neat, with things filed away for easy reference. While Bob could sometimes be curt and perhaps peevish, Doug had the calm, intelligent word and was the smoother of sharp edges. Bob was not without compassion, but Doug knew where it was needed and told Bob of the need. In a trio of metaphors, Doug was the nurturing older brother to the little one, the Tonto to Bob's Lone Ranger and where Bob was the flame, Doug was the lamp. He was one of the ones who made the lab a place where everyone wanted to work. His nickname in the lab was "Mother Izu."

Doug received his Bachelor of Science engineering degree at Stanford University under the GI Bill in 1950 and worked as an engineer at Mare Island Naval Shipyard in Vallejo and Boeing Aerospace Company in Seattle before coming to Lockheed in 1961.

Doug met his wife Mary while taking classes at San Jose State. They had three sons, Dave, Mark and Tom. Doug and Mary were very proud of the boys' interest in the arts. Doug was a good potter and landscaper, loved Big Band music as much as Bob and he and Mary enjoyed ballroom dancing. Doug had a hidden, quiet sense of humor, which he kept for his close friends. He and Bob and Mary and I enjoyed a close friendship until Doug passed away in October of 1989 (his service being held the day after the Loma Prieta Earthquake) and Mary shortly after in 1990.

While his family was interned in California during World War II, Doug fought in Italy with the famous 442nd Regimental Combat Team. His Japanese name, Yamato, was a special in-joke with his friends there.

According to his son Tom: "Regarding my Dad's first name: Yamato is a very ancient word for "Japan." Its actual meaning and history is a bit obscure or complicated. But I have heard that the first non-indigenous people who arrived on the islands and who became the majority ethnic group are referred to as the "Yamato" people. In relation to the story you tell, "Yamato" is part of an expression used in Japan—made famous during the WWII period, "Yamato Damashii," which is usually translated as "Spirit of Japan," and so the name "Yamato" most definitely had to have become connected to the nationalistic fervor of the Japanese militarists of that time period. This link was what Dad was probably ribbed about—here he is serving the US Military fighting the Axis powers with a name like that. As a result, I understand that his army buddies helped him come up with his nickname, "Douglas" as in Gen. Douglas McArthur, which must have been considered an unassailable American name. He then became "Y. Douglas Izu." It is interesting that he never did completely give up the Yamato name—some Nisei I have known tended to stick with the nickname only with no mention of a Japanese name (even an initial)."

Les Shoff recalled that Bob was the BOSS and didn't hesitate to speak his mind if he thought someone was not doing his job. But after that, it was all forgotten. Ed Gzowski who knew Bob in and out of the lab said, "I had a few arguments with him in the past. In fact, one time Morrie Steinberg refereed. I don't remember the details, but we were going hot and heavy. But later Bob asked me to come back to the lab with him and I said sure. I enjoyed working with Bob over the years. I enjoyed fighting with him and agreeing with him. We didn't fight too much and when we did have a disagreement, it didn't last very long because we turned around and started all over again."

Bob always thought that those in the lab should be able to do their jobs in the area of their expertise without his having to tell them how to do it. He usually made suggestions instead.

There was no typical day: new problems, more testing, some guesswork, more testing went on. Bob laid out objectives and everyone worked together on the various tasks, though all had their own areas of experience.

Sometimes Bob would tell them to do something a certain way, but as Harry said, "Bob had his own way of doing things and sometimes it was right and sometimes it was wrong. But if it was wrong, you just kept going. He was usually in the lab—getting his hands dirty—the sign of a good manager."

Bernie Francis, who was the laboratory administrator for a time, was not a materials scientist, so he said his observations were not of a technical nature but more from a human standpoint. He said, "I never met anybody in management at Lockheed quite like Bob who was so kindly. And he was genuinely kindly and you had the feeling like he was really rooting for you personally. And I could see how he would be a person who would create . . . what do they say . . . a group can do things in collection . . . the individual achievements could never be as great as the group. And he could make the group work together. I was very grateful for that experience with him. And I give him a ten in as far as being just a nice guy and a comfortable person to be with."

Bob and Doug didn't merit an office until much later. The others had desks in what they called the "Bull Pen," desks all pushed together. Bob was usually out in the lab and Doug stayed at his desk, writing and keeping everything in order. Everyone appreciated Doug's skill in taking someone's idea, even a nucleus of one and writing it up beautifully. He wrote up all the invention disclosures, of which there were many. All work was written up daily in strictly kept logbooks, a necessary and crucial job and locked away each night for safe keeping.

There was a lab coffeepot. Everyone was supposed to pay a dime a cup. The money would pay for the coffee. Warren Greenway made it every morning, usually in an unwashed pot and with used grounds, but they drank it anyway. Warren would get upset if he found a few pennies instead of dimes in the collection can. Whenever they got enough money, they all went out to lunch on Friday afternoons at the Town Oak, a restaurant in downtown Sunnyvale. Bob enjoyed Japanese food and the group sometimes went to Japanese restaurants. He enjoyed raw fish, hot sauce, tempura and sake. His friends started calling him Beasley-san. He also liked hot Mexican food and nibbled on hot chili peppers as though they were candy.

Like most labs, the atmosphere was relaxed. Work hard, play hard was the motto. There were no set schedules. Everyone knew what needed to be done, what challenges needed to be overcome and so got right to it. Most of the time, until the pilot plant was established, there were only six or eight people working at the same time. Sometimes they cooked lunch for everyone. Corned beef and cabbage was a favorite. There were large ovens that reached over 3000 degrees F, but were capable of baking a hot meal and huge refrigerators to keep things cool.

One time, Augie Ozelin and Les Shoff caught and brought in some abalone and cooked them in beer batter in one of the ovens. The aroma brought people from all over that end of the building.

There was a tragedy when Augie, whose hobby was underwater photography, accidentally drowned late one evening while testing his diving equipment in an indoor pool. (It was like losing a brother.)

When we lived in Palo Alto, our neighbors, who were Sierra Club members, invited us to go on a weekend hike with backpacks up to the backside of Yosemite to McGee Pass—elevation eight thousand feet. Bob was so entranced by the scenery that he organized a trip with a group from the lab, but this time hired a donkey to carry the load. There is a snapshot of Dean Fisher looking like he would love to be somewhere else.

A favorite leisure activity the guys enjoyed playing together was poker—for low stakes. Each year, usually sometime in late spring, they rented a houseboat at Lake Shasta and spent a long weekend fishing all day and playing poker all night and drinking large quantities of beer. They would all "get sick" Friday afternoon to get an early start. Pat and Doug usually did the arranging of details.


This menu was written by Doug:

BILL OF FARE

COAT AND TIE REQUIRED OF GENTLEMEN

NO ALCOHOLIC BEVERAGES ALLOWED ON PREMISES

NO PROFANITY OR BARE FEET ON TABLES

NO TIPPING OR FLIRTING WITH THE HELP

NO COMPLAINTS ON THE POOR FOOD SERVICE

(All meals served with coffee, tea and water. No substitutions. Bag lunches provided upon request).

FRIDAY SUPPER: Stewards on Duty — Tidy Harry and Big Bad La Bleu

Quick Spaghetti (freshly prepared from the can); delicious dinner sausage in the pink, breads aromatically removed from the oven, organically grown fresh carrots and celery sticks; Alka Seltzer on the Rocks.

SATURDAY BREAKFAST: Stewards on Duty — Dirty Griff and Dirtier Les

Southern fried Ham, Eggs Manischewitz (Eggs delightfully scrambled in red and blue wines); hot biscuits delicately aged and reclaimed from WWII; juice affectionately squeezed from attractive oranges.

SATURDAY SUPPER: Stewards on Duty — Sober Bob and Cat Skinner Mac

Chicken and Spare Ribs, a la Hawaiian exquisitely marinated in a sauce delightfully prepared from Friday Night leftovers and barbequed to perfection; rice a la Ireland, (prepared with green Manischewitz nectar with each little green grain fried to perfection); Mysticism Salad—a refreshing green salad with Oriental Dressing and various high protein ingredients (served as nature intended with wings, legs, hair and all).

SUNDAY BREAKFAST: Stewards on Duty — Just Plain Le Bleu and Plainer Harry

Sunday Morning Eye Opener (Snappy Tom with genuine Shasta Lake water); crispy bacon served with or without fresh mountain lake trout, plain old eggs with the aroma of the old West; breakfast rolls (formerly identified as Saturday Morning Biscuit—recycled for your pleasure).

SUNDAY DINNER: Stewards on Duty — Dirtier Les and Griff, the Gambler Barbecued steak (USDA Choice Extra Lean Beef bone) surrounded with bits of Beef—prepared for your individual taste; Chili beans, a la hot—a succulent and traditional dish that will tenderize and digest any bone; baked potato with sour cream that will digest any chili beans made; wilted gray green salad, wilted to exacting wiltedness from Saturday night to exciting shades of green, gray and black.

MONDAY BREAKFAST: Stewards on Duty—Handsome Mac and Still Sober Bob

French toast—made as only the French can; Breakfast Sausage—guaranteed to be fat-free and meatless; sweet and sour fruits—a delicate balance of choice and select fruits to complete an adventure-in-time dining.

YOUR PATRONAGE HAS BEEN APPRECIATED COME BACK YOU ALL

We started having Christmas parties for the group, sometimes alternating with Doug and Mary. They were potluck, informal affairs ending with the appearance of Santa Claus (one of the men) sometimes dressed in a Santa suit or a red nightcap and a pillow stuffed into a large, red nightgown (borrowed from Mary Gentes) and tied with a rope. A beard, made of a roll of cotton batting, held in place with elastic, did not disguise who he was. All the girls had to sit on his lap before they could have their presents. Those were usually white elephants brought by the guests, or things costing less than two dollars. Everyone who had any connection with the workings of the lab was invited. The parties became famous after a while.

We were not interested in climbing whatever were the social heights at Lockheed. We couldn't afford to live in the more exclusive towns on the Peninsula. And Bob, though he loved the game, did not play golf well enough to want to belong to a country club. We were very comfortable in our own niche, our lifestyle.

Early on, I wanted Bob to go back for his doctorate. It would have been hard financially, but I thought we could do it. But as he was learning more and more about this new field of high-temperature ceramics, he realized he would not be learning anything more than he already knew or would be learning in the lab. It would be a waste of time and money. However, that meant he would never really be included in that special society of those with higher degrees. I don't think that ever bothered him.

SAMPE, Society of Aerospace Material and Process Engineers, started the Northern California Chapter in 1969 and Bob became a charter member. He always went to the monthly meetings, usually with Harry Nakano. That was his night to kick back, stay out late and come back home with a slightly apologetic look on his face. I never asked what he and Harry did after the meetings were over. I said if it was a wild time, I didn't want to know, but I knew Bob and Harry and didn't really worry. Once I asked Harry why they came home so late and he smiled and said Bob always said it was too early to leave.

He belonged to the American Ceramic Society and usually attended their symposiums and also to the British Ceramic Society, which was too far away to visit.

He could not tell jokes very well, usually mangled the punch line and made up terrible puns, but he had a great sense of the ridiculous. There is a tale about the time he was flying a boxed-up, three-foot nose cone to its destination. It had its own ticket and was belted in the seat next to him. Bob, several more men from Lockheed and the nose cone were seated in the back in the smoking section. Bob, with most likely the impish expression on his face he sometimes had, poked holes in the box on either side, lit up a cigar, blew smoke in one hole and watched it come out the other. No one ever said what the other passengers thought about it but his travel companions never forgot it. It probably drove the attendants crazy.

Ed Gzowski remembered the time Bob had trouble with the accounting office about a travel expense. The accounting office kept tight rein on expenses. "United had just one class flight called the business class which was higher than coach but lower than first class. Bob, on a trip, finished his business early, wanted to come home and could only get a seat in first class. Well, of course accounting wanted to know why he didn't take coach. So he wrote back telling them that none was available, 'I had to change my schedule and that was the only flight available.' They weren't satisfied with that. They kept going back and forth. Finally he wrote to them and said, 'Look, I went to the airline and asked for coach. They said they only had business and first-class seats.' He said, 'I'm not first class. I'm a Lockheed employee. Can I ride in the wheel well?' And they said, 'no, that is only for overseas flights with stowaways.' Then he said, 'How about riding on the tail?' He sent that in and never heard anything back from them."

He could tell good stories about people he knew from way back, rather like vignettes, which were especially appreciated by Jerry Coy, another Southerner (who claimed to have the largest stomach muscle in Santa Clara County). Though Jerry didn't stay at Lockheed very long, the two remained friends, enjoying each other's sense of humor. Jerry said, "Bob and I started at Lockheed about a week within each other. We were the new guys on the block. I don't think I had anything to do with the tiles, actually, but I did have an electronic microscope over in the corner and a piece of an X-ray florescent and extraction product which eventually got converted on a temporary basis to an X-ray radiography unit. And Bob was bringing in these little windings he was making and I was making radiographs of the samples. We had quite a series of pictures at the time. All I remember about working with Bob was his stories, the incredible number of stories he had. And the way he would take something totally innocuous and make it funny. He had a story he told about some little guy in the navy who was being challenged by some big people in a bar. This little guy was saying, 'I'm gonna throw judo on you, I'm gonna throw judo on you.' You would never think a story like that would be funny, but after Bob got done telling it, it was hilarious."

Jerry also remembered a presentation Bob did at a meeting of the department. He brought with him a long, thin flexible ceramic fiber rope and as he talked about it, he flipped it so that it looped around itself to make a loose knot. Then, of course, it collapsed and broke. It impressed everyone there.

Bob, never told dirty jokes and really didn't like them, but he did make up rather ribald parodies to some songs. "Can't go on, my virginity is gone . . . stormy weather" or "Brassiere, for all the things that I hold dear" or dredged up from his childhood, a tamer, "Toreador, don't spit on the floor. Use the cuspidor. That is what it's for." He couldn't carry a tune, either and had to be dissuaded from singing or whistling in public.

He hid his sensitivity very well, but his emotions were close to the surface for some things, usually experiencing someone else's emotions, especially in the movies. One of his favorite films was *Captains Courageous* with Wallace Beery and Jackie Cooper. He had a video copy of it and when the grandkids came to visit, he liked to play it for them. Always at the end, he would be sitting in his chair choking up, trying not to cry and blowing his nose and the kids would snicker, delightedly.

He was always deeply moved whenever he heard the tune of the Londonderry Air (Danny Boy). It was the tune of a hymn sung at church, "O dreamer, leave thy dreams for joyful waking," and he would always tear up through the first verse. He also loved the romantic "Claire de Lune" by Debussy. It always caught him in the throat when he listened to it.


We often laughed about how everyone in the lab lived in better homes than we did. We really needed a larger one.

In 1966, after looking at new homes and older homes in the area, we saw one we both loved. It was affordable, large and in Sunnyvale—an easy commute for Bob. Sunnyvale was considered a lunchbox community at that time, but it had a reputation for being safe and well run and we loved its friendliness and community feeling. The house in Shaker Heights was sold about this time. We weren't rich, but not poor anymore.

In his letters back home to Florida, Bob extolled the wonders of California so much that Mark and Lou moved out in 1961 and settled close by in Palo Alto. It was quite an adjustment for us and we were grateful that we had had ten years away from all family ties. My parents moved to San Jose from Florida in 1968 to be close to me, their only child.


### *Excerpt from 1994 tape*


Sputnik went up sometime in the last part of 1959. And there was a satellite the U.S. sent up and it would drop back whatever information it had on a parachute which would be caught by an airplane running with a wire. And so, space was a new thought to me. I had never, ever had a thought about that.

Of course, earlier work had been going on all the way back to the missile work at Peenemünde with von Braun during

World War II . . . sending bombs to Britain where its reentry was really . . . I guess covering a warhead . . . its only purpose was to survive the friction of air as it went through it. Because it didn't go out into orbit as it traveled through air and heated up, its only purpose was to survive until it was time to blow up. So that was the background of that.

That technology came over to our country, to the Huntsville Arsenal. They called it Huntsville Arsenal, but that was early NASA—Huntsville NASA. So, they were in this country, all the German scientists. And the next thing that surprised us was the Russians sent up satellites, not just communications satellites . . . they sent a man into space . . . on an up and down. The vehicle parachuted back in after hitting the atmosphere. It wasn't really that much, but they did it.

And then, America decided, "Hey, we'd better get into this." And the first thing that we did was make a missile, which we were going to copy from the Russians. It was called the Vanguard Missile. And that is the famous picture that you see sometimes—that the Martin Company in Baltimore, Maryland made. They were behind that. They were the forerunner of Martin Marietta and that one blew up on the pad. It just became a fantastic amount of flame on the pad.

The next thing after that, they turned to WWII German scientists who had come to Huntsville and had them build the V2 rocket, which was really redoing what they had done in bombing England. And they sent up some things and then the first man . . . Alan Shepherd, the first American into space. This was an up and down and it parachuted back. Then John Glenn was the first man to go around the globe . . . the world and come back. Again, the vehicle parachuted back down. So, the reentry was to come back down low enough to where a parachute would work in the atmosphere. And then it would land in the ocean.

Now, that was Mercury and then eventually, they had Gemini, which is sort of the same type of thing. So, after the Mercury and Gemini programs, there was a long, long pause

and from that then—after a long study of what in the world
NASA was going to do—Kennedy, because of the success of
the Russians and the bad economy in the country and some of
the bad things that had happened . . . almost failure in the first
half of his presidency . . . challenged the country and the world,
that we were going to put a man on the moon and return him
safely. That became NASA's mission.

And so from that they made studies which meant that the
contractors made studies and NASA took the credit. But, they
organized it and brought it all together and from that came
the moon launches. First they launched something to go up
unmanned.

They had a launch while I happened to be in Florida, called
the Paper Moon. I don't know why, but that was a popular song
at the time. And they sent up these flights to see if they could
reach as far as the moon. And this was all leading toward the
Apollo program. And as I said, I was in Florida at the time of
the Paper Moon flight. The reason I was there is interesting,
because it was my first experience in missiles and a really
designed reentry and in this case an exiting body.

The problem had been that when a missile is sent up, its
instruments are almost blacked out during the ascent and they
didn't know why. They thought it might be because of a lot of
debris, yet, they wouldn't know what the debris was because
there's not much heating . . . its very low heating at that time
when it exits. There's not much to contribute to it being debris.

So, I was presented with this problem . . . I don't remember
the temperature, but it really is a temperature rather mild even
by home oven standards, a couple of hundred degrees . . . of
making something that would make a lot of debris, or I'm
going to say, garbage. So, a lot of stuff in space as the missile
exits so that their instruments could detect . . . if that was the
problem or what. So, I was given a little bit of funding to make
something that could be slipped over the pointed part of an
old, out-of-date missile (one that was before Polaris). I don't
remember the name of it, but anyway, they used them and kept

them around for testing things. And so, here in California, I made a filament-wound structure which was inorganically bonded. The structure was rather open to accommodate filling it with a lot of things that would actually sublime at the right heat to make a cloud . . . a debris cloud of stuff . . . so that they would be able to detect that.

And so, I made it and it was flown to Florida . . . I think on the backseat of some two-seat Aris Air Force plane and I was to put it on this missile before the flight. Well, when I got there, the first thing I found out was they had told me the wrong bolt type. They had omitted the information that the bolts were not flush on the missile . . . actually in those days they weren't conscious of it being a problem. They were round-headed bolts. And so, I had to look all over the state of Florida to find some flat-head bolts that would fit on that missile that I could put in place of the round-heads.

And so, I did that up inside this gantry, hugging the nose of this missile . . . changing bolts . . . not knowing much about missiles . . . I had never even seen a missile before. And so, then I did make the exchange and the thing that I had brought, the filament-wound structure, fit down very nice and snuggly over the nose of the missile. Prior to that . . . while at the motel, I had worried about whether it would really work. You know . . . what about it in this Florida sun? It got so hot in the sun I noticed as I was in my motel . . . gosh, it was so hot. So, I made a little sample of it and put it out on the balcony in the sun and I found out, yes, it really would turn to smoke. Particularly if I left the plastic on top it really got hot, so I knew I had to really be careful of it; it was so sensitive. I can't remember what it was, leaded carbonyl or something like that.

So, I put it on this missile. I thought, boy, don't hit the button, don't hit the button, as I'm up there hugging that thing. So then, I came down and we went into whatever they call it, the pillbox or whatever, where all the instruments and the people are. The idea of this missile was to test out a new guidance system. The guidance system was going to be one that would find and zero in on the North Star . . . Polaris. And so, anyway, they were worried about whether the missile would be able to see the star . . . if there was a lot of smoke and garbage debris. So, we were in the pillbox and they shoot it and it goes up, up, sphweee . . . it being a solid propelled one . . . it goes . . . just one minute it's there and about practically the next minute it's not there. It's just so fast. And, it went up and it flipped over and went out as they intended it to go . . . toward the ocean and further out. Then, all of a sudden, it turned around and started coming back . . . headed back at us. And the range officer had to hit the button to blow it up before it came back to the beach.

We later found out what the problem was. Back in the range office, when they were programming it, they A-OKd and they plugged in the coordinates for the North Star, but a guy A-OKd and put in the reverse numbers. And so, the poor missile went up, desperately looking for the North Star, couldn't find it—it was looking in the Southern Hemisphere for the North Star. And of course, there was nothing there, so it flipped over . . . it was coming back. So it had to be blown up. But there was enough telemetry on it to find out that, yes, what I had done had worked beautifully. All sorts of clouds came off. So, that wasn't the problem. They realized that wasn't the problem after all. That was my first introduction of anything going into space.

And, as I said, this occurred at the same time as the Paper Moon flight and that was a liquid rocket . . . a large liquid rocket . . . and going to the moon, not the liquid part, but the part on top. And I was there and I was really impressed because this tremendous . . . it was all the difference in the world . . . here's this tremendous thing rather than this small, sleek thing. And it starts up and it doesn't go zip; it shakes and rumbles . . . the whole state seems to shake. There was so much noise and vibration that I felt . . . from miles away, I felt like my skin was really cavitating, like it was shaking. So that was a liquid fuel flight of a large object.

The group was given a new project, the Reentry Systems Environmental Protection Program (RESEP) and the lab was moved to Sunnyvale, to building 102, a large, long tilt-up, with long metal benches and work stations and not much thought of efficiency in placement of the large ovens, counters and tables. There was a closet of lab coats the men sometimes wore. Pat said they put them on, if they could find a clean one that fit, whenever a publicity picture was being taken, so they would look professional. When working with the material, they always wore gloves to keep it uncontaminated.

The program was classified at the time and therefore in a closed area. A new program manager, Wayne Shannon and Bob proposed to the air force and won the contract for a nose tip for a missile that would enter the earth's atmosphere at a very low trajectory where the environment is very harsh. It was designated as Task Two in the program. Lab personnel under Leo at that time were: Harry Nakano, Chuck Dewey, Bill Ravenelle, Al Pechman, Pat McCormick, Bob, Dean Fisher and, of course, Doug.

Morrie Steinberg went to corporate headquarters in Los Angeles at this time and Bob missed his enthusiasm for what the lab was trying to accomplish.


One Saturday afternoon, in 1968, Bobby fell on a piece of sharp plastic and gouged a piece out of his knee. Bob took him to the Sunnyvale Medical Clinic to have it bandaged. As he was watching the doctor patch the wound, he fainted. The doctor took tests right there, listened to his heart and heard something that didn't sound right. Many tests later, including catheterization, showed that Bob had been born with a faulty aorta heart valve. Instead of three flaps that regulated the flow of blood to and from the heart, he had only two. They had been sufficient when he was younger, but as he aged, they accumulated calcium deposits and something would have to be done about it, or it could prove fatal.

Valve transplants were fairly new. The wife of one of Bob's cohorts had had a valve replacement, which was successful, but it was still considered risky. There were two types of replacement valves: a pig valve (a porcine heterograph as Bob liked to call it), or a plastic valve that had the bad reputation of causing dangerous blood clots. It would never have to be replaced, however. The pig valve was supposed to last about ten years and another one would have to be put in its place.

Several days before the operation, all the people in the lab gave Bob a lunch, just to show him support for his ordeal. It was a traumatic time for everyone with the still new operation to be gone through. The night before the operation, Bobby was to get his Boy Scout Life badge and Bob's doctor gave him permission to leave the hospital and attend the ceremony. It was just what we needed, a chance for us all to be together in a normal setting. That night, back at the hospital, he told his nurse he really yearned for a hamburger, so she sent out for one for him. It was the best one he had ever tasted.

The operation was at El Camino Hospital in Mountain View where young Dr. Robert Enright specialized in this new type of surgery. It was decided, during the operation, that instead of replacing the valve, they would debris it. The valve, itself, was healthy. It would have to be replaced eventually, but science would most likely perfect the operation even more and there would be less of a risk. The operation was a success but unfortunately Bob contracted pump fever, which set back his complete recovery for about a month.

Before they were able to get very far with the RESEP program, Bob had to have the heart surgery, but almost before he had fully recovered, he began traveling to various air force facilities to make presentations. Bob said they just stood him up before a group and he'd talk.

According to Harry, after the first few presentations had been made, Bob became the presenter of the whole program and the program became his. "One thing Bob was great at was whenever there was a monthly meeting with our customers and even if product wasn't made, he would make a great presentation. He became the main character in the new RESEP program and everybody else supported him. In Palo Alto, there was chemistry and plastics. There were individuals there, most of them Ph.D.'s, but Bob outshone them all. When he made presentations, those were the only ones I remember.

Other guys would talk on and on, but I can't remember what they talked about, but I remember Bob's. Bob enjoyed this program because he had the freedom to explore many novel ideas.

"To us, it was a very interesting program because we looked at all kinds of organic materials and also some filament materials and we cataloged it all. Pat McCormick made the program a success because he made all the specimens. We had the ideas, but he was able to put everything into usable test specimens and categorized them all. There was a lot of underground testing in Nevada of the filament-wound specimens gathered from companies all over the country, as well as Lockheed's."

Bob, to some, was considered a genius, but Harry, more down-to-earth and knowing Bob as well as anyone, said he did not fit the accepted model of geniuses. He considered Bob an ordinary human being. He said, "The genius I contributed to him was his early focus on inorganically bonded silica fiber as high-temperature insulation and his belief that a reliable material could be developed and did so in the face of many naysayers in the scientific community. The genius in Bob made him select silica as the fiber and his conviction that a reliable material could be developed made him persist against all obstacles."

The RESEP Program was successful and work on it lasted for several years. According to Ed Gzowski, there was a short follow up, but the air force gave up the project. By the time all the testing had been made, the funding was eaten up, but the program purchased all new equipment and everything was left in the lab. This equipment was very important in the later experiments Bob did without the help of Lockheed funding. Bob received a certificate of commendation for "substantial and important contributions" to the recently completed RESEP proposal. "Excellent technical competence, enthusiastic and devoted effort and ability to meet severe deadlines were clearly visible in Mr. Beasley's performance on the proposal. The excellence of the finished document is largely creditable to this effort."

A letter of appreciation from M. Tucker, Manager of Flight Technology, with copies to Leo Schapiro and Ed Burke said, "I should like to express thanks for your recent effort applied to the preparation of the RESEP Task 2 Final Report. Your unselfish attitude in expending much of your personal time in an effort to meet the publication schedule is sincerely appreciated."

During this time and even much earlier, he was trying, without success, to drum up interest in a material that he thought had unique thermal protective qualities, the pure silica fibers. At lunchtimes and with odd hours borrowed from other funding, or traded with other programs and with salesmen's free samples, he experimented with this idea, but Lockheed was definitely not interested in any of it, at least not then.

Dept. 5230, Materials Technology Lab members, 1968:
1st row, Harry Nakano, Joyce Livingston, Leo Schapiro
2nd row, Chuck Dewey, Bob, Dean Fisher
3rd row, Tom Patton, Pat McCormick
4th row, Bill Ravenell, Al Pechman, Inset, Doug Izu

Bob and Harry, in shirtsleeves, with nosecone, 1968

Escape to Lake Shasta: Bob Griffith, Bob, Les Shoff, Pat McCormick, Harry Nakano, Bob LeBlue. Doug took photo, 1971

Tiger team hero and tiger in our back yard, 1968.

The Dixie, Bob and me, Captain and Admiral, 1995

# Chapter Six

# The Shirtsleeve Invention

*Excerpt from 1994 tape*

I was not funded for anything involved in the space program at this time. My problems were more down to earth, like, how can I get support for today and tomorrow without getting a surplus notice that I would not be continuing my employment? This worry I felt throughout most of my career at Lockheed and even at Corning. However, mostly unknown to me there was activity in space.

NASA, after their successes in the Gemini, Apollo and Mercury programs, had no objectives for continued work in space. But, they did have money, so there were let-out programs to various companies for computer studies about what they should do. And as I say, I was not aware of these; they were completely out of my field. But, I believe one of these studies, Lockheed was interested in, comes to my mind . . . a Space Tug, which I believe was somehow an early thought of a shuttle.

And there was another thing called a lifting entry body . . . a reentry body. And that was something shaped like a bathtub in a way. And I did build one, on bid and proposal money. And this was, because of its shape, if it was going fast enough, there was enough lift without wings . . . sort of like the shuttle is now . . . without wings there would be just enough lift to slow it down a bit.

So these were all early studies that probably led to the evolution of a shuttle type of thought. But, they were very desperate times for me because there was no funding and no interest in anything I had. And as I said, referring to Lockheat anything that I might think of as a more efficient thermal protection system was not of interest at all. As a matter of fact it was sometimes resented because they had things that had worked and had already been used and proven. And so, if you could prove something would work . . . and of course, you had no way of getting out in space and putting it out to test, then they might talk to you, but otherwise, no, unh uh.

Lockheed Management wasn't in the least . . . even Research was not in the least interested in what I was doing or what I proposed. However, Lockheed was part of these let-out programs for computer studies and they really needed a stronger entry point into NASA's activities. They were able to get their studies, but they were leading nowhere. There was nothing concrete there. Finally, I believe, the studies had progressed to the point where they began to wonder, "Gee, let's test something to see how it could perform or how we might be able to utilize something." And along these lines . . . that's when the program office at Lockheed, which had been formed and mushroomed into size, became interested in what I was doing.

Bob's thoughts about a product—a material that could act as a heat shield for any kind of reentry vehicle, starting with Lockheat and its filament winding processes had found some interest within the company, but early on, he had become greatly interested in how pure silica fibers could produce a better system. He had to work on his own time on his ideas without funding, trying to sell it to anyone who would listen in the company. Leo Schapiro and Ed Burke weren't impressed with the idea, not realizing its unique potential.

However, Morrie Steinberg, before he went to corporate headquarters in Los Angeles was very interested in what Bob was doing and tried to get the head of materials for G.E. in Cincinnati interested in the uses of the bonded fibers for use as a frangible seal for HP turbine blades but was not successful.

It was about this time that Morrie asked a former roommate and then a professor at Notre Dame University to determine how the bonding of the fibers occurred. He put some fibers and a few drops of Ludox, a colloidal silica solution from DuPont, on a microscope slide and as the water of the Ludox evaporated, he noted that the charge on the colloidal silicate was attracted to the fibers and the charges actually caused the binding. Later, a high-temperature stage on an electron microscope was used to prove that the amorphous fibers stayed amorphous and did not crystallize to quartz after repeated heating to 2500 degrees F. Now there was proof, outside the lab to show that Bob's idea could do what he said it could do.

Jack Milton, the new manager of the then, small program department saw the silica fibers Bob had been working on, thought the idea might have possibilities and began to promote it himself within the company. Bob was fortunate in that Milton was willing to gamble on his idea. Jack Milton, since 1958, had worked exclusively on space-related activities such as reusable space transportation systems. He became known as the advocate of nonmetallic HRSI materials in the industry. And he had the job of forming the larger program office to meet all the new needs of the company to compete for the shuttle contract.

### *Excerpt from 1994 tape*

And so, it was "We'll give you enough man hours, one or two, to make a sample—shaped like this and this thick and it's supposed to go through this environment and perform—and if it works, why fine! We might even ask for another one. But, this is all done on bid and proposal, so you must always succeed and be a raging success or otherwise we won't ask for another sample." And so, all of this was generally testing, environmental testing. Freezing, heating, no heating, freezing, vacuum, then more freezing, more vacuum, ultraviolet light, acoustic sound vibration, mechanical properties, structural properties, whatever.

Bid and proposal was a system within the company in which ideas for development from various departments were presented to management, asking for development money to carry them out. Sometimes, this was a long process with much funding allocated. At other times, it was done by piecemeal and was not readily forthcoming.

The basic material, itself, the pure silica fibers and the colloidal silica binder never changed, but they were manipulated, that is, arranged, added to, or pressed in different ways, with more or less colloidal silica used to meet certain problems. There were several stringent requirements to be met—withstand acoustical vibration and rapid decompression at launch and rapid compression at reentry for one hundred cycles, withstand temperatures up to 2500 degrees F and still maintain its dimensional stability, withstand the conditions of space, solar heat, extreme cold and total vacuum, get rid of moisture and air without fracture during launch and reentry, be waterproof to cope with earth's water conditions, be ultra-lightweight to add to payload capabilities.

Finally, in late 1972, tests at Lockheed were finished and a report was given at a symposium at NASA Ames on reusable surface insulation for a space shuttle. The report, by S. J. Housten, J. A. De Runtz and D. R. Elgin was on specialized environmental testing other than reentry heating.

The summary said, "Testing to date has demonstrated the compatibility of all the silica RSI system to a variety of space shuttle orbiter environmental aspects for launch, on-orbit and special reentry conditions.

"With continued development, more testing will be performed particularly with combined environments and improved simulation of the orbiter environment. However, the work to date has served to substantiate the LMSC choice of the silica material."

A later article in the thirteenth issue of *Lockheed Horizons*, 1983, written by Doug, Ron Banas and Wilson Schramm, told about other key elements of the system that included quartz windshields, the Reinforced Carbon-Carbon (RCC) leading edges and nose cap, flexible hinge-line thermal barriers and the carrier plate attachment systems. Rockwell International Corporation was responsible for these elements as well as the thermal and structural design of the tile and its attachment system.

In 1968, before the above tests fully proved the tile's utility, LI-1500 was officially chosen by the company as its contender for the thermal protection system for the shuttle. It was usually referred to as the "Tile Program."

As before, because of the government-classified nature of the project, the facility was designated "Closed Area 36" with a cipher-locked door and only Bob's group had the cipher code. This security system proved useful because they were able to control access to the laboratory and they allowed in only the people they wanted to enter. This access control lasted long after the security requirement had been removed. Many outside organizations hated this system, but those inside loved it as it kept outside interference to a minimum and gave them freedom to pursue many oddball concepts.

### *Excerpt from 1994 tape*

We would make samples and they would go test them. And it was always . . . I would have to quote the exact number of hours to make a sample; never was there a way of developing or testing something . . . even receiving chemical tests . . . any test at all. It was just your best guess and this has got to be it and if it looks good, then fine, we might ask you for another one.

Harry said, "It dawned on me that the place was like a miniature Skunk Works in Sunnyvale where Bob had a pretty tight reign on what we were doing. But also we had a lot of freedom to do many things and, in fact, Bob encouraged that, because he never wanted to do ordinary things. He wanted something creative. So he let us do all kinds of crazy things. And I think, because he was always encouraging creativity—and he was himself, of course, a great creator, that the space shuttle insulation was born. It took a lot of creative minds to actually present this concept into a useable material."

Harry's previous career was in paint research and so he was a natural when it came to working with coating and glazes.

George Hamma, senior staff scientist at Lockheed during the early days working on the proposal was involved in testing the material for the company. He said:

We were trying to help the systems that did the dimensional confirmation of the machined product. So I got involved in two different areas. Some of the people I worked with were Alan Holmes, who designed the mechanical tests; Mike Duggan, an engineer who made up the test systems; and technicians, Les Fisher and Rich Yee. We had to make some pretty different kinds of machines in order to test the materials. We had a couple of tasks to deal with. One of them was to determine the mechanical properties of the material itself. So we would get samples and we had to build a machine that could both crush it and pull it apart and then carefully measure everything. We also worked with application of heat. We had these little samples glowing away and then we would pull them apart. Also, I remember doing biaxial tests on little cylinders of this stuff. It was kind of like doing tests on tissue paper and glass at the same time.

I know we tested little rectangles of material for mechanical properties and we had to do it under all shock conditions and everything. So basically we had to create a whole new set of tools in order to be able to explore what this thing was that had been created. So it was very interesting.

On the Sunnyvale side of things, the biggest problem I dealt with was trying to get various computer makers to talk to each other because you had Hewlett Packard here and Digital Equipment there and then you had numerical control machine tools and none of them wanted to communicate with each other. But it was needed in order to be able to try to automate the testing process. Each company had done its own proprietary style of working together with communication lines. So, all these different systems had to be disciplined so that they could eventually come up with a common means of talking. I think this was probably the first time we did that in the company . . . was, in order to get this system going, to test the tiles once they were manufactured.

Bob originated an idea to make some unauthorized test equipment and Harry Nakano and Chuck Dewey rigged up two high-temperature heat lamps that exposed two tiles alternately to 2400 degrees F at a heat-up rate simulating reentry. The use of this rig allowed them to heat up to one hundred cycles with no one in attendance. This, of course, was not a sanctioned test, so it was never reported, but it gave them valuable information. Those in the lab did many improvisations like that, either at Bob's suggestion or their own.

### *Excerpt from 1994 tape*

This all came together into a period of my life that I sort of look at and I have named "yes, but." Yes, but, what if . . . yes, but, what if it rains? OK. Yes, but, what if it vibrates? Yes, but, what if there is a lot of sound . . . which there is, what would you do? Well, for each of these questions I would have to make a sample and have to answer it. And so, when it came to the moisture, yes, but. I made the material hydrophobic. I treated it so it absolutely repelled water. And that was interesting because, later one day, that property would come to help me . . . that capability.

But, with each test, I would make my best guess and make a test specimen, with maybe an hour's support of time, maybe two hours and then, some of that better be from the machine shop or whatever, if it's got to be made a certain shape. And if it doesn't work, since this is bid and proposal money, we won't be asking for any more. You will have failed and that's it. This went on for a long, long time.

We even had to make samples that NASA put on one of its airplanes and flew around the country. I don't know what test that was, but it was on the wing . . . or some part of the body of an airplane as it flew around. I remember the name; I think it was Gulf Star. And another one . . . a NASA test, there was a short missile firing up in Virginia someplace. We had to make a sample for that. And that was our first missile. There was a lot of importance attached to that. And even now, I still see it quoted that it had flown on a missile.

LMSCs proposal included the preliminary idea for the orbiter resembling a Delta body with all engines buried in the interior and carrying throw-away liquid fuel tanks and much different from Rockwell's concept, which eventually won the contract. The company was not involved with any tile design Rockwell had for its orbiter.

The Lockheed program office, with its many people, had a tremendous task in designing their proposal for the orbiter and later, when it had chosen LI-1500 as its TPS, had to figure out just how the material could be placed on the orbiter body, itself. Murat Kural, who had been doing structural design studies to support the system proposal funded by the Johnson Space Center, was one of the members of that team. Everyone recognized that tile size and its attachment to an aluminum substrate presented challenges due to the high differences in the thermal expansion between silica and aluminum. If the tile was bonded directly to an aluminum substructure, it would break apart the first time it was heated. A flexible rubberlike material was needed to bridge the gap in thermal expansion between the two materials and the tile size needed to be small enough to limit the actual linear differences in expansion. Through Kural's analysis, $6 \times 6$ inch tiles were established as the optimum size. He also determined the engineering requirement for the strain isolation pad (SIP) and determined the spacing requirement between tiles when bonded to the aluminum substrate. His concept also included a strain arrester plate (SAP). The final engineering requirements were established later by the winning prime contractor, Rockwell. According to Harry, Kural's work was valuable and a starting point for Rockwell.

In the 1983 **Lockheed Horizons** magazine article about the early tile program, it was discussed why the insulation system was subdivided into individual tiles. In the article it stated that, "They had to be able to accommodate the complex contours of the aluminum airframe as well as to absorb large differential thermal expansions over extremes of temperature during the mission—from minus 170 degrees F in extended orbital cold-soak conditions to 2300 degrees F during reentry. Pure silica LI-900 tile spans are typically in the six—to—ten-inch range (LI-900 was a lighter weight development of the material). The strain isolation pad (SIP) and bond system supports the tile in flight, absorbs the internal cold-soak thermal differential stain and floats the tile on the aluminum airframe structure as it flexes under dynamic loading conditions."

According to the article,

The tiles accomplish three major tasks:

1.  The tiles dissipate 90 percent of the reentry heat energy by radiation to the earth's atmosphere and deep space from the Reaction Cured Glass (RCG) coating which is only 1-2 mils thick. The energy is transformed into surface heating at incandescent temperatures and is dissipated because of the high emissivity inherent in the coating's optical properties. The RCG coating forms the aerodynamic skin of the Orbiter vehicle and rapidly heats to 2000 degrees F for ten minutes during reentry. The peak heating rate typically is 25 Btu/sq ft during this critical period.

2.  The tiles provide the unique fused silica fiber insulation structure that allows a rapid surface temperature response and supports the glass aerodynamic skin of the vehicle. The structural insulation delays in-depth temperature response and takes the thermal shock and acoustic impulses. Each fused silica tile transmits the aerodynamic loads into the orbiter airframe structure through a Strain Isolation Pad. About 5 percent of the incident energy is dissipated by convection back to the cooler atmosphere during let-down for a landing.

3.  The tiles delay the remaining 5 percent incident energy from reaching the aluminum orbiter airframe structure until after the landing is completed. The low thermal diffusivity, a unique property of density, specific heat and thermal conductivity delays this heat pulse typically for thirty minutes while the aluminum structure never exceeds 350 degrees F.

Later on, as more was realized about problems of reentry, parameters were changed but for the most part, Kural's ideas were still used by Rockwell throughout the program.

### *Excerpt from 1994 tape*

Lockheed had no interest in materials, but built a tremendous proposal staff with many men at drafting boards and that was the program office—a big activity. There was a great interest in that. And there was an interest in cultivating the NASA agencies, because at this same time, all the NASA agencies were among themselves competing for who was going to get the big piece of pie. Even NASA Ames and NASA Lewis which were two small, relatively small places, were really in there to get a piece of the pie. I don't know the capability Lewis had, but Ames at least had a wind tunnel and so they were ultimately able to use their wind tunnel to test thermal material.

But the real entry point that Lockheed had, even though they desired the engineering contract, was the material. And so, I had to go to all the agencies of NASA, including headquarters and make presentations about the material, LI-1500. I remember at one presentation I was giving, a man sitting in the back got up and stomped out of the room. He eventually came back with a large volume which he leafed through furiously. He must not have found what he wanted in order to refute my claims because he finally gave up and just glared at me.

Lockheed early on decided they would have a competitive advantage . . . the program office . . . if they took the position that the material had been the result of years of research and development, with a great deal of money and effort put into it. And that if they were to get the contract, then NASA would save much money . . . the government would save money by not having to develop anything. And so, really they took that position—that it had already been done with in-house money. That the only things that needed to be done, maybe a few vehicular tests that NASA might want, but no development would be needed whatsoever. Well, this presented a problem for Lockheed really. It sounded very good, but almost immediately they realized that they couldn't let anybody know about the material. So they became very secretive. I had a secret laboratory where, individually, the employees signed drawn agreements of nondisclosure. It meant I could not write, I could not report, I could not talk about it to anyone since it was a secret for the government. And so there was a cloak entirely on my work. And Lockheed was very careful not to let the material get out of their hands. They would make a sample just for a test and then be there for that test. And although they did sell a few test specimens to NASA, there was a thing that would make me smile. It was that if you got the specimen, you could look at it with a microscope and see that it had this structure of fibers and whatever, but you couldn't see what was holding them together. And if you tried to chemically analyze it, or even analyze it with X-ray, it would all come out as only silica. It was sort of maddening. It wouldn't necessarily tell you what kind, but anyway it would be silica.

I later became aware, sort of on the peripheral of all of this that the various NASA agencies as they were trying to vie for the position of having the main program, each also sort of seemed to champion various potential thermal contractors. And some of the contractors really had no more than really a desire. I can't even name a product they ever had. For example, McDonnell Douglas was one of them and G.E. was another one. Of course, NASA Langley was a champion of G.E. G.E. really had the raw material which they didn't realize was the raw material. In other words, the same silica fiber I had used

on the Apollo Radome. And then there was Martin Marietta . . .
had a desire, I don't recall the product. Those companies that
didn't have products generally were trying to discredit the
one product that was out which happened to be mine. I later
became aware that NASA Langley, which had, I believe,
an in-house ceramist, Dr. Somebody . . . I've forgotten his
name . . . well, they purchased some materials of LI-1500 at
the time, presumably for a particular test. Later, I was told what
they did . . . that the ceramist told them that if it was silica,
it wouldn't be very good in a salt water environment. Well,
what they did was put racks of it out on the beach in Virginia
and after it was in a lot of the sea fog . . . sea atmosphere,
they would test it. I was told that they even went so far as to
physically put salt water on it, but what they didn't realize is
that yes, during the "yes, but," period I had made the material
hydrophobic and that meant it rejected atmospheric moisture as
well as painted-on moisture. So, it was of no value, their test.
The material performed as it should perform.

During this time, the computer studies were identifying
potential problems. And as it did, new tests were devised and
then I would be contacted again to produce an item to be tested.
I was not funded at all. This was all strictly in-house. It was bid
and proposal; therefore, there was nothing continuous for me; it
was just in terms of we have a test we're going to do and what
will we do? Make a sample and what would the sample be? No
development, no research, nothing. Just whatever I could think
of out of my head and how I could apply the material. Mostly,
by and large, the LI-1500 applied very nicely, but there was
always this underlying fear that each test must be a success, or
it is the last test.

And the program office positioned very well in front of
NASA that it had developed this marvelous material, strictly
on its own and without anyone asking and without asking for
anyone's money. It was entirely our own money. It was very
secret. The program office grew to maybe several hundred
people. My lab and my helpers stayed the same size. Always
starving for support, never knowing where the next hour's

support would come from. I was running around the company, begging other departments to let us support them in whatever they might think they needed. And that was a continuing effort throughout my entire career at Lockheed.

May 1971, Bob's boss, Ed Burke, still wasn't sure about the material and took Bob and some tile material up to the University of Washington in Seattle for a consultation with Dr. James Mueller, head of the Department of Mining, Metallurgical and Ceramics Engineering. His tests proved that Bob's claims about the material were correct. Because of Dr. Mueller's excellent reputation as an expert in the ceramics field, the material gained more acceptance within Lockheed. But still, the testing came only through bid and proposal money.

In July 1971, Ed Burke sent Bob a letter of commendation for his personal file:

The LI-1500 TSP program for the space shuttle is one which is extremely important to the company. The LI-1500 Tiger Team during the past six months played the key role in the successful establishment of a manufacturing process for the LI-1500 material. The recovery program conducted by the team resulted in on-schedule performance on contractual obligations and maintained LMSC's leading position in the space shuttle TPS materials. Additional contracts totaling $560K, starting in July 1971, have been awarded based upon the LI-1500 material system and pilot plant performance.

While we may take justifiable pride in this team effort, it is a pleasure to acknowledge your outstanding individual performance as the team leader. Your unselfish attitude in expending long hours under pressure, as well as your technical direction to overcome the many vexing problems encountered, were the essential ingredients for the program's success.

I am personally aware that your invaluable technical insight and outstanding leadership throughout this program contributed immeasurably to the success of LI-1500.

Please accept my sincere appreciation for your exemplary performance and outstanding contribution to this important program.

E. C. Burke, Director Materials & Structures

There was still great resistance about the material. In fact, early on, there were still some people in the company trying to put together other thermal protection systems to compete with LI-1500, mostly those who had worked with and trusted the proven ablation systems.

At the same time a lighter weight version of the LI-1500 material, designated, LI-900 was being tested along with a denser, heavier material, LI-2200. LI-2200 was later taken over by NASA Ames. Later, in 1971, LI-900 became the prime tile material for Lockheed's bid for the shuttle's thermal protection system. A coating for the tiles, 0042, was also being developed in the lab.

### *Excerpt from 1994 tape*

Meanwhile, the program office decided that it cost too much for the specimens they were asking for. And I believe they felt that they were being cheated. It was obvious they felt that way because they got some auditors, even had them come to my lab and make time studies on our activities. And so, this was really rather upsetting, quite upsetting, for them to think that, while there were a few hundred of them, they thought we five or six were cheating them out of all this money and time.

Well, the auditors spent about a week there observing, never quite understanding what was going on, I'm sure. They would study the motion of a man moving across a room or lifting an object . . . how long it would take him to do it. And the final thing of it is, I believe the report must have gone back favorably for me because, it was just sort of one of those things that died and no one ever dared mention it again.

There were some people in the program office that fully supported Bob. One was Bruce Burns, who everybody respected and who everyone in the lab, including Bob, trusted and appreciated. Bruce had become chief engineer under Kevin Forsberg when he started working with Bob on the tile program.

Bruce at one of the get-togethers said, "My feeling for this program . . . I felt it was a rare opportunity that doesn't come along often. And in the Rockwell people I sensed were really focused on the success of the program. I'm sure there was politics going on in their organization just like there was at Lockheed, but they were pretty focused and objective in what they were doing and I thought Bob was that way, too. And as long as you could focus on your problems and set aside these other aspects you got along pretty well with Bob. Bob was a good man. You know, he stuck to his word when it came to budgets and deliveries and all that good stuff, which eventually drives almost everyone crazy."

Another person was Ron Banas, who had great faith in Bob and the material from the beginning.

### Excerpt from 1994 tape

Meanwhile, I had to make sure everything was absolutely perfect always. About this time the company thought it would be good if we had a pilot plant. We could get a few people to help us. So next to the lab we opened up a pilot plant. This allowed us to have a couple more men to help us. But also, since it was next door to the laboratory, it meant that we could do it cheaper by working it in while we were doing in the lab whatever it was that we did that paid our checks weekly. And it meant that we were able to handle things in larger volume, get out of the big bucket stirring for dispersion and also to get larger equipment and have more help and turn out, of course, more and more samples. But at the same time, the program office was mushrooming by a factor of probably fifty to our one. And so, the studies became greater in size and more involved. Mechanical properties became a real concern . . . somebody would be more concerned of our making materials to be tested for mechanical properties and someone would be interested in vibration and one would be interested in acoustics . . . sounds . . . in acoustic tests. It just meant more and more performance on our part. And always with the standpoint that if there is a failure, that's the end of it. It was all bid and proposal activity.

Most of the tests were non-thermal tests . . . environmental tests. The shuttle was still being defined and its environment requirements by the computer studies and so they were continually evolving. Never in this program was there an initiation of 'here are the properties we want met and you invent something to meet them.' It was the other way around . . . of we will evolve them each step of the way. That's the way the shuttle was evolved, it came out of computer studies.

From the *LOCKHEED STAR*, Friday, July 30, 1971

### LMSC DEVELOPS A NEW TYPE INSULATION FOR SHUTTLE APPLICATION

A featherweight material, candidate for the external heat shield on the Space Shuttle orbiter vehicle, has moved from the laboratory development stage to a pilot plant operation.

Called LI-1500 (for Light-weight Insulation, 15 pounds per cubic foot density), the rigid inorganic composite material is made by an LMSC proprietary process and can be cast or sculptured to required shapes. The silica fiber raw material, prior to processing, resembles newly-picked cotton.

A major technical problem in the Space Shuttle program is developing a lightweight, low cost, reusable reentry heat shield. LI-1500 material shows great potential in solving this problem according to Robert L. Hammitt, project manager for Thermal Protection Systems in the Manned Space Programs organization.

Used as the thermal protection system for the orbiter, according to a seven-month study recently completed here for NASA, the LI-1500 can be bonded to panels attached to frames that will keep the insulation six inches from the fuselage skin. LI-1500 probably will be bonded directly to the stabilizing and control surfaces.

Although temperatures on some surfaces of the orbiter are expected to reach nearly 2500 degrees F. during reentry into the Earth's, atmosphere, the temperature on the panel behind the LI-1500 will not exceed 600 degrees F.

LMSC has spent more than 10 years developing the silica composite process under the guidance of project leader Robert M. Beasley, known among his co-workers as the "father" of LI-1500. A chemical engineer, Beasley said LI-1500 is an unusual insulation material. "Tell us what you want it to do," he said, "and LI-1500 can be custom mixed to your requirements." It may be this flexibility for designed inorganic composite that tends to confuse designers who are accustomed to fitting the design requirements to the properties of the material, rather than "tailor-making" a material to fit the design requirements.

Here are some of the facts on LI-1500:

- It is all silica, both basic fiber material and the binder.

- It can be formulated in extremely lightweight (low density) configurations. This material tested on the outside of a NASA jet and on a NASA sounding rocket nose cone, is about 89 per cent air.

- It can be made with greater density—and hence greater strength and weight—so that it approaches the feel of glazed earthenware.

- It exhibits excellent electromagnetic transparency characteristics—and the dielectric properties can be altered for the application.

- It also is a good insulator at cryogenic (extremely low) temperatures.

- It has been tested for its ability to withstand vibrations that might shatter ordinary, brittle ceramics.

- LI-1500 can be cast in molds and can be shaped to the contours of the object it will protect.

### *Excerpt from 1994 tape*

The demand was quite heavy on the pilot plant for materials . . . samples for tests. It wasn't very long before it was apparent that even the pilot plant couldn't keep up with the demand. So, next to the lab an Initial Production Facility was built . . . a good name chosen for sales reasons. This was adjacent to my lab. In this, things were done on a larger scale and so, instead of stirring in big drums or buckets to get a dispersion of deionized water which we used . . . deionized water and the fibers to disperse them prior to casting, why I was then able to get what people like to call centrifugal casting. I had an industrial clothes washer and I could use it on the spin-dry mode. Using the spinning cycle I could disperse the fibers in the water and then from the second floor, dump them down into the chamber. And in the process that I had developed, it was necessary to take the fibers, which were fascicular . . . porous silica . . . take them first and sinter them so that the pores would close and shrink and then would become dense fibers. And to facilitate doing this, I first dispersed the fibers in deionized water and then poured them into a form to make a block, or in the case of the centrifugal cast, it was a large, round cylinder shape. And from that I could cut out big sections of the material in block form so it could be handled, put into a furnace and heated to close the pores. The material would shrink as the pores were being sintered shut. The fibers would then be re-dispersed in deionized water and then cast to the block shape to form the blocks. These two pretreatments were designated PT1 for the casting . . . original dispersing and casting and PT2 for the sintering of the dried casting. The pre-sintered fibers, which had shrunk approximately one-third of their volume during PT2 represented the initial source of raw material later used for the LI-900 process.

In May 1973, a report on the Initial Production Facility (IPF) was written up by Doug and Bob and included Dean Fisher, Ed Law, Harry Nakano, Al Pechman, Bill Ravenell and Les Shoff. It was titled:

## LMSI HRSI Initial Production Facility Organization and Operation

The IPF is planned to satisfy the material needs for the initial 18 month DDT & E phase of the Rockwell Space Shuttle TPS HRSI Program. Early in 1975, production for the shuttle will be shifted to a larger, new facility under SSD manufacturing. The IPF will be maintained as a pilot plant at a reduced capacity as part of the R & D Laboratory for development and verification of improved processes and/or new materials for business enterprises. The planned IPF organization, scheduling, production operations, engineering controls, traceability and financial accountability resulting from this and analysis are presented. Although the intent is to operate the IPF as described, actual experience and time will determine necessary modifications and changes to be incorporated in future IPF operations. The IPF operations will be under the direction of the Thermal Protections Laboratory (52-34), R. M. Beasley, Manager; Y. D. Izu, Assistant Manager; C. Burke, Director.

The successful operations of the IPF is highly dependent upon the services provided by supporting LMSC organizations. Full cooperation and rapid response will be required in order to meet the Rockwell HRSI program schedule.

The organization chart lists Ed Law as supervisor of IPF operations. Doug was to oversee research and technology, pilot plant support and technology contracts; Dean Fisher was to supervise forming, drying and sintering; Al Pechman, binder and fiber; Harry and Les, machining, coating, waterproofing and attachment. Tom Budinot and Bernie Francis came in to keep track of the purity of incoming materials. Fabrication, chemical process, finishing and process analysis would be carried out also.

A daily meeting was to take place, a weekly oral report given and a written monthly status and progress report. (According to the lab team, these meetings became very boring).

### The *Lockheed Star,* February 4, 1972

LMSC TECH TEAM GIRDS FOR NEXT BIG SPACE EFFORT

President Nixon's recent decision to proceed with the development of an entirely new type of space transportation system has increased the already hectic pace at LMSC's Manned Space Program organization.

Reaffirming a pledge made earlier by SSD General Manager, Jim Plummer, Jack Milton, director of Manned Space Programs, said the LSMC space shuttle team "is ready to go all out" to win the leading role in this most challenging new program.

"The space shuttle," Milton said, "is the next logical and essential step in NASA's manned space program. It is needed to make space operations less complex and less costly."

He pointed out that the airplane-like spacecraft will make a launch into orbit almost routine—at a cost approximately one-tenth that of today's space operations.

"We've got some of the top people in the aerospace industry on our shuttle team," said Milton, "and Lockheed has been studying reusable space transportation systems since 1958. In addition, we have been working hard for many months and have in sight some solutions to some of the most difficult new technology problems facing the shuttle program."

The space shuttle, as presently envisioned by NASA, will consist of an airplane-like orbiter about the size of a DC-9, capable of carrying into orbit and back to earth, payloads up to 15 feet in diameter by 60 feet long and weighing up to 65,000 pounds.

The orbiter, which will be launched by an unmanned booster, can operate in space for about a week. Crewmen will be able to launch, service, or recover unmanned spacecraft; perform experiments and other useful operations in earth orbit; and in the future, resupply with men and equipment, space modules which themselves have been brought to space by the space shuttle. When each mission has been completed, the space shuttle will return to earth and land on a runway like an airplane.

LMSC is one of four major contractors currently working on the "Space Shuttle Program Definition Phase B Extension Study." NASA last year alone awarded LMSC nearly $6 million for work on the space shuttle and supporting technology.

The company has studied systems since 1958, both under contract and with its own money. In 1968, Lockheed and three other contractors were awarded $450,000 each to aid NASA with concept evaluation studies of the space shuttle. Since June 1970, LMSC and other companies have been under contract conducting design studies which led to the present shuttle configuration. The current contract extensions run until March 15, 1972.

Milton pointed out that in addition to the prime orbiter and system integration role which will be the central focus of the shuttle competition, there will probably be a number of supporting systems contracts, some worth up to several hundred million dollars.

Early in the space shuttle program, he said, LMSC determined the key technical areas it thought should be explored—such as orbiter external thermal protection, the avionics system, advanced lightweight materials, methods to produce low cost external fuel tanks and optimization of a cryogenic fuel supply system.

As a result of these studies, Milton said LMSC has a candidate material—LI-1500—for the orbiter external thermal protection system; has suggested for the orbiter avionics a low cost combination of systems on such Lockheed airplanes as the L-1011, the S3-A and the C-5A, plus those on the Agena and Apollo spacecraft; has developed Weldbond techniques, which could be used for economical fabrication of external fuel tanks; and has studied the use of beryllium in the orbiter to save weight.

The timetable for the program called for NASA to issue a request for prospective contractors that spring. The shuttle would be placed under contract that summer and development work would begin. The system was expected to take six years to develop and would be operational by the end of the decade.

Development costs over the six year period were estimated at $5.5 billion.

**The *Lockheed Star*, March 3, 1972**—Front page

Photograph under the heading: Tours Facility—von Braun Reviews **LMSC's Space Shuttle Insulation**

Under the picture, the caption reads: **INSULATION GLOWING HOT BUT TOUCHABLE**—

Dr. Wernher von Braun of NASA toured the Lockheed Missile and Space Company's pilot plant and laboratory where a Lockheed developed candidate material for external insulation on the space shuttle orbiter is being refined under NASA contracts. A white block of the LI (for Lockheed insulation)-1500 just removed from a 2500 degree F oven, can be touched by the bare hand—though the inside is glowing red—as Lockheed employee Charles A. Dewey demonstrates. James W. Plummer, Lockheed Space Systems Division general manager and Lockheed vice president, can feel with his hand the heat radiated. Others in the photo are Dr. J. I. Dodds of NASA, Robert M. Beasley, Lockheed inventor of LI-1500 and von Braun, NASA deputy associate administrator.

When he came home that evening, Bob told me that when von Braun asked about the tensile strength of the tiles, how fragile were they, Bob told him he could walk on them with his regular shoes but never in high heels. He said von Braun thought that was amusing and chuckled satisfied with the answer.

From the *Journal of Materials Education,* Pennsylvania State

Volume 17, Numbers 5&6, 1995, *"Rigidized Structural Ceramic Insulation"*

Robert M. Beasley Sr. (retired) Lockheed Missiles and Space Company

In this article, Bob wrote:

Visitors like to watch one of our team take a 2500 degree F cube straight from the oven and hold it at its corners with his fingertips. This was of no scientific significance, but it almost became the symbol for the LI material. Wernher von Braun, by then Deputy Director of NASA, visited our lab in February 1972. We were especially pleased, after he expressed great interest in our work, in hearing him say, "This is it! This is it!"

In fact, the tiles, properly engineered, were tougher than most everyone thought. Not one has failed thermally in all the flights of the five orbiters. Damage had been caused by failure to protect the tiles from external tank foam debris, runway debris, hailstones, frozen moisture and manhandling. Early in the program, when tiles were falling off, the problem came from the attachment system, which was later overcome. Tiles damaged by ice impact showed remarkable fail-safe characteristics.

A later article in the 1983 *Lockheed Horizon* magazine discussed the competition the LI material faced:

By 1972, the Space Shuttle was in a full-blown competition for the prime system contract. The many alternative system concepts had narrowed down to the solid rocket booster and external tank configuration now familiar as the Space Shuttle. As a major contender, LMSC continued with heavily funded in-house component preliminary design effort as well as the NASA funded system definition contract studies. Technical attention turned to refinement of TPS installation design details as well as the total logistics and space operations environment. Areas of analytical design and test included: strain isolation system, cold soak of aluminum primary structure, tile gaps, Room Temperature Vulcanizing (RTV) bond system, filler bar, compound curvature, sidewall coating, gap filler and many other real world technical constraints. These concepts were well established in time for the competition in 1972.

On July 26, 1972, NASA awarded the Space Shuttle prime contract to Rockwell International Corporation. Principle focus for LMSC then became the TPS itself. LMSC continued through the spring of 1973 with an unbroken string of TPS development contracts with NASA, supporting evolution of the system design and installation concepts and materials characterization. LI-900, LI-1500 and 0042 coatings were produced in the LMSC pilot production facility. Numerous test articles were manufactured for the expanding TPS competitive evaluation program in NASA research facilities.

With award of the system prime contract to Rockwell International, a new phase of competition opened between the silica LI-900 and LI-1500 developed by Lockheed and the General Electric mullite system baselined in the NASA award. Other competing fiber ceramic material candidates were introduced by McDonnell-Douglas and Martin-Marietta. An extensive series of tests of these competitive materials extended from August through November of 1972 and were undertaken by NASA to resolve the final selection. The arena was in NASA test facilities at JSC, ARC and KSC, backed up with Battelle and other supporting facilities. The LMSC LI-900 and LI-1500 demonstrated 100 thermal cycles to 2300 degrees F within specified thermal conductivity and backface temperature response requirements. The G.E. mullite system exhibited excessive backface temperature response and high thermal conductivity, especially in the high-temperature response requirements. Indications of coating cracks and potential substrate fracture appeared along the way as testing became more severe and acoustic cycling to simulate ascent dynamic loads was introduced. Testing was then extended to a program of sequential thermal-acoustic cycles simulating the full ascent and reentry environments.

By mid-November, LI-1500 had demonstrated the equivalent of 20 sequential thermal-acoustic cycles of 2300 degrees F and 160 dB. A sudden death shoot-out was commissioned in December 1972 with all the competitive materials in a single large 24-tile array in sequential thermal-acoustic tests at NASA-JSC. After 20 equivalent cycles, only the LI-900 and LI-1500 tiles remained intact.

The NASA tests demonstrated compelling technical superiority of LI-900 in every conceivable aspect from sequential thermal-acoustic cycle performance to coating integrity in salt and seagull dew. In addition, LI-1500 had achieved remarkable performance in demonstrating 100 thermal cycles to 2500 degree F, thermal overshoot to 3000 degree F and acoustic overshoot to 174.5 dB.

Subsequently, the density of the LI-1500 formulation (15-lb/ cu ft) was considered to be too low for use in some specific areas of the Orbiter—such as control surfaces, landing gear door frames and access panels—which were sensitive to mechanical damage. The higher density LI-2200 formulation (22-lb/cu ft) was introduced for use in these areas. (The LI-900 formulation was used for most of the Shuttle area.)

At the critical Symposium at NASA Ames, where the TPS contract was to be awarded to one of the competing companies, Ron Banas, a bright, young, thermal engineer, presented a strong argument for LI-900 that left no doubt as to the superiority over its competitors. It was an easy argument because the lab had already solved the fiber problem.

Ron, later, was the program engineering manager of the Thermal Protection Systems at LMSC's Space Systems Division. He was with Lockheed over eighteen years and was on the staff responsible for various NASA TPS technology contracts. After getting his degree in Aeronautical Engineering at University of Illinois in 1960, he worked at NASA's Flight Design Center at NASA Dryden Flight Research Center for flight tests designed to measure turbulent heat transfer on the X-15 research airplane.

The company bid for the thermal protection system contract (TPS) and won it in April 1973. NASA Houston directed Rockwell to use the Lockheed TPS material. (Rockwell originally had G.E. and their TPS material on their proposal team.) The initial contract was for $20 million. NASA Ames was directed to work with Lockheed and with the Materials Sciences Laboratory.

Perhaps one reason why Lockheed wasn't awarded the full contract might have been because of the problems they had producing the CSA cargo plane they were building for the air force since 1965. There were not only costly overruns, but the planes themselves had many flaws. It had been a nightmare for Lockheed, according to an article in the *Palo Alto Times*, Tuesday May 15, 1973.

Leo Shapiro had resigned early in the year and on February 12, 1972, Bob was promoted as manager of the Thermal Protection Materials Laboratory. His takeover didn't start until the middle of May. He had been unofficial lab manager for quite some time while Leo had been working on his other programs. It wasn't until February 1976, however, that he joined the National Management Association.

Doug and Bob became aware that there were others, higher up in the company who wanted to take over the running of the lab, but they were not successful

### *Excerpt from a letter to Mark and Lou who had moved back to Florida*

June 6, 1972

Things are going better (easier, I hope), for me at work. They have made me manager, given me over $700,000 for expansion and an administration assistant (my choice)—all in May. They went all the way for corporate (Haughton) approval for this new department (unusual). Be interesting to see what happens—particularly if things can ease up. I am doing everything I can do to make it come true—easier, that is. I would like to play a game of golf again, sometime—Ha!

We are all fine, busy in many different things and think of you two often.

Love,

Bob

### From the *Journal of Materials Education*, 1995

Production of the tiles was almost as simple as the tile material itself. Staple fibers from the manufacturer had been made pure by leaching the sodium silicate glass fibers. At this stage, they were porous. Pure monofilaments, seldom used, were not porous. Upon receiving the pure fibers, we dispersed them in deionized water. (We could not afford the distilled water we preferred). They were then centrifugally cast in the spinner to remove the water. This left a freestanding structure, somewhat resembling dense felt. After this structure was dried and cut into pieces, it was placed directly into a 2500 degree F oven and held there long enough for roughly one-third of the void area of the porous fibers to close to achieve a theoretical density. These were removed directly from the oven to room temperature and when cooled, were broken up and redispersed again in de-ionized water, thus making a slurry. The slurry was molded into blocks which were then almost completely dried by use of compressed air driven through the block, still held in its frame.

### Excerpt from 1994 tape

Early in 1969, we were sent a supply of raw silica fibers for making samples for testing in the lab and also material for the pilot plant and its experiments. It was during this time that all of a sudden, surprisingly, it was found that the material couldn't be cooled from a high temperature without cracking. You could hear it crack all the way across the room. It was a long room, maybe 100 feet and yet, when you went to look for what made the noise, you couldn't see anything. Well, after observing enough of them, you really saw as it cooled down it would crack. A large crack would occur—sometimes large enough to put the end of a pencil into it. And as it cooled further, it would open up further. And then when it got back to room temperature . . . when it finally cooled down . . . it would then shrink. The crack would close and you couldn't see it.

This was really evidence of the fibers going through the polymorphic inversions which are so common in silica and in glass. In other words, when they are at a very high temperature, they have expanded and as it cools down, if it is impure, it will slip over from being in the amorphous state or non-crystalline state . . . it will slip over into being cristobalite and eventually as it cools further, tridymite and eventually as it cools, it will shrink a little bit and then . . . first expand, shrink, expand and then shrink further and finally close. And at room temperature it would be cristobalite and not non-crystalline silica.

This description is taking advantage of hindsight in a way. At the time it was a horrifying happening because of the intensity of the program and the no-failure policy. I had noticed as I looked at the materials and tried to trace back through to see what was happening, I noticed that in the PT1 operation which was the dispersion into the block form . . . into the deionized water and then made it into a block form, you could see something appear in this sort of translucent, wet material. The best description that came to my mind . . . was there was a water mark or a line on it and I didn't know what that was. It was hard to get a sample of it. You could try to get a sample, but you really couldn't get a good sample of this fiber mass and water to determine exactly what it was. But, I did get some and dried it out and had it X-rayed to find out what it was . . . couldn't quite find out what it was really, ever.

Finally electron photomicrographs were taken and lo and behold . . . the fibers, you could detect, what appeared to be almost like a scale . . . or a film was stripping off of the fibers . . . didn't know what that was. And I brought this to the attention of Johns Manville, at their Waterville, Ohio plant and they tried to act very intelligent. They stonewalled me. I made numerous trips back to try to find out what it was. And still they had this stone wall attitude. They had a very proprietary process so that I couldn't see it. They were afraid to let me see their process or know anything about it. They brought in a bunch of people I had never heard of, but they were all Ph.D.'s. My contact, when he talked about them, talked in a hushed voice as though they were somewhat sacred and they were such high-powered, intelligent people. And I was supposed to give them a great presentation to impress upon them that something had to be done, or they might not do anything at all. This was just a smokescreen and nothing was meant by it.

And eventually I discovered what had happened when I found out that the Maumee River had overflowed its banks and had flooded. That yes, indeed, there had been a flood and it had wet—with muddy water—a big supply of their manufacturing material. And so, what they did, they just dried it and randomly

worked it into their production over a long period of time
without keeping any record at all or even notifying me. To the
contrary, they tried to stonewall me and hide it.

Of course, I was frantic because of the test demands. I had to
do something. I had to find another source of silica fibers. The
only other domestic source that I knew, G.E. was a competitor
in the TPS competition, but they didn't have a product yet.

But luckily there was another product that I found . . .
another source in France. A company by the name of Quartz et
Silice made silica fiber . . . continuous silica fiber. A product
they made by melting and attenuating Brazilian quartz. And
we were able to get some of it. The only problem was . . . it
was such a beautiful product with long fibers and it would
have to be macerated or shortened to small fibers so it could be
dispersed and cast. That presented a great problem. We really
didn't have time in our process . . . our program . . . any time to
really sidetrack any efforts into learning how to disperse them
well. We just had to do the best we could. It was difficult, but
we did it. And it kept our test program running. We didn't dare
use the Manville material because who knew when it might be
defective. Manville had kept no records whatsoever, so no one
knew. You might be able to cool it down to room temperature
without cracking and you might not. But the Quartz et Silice
fiber was a beautiful product. It worked just wonderfully and it
helped us through the tests.

Bob went to Paris to discuss fiber needs with the company. It
was strictly a business trip and a productive one. He didn't see much
of the city. The company headquarters was in the suburbs where he
spent most of his time. But they did suggest first-class restaurants in
Paris and arranged for him to go to the Folies Bergère one evening.
To his great disgust, he was so tired that he slept through most of the
performance. It was his first trip to France. I taught him how to say
please and thank you in French and he decided, if he had to, he could
always ask for omelets in restaurants. It was a surprise when he asked
for a Martini and was served wine, (he never became sophisticated

about wine). He was intrigued by his hotel porter holding out his hand and saying ingratiatingly, "S'il vous plait." Bob finally tipped him. (Ces Americains!)

### Excerpt from 1994 tape

Unfortunately, later, as the program was coming to an end in the proposal stage, Manville went to Washington and got a ruling of 'Buy American,' through NASA and applied it to us. So, when we received the contract, we would have to use the Manville material and no other. At least now that we had the contract and the government was paying for things, Manville would pay attention to the problem of trying to make a good product . . . a controlled product, which they had never, ever done.

I was finally allowed to observe their process and it was very primitive. In fact, that's almost a too sophisticated word to use. It comprised of melting sodium silicate in a crucible with a hole, an orifice in the bottom, letting a stream come out. And the stream would be fed a blast of hot air . . . gas, which would blow it down an enclosure and they would collect the fibers.

Then the fibers, which looked quite uncontrolled, since some stuck together and some didn't . . . it looked like cotton . . . these fibers would then be put into a large vat . . . from a second story . . . a large vat of hot acid. The fibers would float on top and a man would stand at the top, over the vat and poke at the floating fibers, trying to get them wet. And finally, after some length of time all of the fibers would have gotten wet and sunk. At that time, it was considered that the etching process . . . or leeching process had been completed. And so, then a man would stand at the top with a garden hose and hose down this mat of fibers that looked like wet cotton. And then it would be dug out of there with shovels and put on a belt that ran into an oven where they were dried. Then the fibers would be put in cardboard boxes and shipped to people who would use them, like us.

Well, with our past experience with Manville, we knew that some control would have to be taken over this and also they really could not ever be trusted again. So we had our own engineer sent and made a resident of him at their manufacturing plant in Waterville. I found out that they never even took the chemistry of their material even though they had cited the chemical purity of their fibers. They probably had taken a chemistry when it was originally developed and never again.

I had to go to Ohio with our analytical chemist and find a commercial source for conducting chemical tests and set up for the fibers to be tested. And also, in testing the fibers, we found out that they were contaminated with a lot more than we had ever thought. So there was a need to find a source of sand to be melted for sodium. And so core samples were taken of possible sources of sand . . . for mining sand . . . and a good sand mine was finally found. The government bought it and that became the source of sand for Manville. Under the watchful eye of our representative in Waterville, Ohio, the leeching process was made a lot better by making sure that it stayed in for a proper length of time and that it was actually completely wet—had become wet for the proper length of time, which would remove all of the sodium by measure of a chemical test. The resulting process, in which practices only vaguely were representative of what had gone on before, appeared to make a good enough material. I still don't think it was as pure and good as the continuous filaments from Quartz et Silice, but certainly adequate. And good enough to pass what I had established as the receiving test at Lockheed.

The Manville facility had been completely rebuilt. It no longer was an open tin shed. It was a nice, clean place as one would expect that it should be. And there was control exercised and certainly, traceability. They had never had traceability, but now they did. They could know which day the fibers were made and which shift. But much time, money and energy had been wasted and almost caused the 'end to further development of our material.

Harry later said about this time, "We did not know why our first samples worked or why the others failed. We couldn't duplicate the first tiles until much later. I remember Bob Hammitt from Jack Milton's program office coming to the door of the lab looking for a sample to give to the customer and we had to turn him back each time. It wasn't until much later that we were able to give him a good specimen and it was much later when the tiles were produced consistently."

There was a lot of the long staple Quartz et Silice fibers left over. Bob asked Pat McCormick to get rid of them, so Pat took them home and insulated his attic with them. He has the most unique and costly attic in Santa Clara County, thanks to Johns Manville.

### Excerpt from 1994 Tape

The next problem was to purify the colloidal silica, enough to remain non-vitreous as the product went through high-temperature cycling and holding for long, numerous hours. There was nothing wrong with the process or control of the process for Ludox; however, that material was just not pure enough. It did have contamination of sodium in it still. Ludox was the raw material coming in the door, but that is about as far as it got. It got from the door to where it was reprocessed and purified by deionizing and removing all alkalis. And to this date that is the process . . . people may call it Ludox, but it's not Ludox, it had been deionized many times . . . passes to get it pure enough. Otherwise, it too devitrifies to become cristobalite. But, if it's pure enough through deionizing it will remain amorphous silica . . . the dried product would be amorphous silica.

NASA encouraged its technical staff to write papers and acquire patents. Their goal then was to get sufficient funding from Congress and to be pioneers in space projects. Lockheed, on the other hand, just wanted the contract. They had the material as an "ace card" as Harry put it. They also wanted to keep the LI material as a trade secret. Later on, though, during the competition for the TPS system, Ames and LMSC were on the same side and policies changed.

Bob was perhaps grudgingly respected by the company's management, but he had gotten the reputation, by some, as being uncooperative and secretive. He had no interest in company politics or of going higher in the company hierarchy. He wanted only to perfect the material as he knew it must and could be done. The LI material was his baby and he was passionate about its well-being. He felt strongly that the integrity of the material could easily become contaminated by those who didn't understand the need for the silica fibers to be as pure as possible. The safety of those inside the orbiters depended on it.

To Harry, Bob was fiercely independent and though he was accused by some outside the lab as being uncooperative, those inside found him quite different. He allowed his men to explore many different concepts and encouraged their creativity.

Usually, programs being developed at Lockheed weren't known about outside their own areas, but the tiles, with all the publicity, became a source of pride throughout the company.

The laboratory also provided development services to many organizations. Quite often, these people wanted to control Bob, but he refused. Some even made attractive offers for him to join their organizations, but he would not "take their bait" as Harry said and so the lab remained as the last outpost in the R&D Division in Sunnyvale.

Bob knew his faulty aorta valve would have to be replaced sometime or other, but not quite yet. He was being monitored closely by his doctor and had a catheter procedure every few months. Bob said he did not really mind them too much. In fact, he liked to watch the screen as the probe ran up a vein in his leg and searched his heart.

He was always tired and appreciated the opportunity to lie down in the middle of the day. One time, at El Camino Hospital, he was left in the catheter room on a narrow cot in his hospital gown with a thin sheet over him. The wait was long and the room bright and chilly, so he pulled the sheet over his head and fell asleep. He was awakened by his doctor shouting, "MISTER BEASLEY." Bob sat up chuckling, but it took the doctor several minutes to get over the thought that he had lost his patient.

More and more work went over to Ames and the scientists there, privy to the classified formulations, started working on their own to try to improve the material, thinking to make it stronger. One man at Ames, whom the men in the lab respected, was Dr. Daniel Leiser, who had come from the University of Washington where he had worked under Dr. Mueller. He contributed in perfecting the thermal glazes for the tiles, among other things.

In the middle of the program, Bob was suddenly taken out as manager of the pilot plant and the work was given to another department. There was no publicity about it. Probably, because the safety of the tiles was being questioned, Bob must have made a heated remark at a big meeting with Rockwell that the manager and others there considered inappropriate. The remark was said to be very offensive in that he supposedly brought up the negligence for the fire and deaths of three astronauts in a practice *Apollo* module some years before. A man was there who had been part of that tragedy, someone later told me. If this was so, there was no excuse for Bob's remark, but he might have been trying to defend the material in what may have been a hostile atmosphere. And he had been greatly troubled by the *Apollo* incident at the time it happened. He never talked to me about what happened at that meeting.

The program manager, at Rockwell's bidding, went to one of the vice presidents, Fritz Oder and the program was given to the Manufacturing Research Division. This was another very unhappy time for Bob, so much so, that at times he would have tears of frustration when telling me what he was going through. There were still problems to be solved in production, but he had no way of solving them.

One night, after dinner, after he had had a very harassing day, he felt he just had to get away from everything, so he went to a small bar a few blocks away, the Blue Max, where there was a lot of noise and no one to bother him. Some minutes later, a man he didn't know came up and sat on a stool beside him and told him he had been at that meeting. He said he thought Bob had been given a raw deal, that he was a good man and more or less gave him words of encouragement. Bob came home that night much comforted. Someone knew; someone was his friend. That night he slept better than he had for months. I said this man was an angel.

Bruce Burns was sent down to Rockwell in Downey, California, for nine months as a liaison between the two companies. There was a DDT&E contract task called "Buyer Support" where LMSC sent about fifteen TPS people to work on-site. The team included people from design, stress, test, therms, etc. Bruce said that the relationship and working conditions between the two companies were cordial and productive. They did, however, ask that several others at Lockheed be taken off the program for one reason or another and with every right to do so.

And so the pilot plant was taken over by Manufacturing Research. For about a year, the new manager tried and failed to do Bob's job. Part of his problem was the inferiority of the fibers they were still receiving. The problem with Manville had not yet been resolved. That precluded producing tiles good enough to send to the customer. It was a big problem for the program office needing and demanding tiles for the customer and the tiles still not perfected enough to be used safely.

George Hamma, who did testing on the material but was not one of the lab personnel said, "I have a recollection that's more vague now than it was then, about a sequence where the lab pretty much demonstrated the technology . . . everything seemed to be working . . . the materials tested out, but we were working with small batches. Then it was time to go into a production mode and as I recall, the decision was, Bob was just kind of moved out of it at that point and it was taken over by a manufacturing kind of operation.

"But the sequence I remembered was that it didn't work. When you got through trying to make it in larger batches and stuff like that, it just wasn't successful and the material wasn't turning out properly. They weren't having the projected success that they were hoping for with this thing and so finally brought Bob back in and it finally took. If I remember correctly, as legend went, it took Bob's personal touch to the extent that he even used to taste the material to make sure it had the right consistency and it was appropriate for use."

Pat McCormack said, "Bob used to say 'you can mix it up in a 100 ml beaker, but try to mix it up in a five-gallon bucket and you have a problem.'"

When he came back, the company made Bob the head of another "Tiger Team." A Tiger Team effort was just a way to satisfy the customers (NASA and Rockwell) that Lockheed was concentrating on solving their problems. With Bob back on the job, things started going well again and the lab personnel were glad to have everything back in working order. They honored him with a very large card made by Joe Cappels at Tech Pubs and signed by all the men and as an added present, gave him an almost life-size toy stuffed tiger that took up a lot of space in the office.

Ed Gzowski came into the lab at Bob's request. He had been buffer between Manville and the program manager. Bob also asked Ed Law to come in as IPF supervisor. This worked out very well because Ed Law was good at attention to detail and was Bob's voice, his representative at the many meetings with the program office. As Ed said, this left Bob free to get on with the job of further perfecting the material. Ed remained a good and loyal friend even after he left the IPF.

Bernie Francis and Tom Budinot worked together as program planners and after that they left to take up other duties. Bill Short, whom Harry said knew everyone in the company, was asked by Bob to come in as administrator. Bill was also the mayor of Monte Sereno, an exclusive little town between Los Gatos and Saratoga. He ran on a no-growth ticket and stayed in office for quite a few years.

Tom Tanabe, Jack Creedon, Ed Bahnsen, Warren Greenway and Bill Wheeler joined the team to work on the problem of the coatings as well as other problems that came into view. Les Shoff worked, among other things, on adhesives as well as the original waterproofing as did Joe Gentes. Augie Ozelin worked in the pilot plant and was one whose enthusiasms, such as cooking abalone for lunch in one of the big furnaces, was enjoyed by the crew. Chuck Dewey, one of the original team, was a tinkerer and as Harry said, "was a genius in his own way, coming up with innovative ways to solve problems." Dean Fisher was also innovative and knew all about furnaces and had a practical sense of things. Carl Luchetti, Rudy Vasquez, Herb Allen and Paul Ferguson worked their expertise as hourlies in the pilot plant. Carl, holding a red hot cube by his fingertips was on the cover of the October 1981 *National Geographic*. Bob LeBleu worked on mechanical problems. Bill Ravenelle was an evaluating technician. Working separately and together, loyal to the program, each one had his special place—his thumb print—in the perfecting of the tiles. To use a cliché, it was a "heaven sent" team.

**INTERDEPARTMENTAL COMMUNICATION** February 28, 1973

To: R. N. Alleman

From: J. W. Plummer

Subject: **HRSI PROPOSAL DISCLOSURE OF LI MATERIALS PROCESSING DATA**

We have evaluated our posture for the current proposal to Rockwell International for the HRSI portion of the Thermal Protection System for the Space Shuttle. We have concluded that the best strategy for us to follow is to expose our proprietary processing methods in the proposal itself. The proposal will be protected by the proprietary data notice.

We recognize that this will not necessarily protect our process, but the value of protecting the process beyond the proposal evaluation and possibility is considered negligible.

J. W. Plummer

cc: J. F. Milton; H. W. Huntley; F. C. E. Oder; W. D. Snow; S. I. Weiss

## INTERDEPARTMENTAL COMMUNICATION

March 1, 1973

To: R. Beasley

From: H. Donald Volk

Subject: **Disclosure of LI-900 Proprietary Data to North American Rockwell**

Ref: (a) IDC, Plummer to Alleman, 2-28-73

    (b) IDC, Beasley to Volk, 2-28-73

As you know, LI-900 manufacturing information is proprietary to LMSC and has, in the past, always been protected as such. In prior dealings with NASA we have been careful to protect the data and have concluded with NASA an agreement that we do not have to reveal or disclose the data to NASA except under certain conditions. The conditions of that agreement are that we would first, prior to disclosure of the data, have to receive from NASA or NASA prime contractors, contracts or subcontracts in an amount totaling one million dollars within a two-year period. After disclosure of the data to NASA, NASA would not have the right to use the data but could acquire such rights upon payment to LMSC of an amount not to exceed $500,000.

In response to your reference (b) IDC, it has been determined as evidenced by reference (a) IDC that Lockheed will disclose the LI-900 proprietary information to NAR (North American Rockwell) in connection with our proposal in response to the NAR RFP for Thermal Protection Systems without having received contracts totaling $1,000,000. However, in order to continue our protection of the data and to reserve our position with respect to payment of the royalty of up to $500,000, reference (a) recognized that such disclosure to NAR must be with appropriate restrictions on use and disclosure. Therefore, prior to disclosure of any LI-900 proprietary data, such data must be appropriately marked in accordance with NASA PR 1.304-2 (d) with the following legend:

"Technical data contained in pages of this data shall not be used or disclosed, except for evaluation purposes, provided that if a contract or grant is awarded to this submitter as a result of or in connection with the submission of this proposal, the Government and NAR shall have the right to use or disclose this technical data to the extent provided in the contract or grant. This restriction does not limit the right of the Government or NAR to use or disclose technical data obtained from another source without restriction."

This procedure of marking the data with a restrictive legend will implement paragraph 2 of Mr. Plummer's IDC which directs that we include appropriate restrictions. Further this procedure will protect our position with respect to the prior agreement with NASA that NASA shall not have the right to use such data until NASA has purchased such rights from LMSC. We are presently reviewing the terms and conditions included in the NAR RFP to recommend changes to reflect the above restrictions and agreement with NASA. Although this procedure will not provide to LMSC the absolute protection of its proprietary data that it has had up to this time, it will provide some reasonable protection for our position with respect to the proprietary information and with respect to our rights to payment for the use thereof.

H. Donald Volk

Patent Attorney

cc: Alleman, R. N.; Burke, E. C.; Eger, F. E.; Forsberg, K. J.; Hoover, R. K.; Huntley, H. W.; Milton, J. F.; Oder, F. C.; Plummer, J. W.; Snow, W. D.; Twomey, J. D.; Weiss, S. I.


Kevin Forsberg, writing in *If I Could Do That, Then I Could* . . . said, "When Lockheed continued to treat the producing of the silica material, as a 'trade secret,' NASA directed that the process be duplicated, so NASA would not be 'held hostage' to a sole-source vendor of a mission-critical item."

Harry believed that people in the program office talked with NASA and probably indirectly gave them the information needed to apply for a patent. According to him, Lockheed probably didn't have a mechanism for keeping the material a trade secret, but on the other hand it would have been easy for any organization to know the chemical composition and its physical makeup. But it was difficult to duplicate it. Harry believed vendors such as Manville or Corning supplied the information.

Over at NASA Ames, on the day after Christmas in 1973, a patent on LI-900, under a different name, was applied for by Dr. Howard Goldstein (who had formerly worked at Lockheed) and it was awarded a short time later.

On May 18, 1973, in the lower right hand column, The **Lockheed Star** announced that:

LMSC's remarkable High-Temperature Reusable Surface Insulation (HRSI) has been selected as the protective blanket for NASA's Space Shuttle Orbiter.

Space Shuttle prime contractor, Rockwell International Corporation made the announcement of the award last Monday. At the same time, they noted that the subcontract will have a peak year funding of about $8 million and will be in effect for several years.

The special insulating shield will be applied to the orbiter as small tiles covering about two-thirds of the vehicle's outer surface and will protect it from the 650 to 2500 degrees F heat generated by the craft's reentry into the earth's atmosphere.

HRSI is presently being produced in LMSC's pilot production plant. However, according to Robert Beasley, who led the team that originally developed the material and is now manager of the production facility, an expanded plant capable of producing 220 cubic feet of HRSI per month will be ready for production by February 1975.

The extremely light insulating material is formed of pure silica. Beasley said that one cubic centimeter of pure silica crystal will produce 94 cubic centimeters of the finished product. Other unique features of the material is that it can also be manufactured as a very dense material that has the look and feel of glazed earthenware; it also maintains its insulating properties at cryogenic temperatures; it exhibits excellent electromagnetic transparency characteristics and its dielectric properties can be altered to specific needs of application.

Lower down on the same page Lockheed President Stan Burris and Vice President James Plummer expressed their gratification with the shuttle contract. Plummer stated, "We have supported the space shuttle program since its inception and now look forward to working with Rockwell on this critical element of the shuttle orbiter."

A few years later, in 1975, John Milton went on to other things in Palo Alto and his assistant, Dr. Kevin Forsberg, took over the job. Kevin Forsberg had twenty-seven years of aerospace experience and a background of both technical and management aspects of composites. He was a graduate of MIT and received his Ph.D. from Stanford in Engineering Mechanics. For five years, he was involved in the development group of HRSI and the last two years under John Milton in the program office. He received the NASA Public Service Medal for his contribution to the Space Shuttle Program. After leaving Lockheed in 1979, he cofounded the Center for Systems Management.

He was respected by the men in the lab. Harry said of him, "He was quick to learn technology beyond his training. When I pointed out that the problem of sintering frits was its particle-size distribution and suggested a method to measure this, he was the one who quickly dispatched me to a manufacturer of sedigraph instruments and adopted its use for quality control. He could listen once to Bob's presentations and repeat it the next day to a customer. Comparing Milton to Forsberg, Harry said, was the difference between the 'old guard' and a 'new star.'"

At one of the get-togethers, the subject of management styles was brought up. The styles varied, some pleasant, some not, some hands-on, some laid back; but early on, confrontation seemed to be the norm. George Hamma told of his experience at a management seminar. "I was at Sunnyvale at that time and why they sent me I think was to avoid a threat. Anybody else would have been more of a threat. Kevin Forsberg was there, too, I remember. So here I was going with department heads all over the company to this institute at Santa Clara University.

"You guys would have been amused at the exercises we did at the Management Institute. One of the things we did was the effective use of rage or anger. We had little theatrical exercises that we did where we would pretend to be angry because that seemed like that was what was necessary to motivate the workers at that point of time."

George said that policy changed later on. He remembered one manager choking on an expletive he was about to let loose and said, instead, "I'm sorry, I just can't agree with you on that."

There was also a good bit of contention between Bob and the new program manager. Bob still distrusted most of the motives of the program office's interference in the work of the lab and the program office still resented Bob's desire to be secretive about what was going on. Kevin wanted to have control of the lab and Bob was still afraid that the integrity of the material would be compromised if it got out of his hands.

However, Kevin Forsberg so admired Bob's creativity and work habits that he used him as an example in a paper he gave in 1996, *"If I Could Do That, Then I Could . . ."* *"System Engineering in a Research and Development Environment."* It gave both sides of the problems they had working together as he saw it. In a cover letter he sent to Bob, along with the abstract, thanking him for his input, he said, "I included examples of instances which caused me considerable heartburn at the time. I tried to also include problems which caused you heartburn as well. I think your contribution will greatly strengthen the paper and sharpen the message on how to resolve teamwork issues."

Much later, in May 1979, shortly before he left his position as Program Manager, Kevin sent this letter to Bob:

Dear Bob,

We recently completed delivery of the last flight tile for the Space Shuttle Orbiter 102 which will be the first vehicle to be launched into orbit. That delivery was the final step in a long road which you began back in 1962. We have received praise for our performance on this program from Chris Kraft, Director of Johnson Space Center for NASA at Houston and from Ed Smith, Vice President and Shuttle Orbiter Program Manager at Rockwell. I want you to share in their praise since without your efforts we would not have achieved our goal.

You were father of the basic insulation material and without your insight and judgment this whole program and in fact the Space Shuttle itself, would not have become a reality. While a great deal of work has gone on to modify and revise the process to eliminate minor difficulties, no one has been able to make any substantive change that improves the basic concepts you developed over a decade ago.

The engineering implementation of your materials has involved many challenges and required many frustrating weeks and months of effort on the part of our personnel. Aside from Rockwell engineering data problems which caused us agony in the machining of the tiles, we have encountered from time to time process related problems involving both the coating and the basic LI-900 material. Personnel from your research laboratory have played a key role in helping us rapidly resolve these process problems and have provided instrumental and vital guidance right up to the time of the delivery of the last tile. You should be very proud of the organization that you created and very pleased with their continued excellent performance.

You may have read of the many difficulties encountered in installing tiles at the Rockwell Palmdale or Rockwell Cape Kennedy facilities. The basic difficulty is that there was not sufficient time to bond all the tiles onto the vehicle at Palmdale prior to shipping to Cape Kennedy. As a result, they decided to install low-density (4 lbs per cubic foot) foam in areas where they had not yet installed tiles. Approximately 3,000 dummy tiles were installed. During the test flight at Edwards Air Force Base made just prior to the planned transportation of the shuttle on the back of a Boeing 747 to the Cape Kennedy facility, a number of the dummy tiles fell off and in the process some damage was done to the permanent LI-900 material. The dummy tiles were repaired and the Shuttle was successfully flown to the Cape, but a lot of bad publicity surrounded that event. Rockwell has had difficulty in applying tiles to the vehicle at the Cape at the rate at which is needed to support the launch date, but the problems are entirely beyond Lockheed's participation or control. You should be aware that we have completed our job in a timely fashion and that all concerned are pleased with Lockheed's role.

Again, I want to express my appreciation for the many contributions you made to the program and to let you know that all of us here at Lockheed still remember you as the father of LI-900. Without you there would not have been an HRSI Program. You can be very proud of your major contributions to the nation's space program.

Sincerely yours,

Kevin Forsberg

K. J. Forsberg, Program Manager Thermal Protection Systems

*LOCKHEED MISSILES & SPACE CO. INC.*

*SPACE SYSTEMS DIVISION*

Bob appreciated this letter from Kevin and they kept in contact. In another time and in a different place, these men could have become good friends.

## From the *Journal of Materials Education*, 1995

I was asked to set up a 43,000-foot manufacturing facility which eventually employed 400 people. The plant had the latest in automated fiber-blending and slurry-casting facilities, precision-controlled kilns and computer controlled inspection equipment. Numerically controlled machining techniques and array-framing tooling concepts were brought in 1977. The vehicle configurations were translated into computer tapes which drove numerically driven mills to machine each different, numbered tile. Later, Rockwell, at its Palmdale plant and others, also produced tiles.

After manufacture, the tiles were coated, waterproofed and then gathered in arrays that contained an average of 22 tiles. The arrayed tiles were held in place with their coated sides down against the outer mold line in the same position they would later assume on the Shuttle. Then they were machined as a group along their inner mold line.

First, a strain arrestor plate (SAP) and then a strain isolation pad (SIP) were developed to be used as protection between the tiles and the orbiter body. This was necessary to isolate the tiles from expansion and contraction of the aluminum skin. The SAP idea was discarded and SIP (brand name, Nomex) was used. It was bonded to the Shuttle by common RTV and the tiles were bonded to it. We developed filler pads to be used in the minute gaps between the tiles. Our pads, made of LI material, were anisotropic, rigid in one direction and resilient in the other due to fiber orientation. RTV is used as a filler now.

The tiles received certain notoriety when they began to fall off or crack and it was suggested by many that the whole LI material concept should be discarded, but the tiles were innocent bystanders. Problems were caused by undiscovered SIP flaws that caused it to slide on the orbiter skin and faulty adhesive caused them to fall off.

Though Bob's account in the journal about the problems of falling tiles was written dispassionately some twenty years later, then it was a harrowing time. People at NASA Ames were very much part of the decisions concerning how to attach the tile arrays to the orbiter. Nomex was a decision that came from Ames. Carbon-carbon on the leading edges, however, was suggested by scientists at Lockheed Corporate Headquarters.

Later in the program in 1973, Bob and a few others who had no influence over the program office were becoming concerned that the government's money was being wasted in unnecessary programs instead of it being used for simple, commonsense solutions. NASA was worried about how to replace a single tile fallen from an array and was going to give Lockheed a million dollars or so to make a study on it. The men in the lab did it all the time. Bob was going through another hard patch with the program office and NASA people always underfoot. He knew it was very easy to replace a tile in an array. He could get hyper occasionally when he didn't like something, so one day, without telling anyone in the lab and perhaps against his better judgment, he went over to the administration office lobby, when everyone was out to lunch. There was a large array of tiles on display and he whacked a hole in one of them with a hammer and left. When they came back from lunch there was a big uproar, especially from the program manager. According to Bruce Burns, who was there, the damaged hole caused a lot more theatrics than an empty hole would have. This was before the contract had been awarded.

Bob came back a short time later with a new tile and some adhesive, took out the damaged tile and put in the new one with no problem. It didn't make any difference, of course and the study went forward. Some people were amused by the whole thing but all he got for his exploit was a chewing out by Jack Milton and a good bit of notoriety. At this point, he didn't care.

Thinking back on this, myself, I think Bob unconsciously wanted to show he was still the "Father of LI-1500."

Bob was still manager of the lab after he had been taken off as pilot plant manager. They had been able to survive with funding for work on fiber-reinforced composites, electronic windows, kinetic energy flywheels, high-modular composites and coatings made of high-strength glass and high-modulus graphite. He had always tried to keep the work in the lab diversified. Pat McCormick, except for making samples, was kept separate from the tile work to be available for whatever funding that came up.

He also spent about twenty-three days on business trips attending meetings and in consultations with the air force and other aerospace companies during that time. What he liked best was to be in the lab with his coworkers, shirtsleeves rolled up, working with his hands, listening to other's ideas and sharing his own.

There was always time in the lab to work on far-out ideas. One of these ideas was the continuous filament-wound pipe, which could snake out for many miles on site, if need be. It could be used to transport oil from Alaska or water from the Northwest to Southern California. They were asked by the city of San Francisco to build a kinetic flywheel to put on a cable car but it was later put on a bus. It was a way to conserve energy while driving. One of the newer young men in the lab, Steve Garofalini, tried to get Red Adair, the famous man who put out oil well fires, to use the material as a human heat shield. A good idea, but nothing came of it. There was also a lifting device using the material and forcing air through it. In the lab they lifted a refrigerator and much to the enjoyment of everyone there they lifted themselves and floated around until they had to get back to work.

Doug wrote up all the disclosure of invention notification submissions and sent them to the patent office. Since everyone worked together on projects in this close-knit group, Doug usually spread the honor of whose names should be put on the submissions. No one really expected any patents to come from the disclosures, but Doug sent in every new idea that came up. The one for the continuous pipe, D-03-5422 dated 4/30/69, was apparently evaluated and found to be of no interest to the company.

There were a lot of people coming into the facility escorted by the program office and other Lockheed personnel. In 1971, alone, there were more than seventy-one outside visitors. Work would stop while these people, some of them very important to the Space effort, were shown around. Everyone liked the Hot Cube presentation.

Ed Gzowski had a tale about a Lockheed man who sometimes brought in visitors to see the famous demonstration. When Dean Fisher did it, he would take a cube out of a 2400 degree F oven, hold it barehanded by two corners with his fingertips, put it back in the oven, take it out again and immerse it in a container of water. It was very impressive.

Thinking to even further the show, the Lockheed man took out his penknife and sliced the cube in half so everyone could see the red hot inside of it. But he made the mistake of closing the knife and putting it back in his pocket—a very hot mistake.

Most of these people would be honored visitors and would be treated very well by the program office with high-class dinners and perhaps, entertainment. It was rumored that the air force people, especially, liked to be entertained very late into the evening.

All the way back, long before the *Apollo* program, Bob realized he had a "feel" for the materials he worked with and could sense, almost physically, what was needed to make them comply with almost any requirement. He could feel in his body how the materials would react. Many other inventors have this same "feel," too.

Many times the creative process would be so strong in him that he would be awake all night thinking about ideas and making them work in his mind. He was able to open his thought beyond what conventional science decreed. No one in the company management was interested in these far-out but workable ideas. The company at that time, it was said, did not want to spend any money on something that would not bring in at least $100 million dollars in profit. Later, that policy would change.

Early on it was seen that it was necessary to develop a glass surface coating for the tile's reuse under the rigors they would be facing. It had to match the thermal expansion of the composite silica structure, have high thermal remittance at all temperatures in critical wavelengths below three micrometers or three microns and be capable of surviving cyclical heating to 2500 degrees F.

Tom Tanabe talked about the early days working on coatings. "I remember we had a competition against G.E. and we had to come up with something special. We started making tiles and coating them with a silica carbide type of coating. And we did win the contract. I remember, Jack Creedon and I were responsible for the various coatings and we had to get the right emissivity for the coating of the tiles we were working on through the 2300-2500 degrees F area. Every week Bob would call us in to see what kind of progress we were making because we had quite a short deadline to get this done—I think it was a year. And so, every week Jack and I would go in there terrified. The type of progress we were making was very slight and he would chew us out. We kept at it and eventually came up with a good coating—Jack for the top tiles and I came up with one that worked for the lower tiles—and it was the greatest program I ever worked on."

Work went forward on the problem of special coatings and glazes, for both the black coating of the tiles on the bottom of the shuttle and the white coating, for the tiles covering the top side. The first coating was based on a borosilicate formulation with a $Cr_2O_3$ admixture.

Ed Gzowski, Tom Tanabe, Jack Creedon, Bill Wheeler, Al Peckman and Warren Greenway worked on solving coating problems, along with Harry Nakano. The top of the shuttle had to be protected from the intense heat of the sun and the underside had to withstand more extreme temperatures caused by friction during reentry into the earth's atmosphere. The first heat-repelling tile was a soft gray-green color, but NASA made a better black coating that was finally used.

Harry added: "The black coating developed at Ames had several problems when Lockheed personnel tried to apply it. On some batches the coating would not fuse or sinter and on the others the applied coating would 'mud crack.' Also, it did not spray well and the spray gun became clogged with frit (finely ground glass) particles. I knew from my experience in highly pigmented coatings that particle-size distribution was an essential requirement for proper nesting of the particles. Warren Greenway found that frits that were not fusible became fusible when subjected to dry ball milling.

"Microscopic examination of the particles revealed that the mix contained particles ranging from submicron to larger—fifty to sixty sizes. I then decided that an instrument called a sedigraph would be able to monitor incoming frits. The program office immediately accepted my suggestion and purchased the instrument and particle-size distribution has never been a problem since then. This also solved the mud cracking problem, which occurs when there are excessive small particles. As for the spray ability problem, it was solved by adding an acrylic gel, which helped suspension of the particles in the coating mix but also helped in its spray ability."

Al Peckman was able to match the expansion coefficient of frits with that of the substrates and was able to form them by mixing frits with of different boron content and was able to make it water impervious. This led Bob to accelerate his effort to get Corning to tailor-make frits of correct boron content for the coating.

Bob had visited Corning Glass Works Research Department for making frit to certain specifications that would allow for the spraying of better coatings on the tiles. The frit was ground Vycor, a glass developed at Corning by Dr. Stookey when Bob worked there. It was used as laboratory ware that could stand very high temperatures and it was very expensive. Corning came through with the perfect frit.

Lockheed was worried that Corning might claim that what Bob did back in the '50s might still belong to them. In February 1976, Tom Elmer, a long-time friend and coworker at Corning, wrote back that the company decided whatever Bob had learned at Corning belonged to him and they wished him well in his endeavors.

Patents were finally given to Al and Bob by NASA for the "Two-Component Ceramic Coating for Silica Insulation" and the "Three-Component Ceramic Coating for Silica Insulation." As the patent disclosures said, they "covered the tops and sides of the tiles with two and three coatings of ceramic glazes of essentially high-silica glass, an emissivity agent and borosilicate glass."

These coatings provided a moisture-proof insulation, which had high emissivity and was resistant to delamination and spalling at repeated cycles of thermal shock. Later, the tiles were densified by spraying on a heavier coating. Now the thermal protection system was ready to provide "shirtsleeve weather" for those inside the shuttle going into and coming back from space.

Under the Lockheed Patent Plan, employee/inventors were supposed to receive 20 percent of the first $100,000, 10 percent of the next $400,000 and 5 percent of all other royalties received when their inventions were licensed to other companies. But there was a Special Invention Award provision that was instituted to provide something for employees whose inventions were manufactured and sold by Lockheed, but not patented. Lockheed had given just two such awards in the past, one in 1964 and one in 1968.

On August 1973, the subject of an IDC was brought up to the members of the Lockheed Inventions Awards Committee by B. G. Corber, Secretary of the Committee: "Fact Summary and proposed Special Invention Award for Robert M. Beasley, Employee No. 605597—for Insulation Materials." It gave the technical background of the invention and Bob's additional invention disclosures. It also gave many reasons for not patenting the material. (And though it was never stated, it could cost the company a lot of money to go through the patenting process and it was thought by some of the men from the lab that perhaps this had some influence on the decision.)

Further down in the summary was a paragraph titled "Use of the Invention." Over the years government contracts have been obtained by Lockheed on concepts developed by Mr. Beasley totaling $48,555,400 as listed below." After listing the contract titles and their contract prices or negotiated values, it concluded, "The most recent and meaningful contract for thermal protection materials for the NASA Space Shuttle is PO No. M3J3XMA-483011. This contract totals $45, 213,000, including fees, plus potential award fees of $869,000 performance and $1,087,000 cost."(This also included about forty change notices to the basic contract.)

## Interdepartmental Communication, September 21, 1973

To: R. N. Alleman/LMSC

From: B. G. Corber

### Subject: SPECIAL INVENTION AWARD FOR ROBERT M. BEASLEY

The Special Invention Award as proposed in the IDC of August 30, 1973, for Robert M. Beasley has been approved by the Invention Awards Committee.

It is noted that the Award provides for more than one payment to be made to the inventor under certain conditions. Please see to it that these payments are made in a timely manner.

B. G. Corber, Secretary Invention Awards Committee

cc: J. E. Cavanagh, Chairman Invention Awards Committee

## Interdepartmental Communication, September 26, 1973

To: H. L. Graham,

From: R. N. Alleman

Special Invention Award—Robert M. Beasley, Employee No. 605597

Attached is a copy of the IDC from the Secretary of the Corporate Special Invention Awards Committee dated 21 September 1973 indicating that our request for a Special Invention Award for Bob Beasley has been approved. A copy of the request is forwarded for your use in connection with providing any special controls necessary to assure that the second increment of $10,000 will be made at such time as LMSC's receipts under the M3 J3 XMA-483011 Contract reach $25,000,000.

cc: E. C. Burke

J. F. Milton

On October 2, 1973, at 8:15 a.m., in the office of the president of Lockheed, S. W. Burriss, were Robert Yates, inventor of CLEAN SWEEP, an oil recovery system and Bob. Pictures were taken of the three and published in the *Star*. On October 23, pictures of Bob Yates and Bob were published in the *Palo Alto Times* over the headline, **Peninsulans Win Lockheed Awards.**

Though the CLEAN SWEEP invention was of importance, publicity was perhaps unfairly centered much more on the award for the LI material. Congratulations came from all over to Bob.

A letter from:

D. L. Schmidt, **Technical Manager for Ablative Materials at Wright Patterson AFB**

> ATTN: Mr. Robert Beasley
>
> PO Box 504
>
> Sunnyvale CA, 94088

Congratulations on your recent award for pioneering the development of siliceous insulation materials in direct support of the Space Shuttle vehicle. The technical significance of your work will be most apparent in transcending the difficult reentry flight corridor. The monetary significance of your work is apparent from the initial $10,000 award. Your friends share with you pride in this award.

Another letter, closer to home, from Willis Hawkins, senior vice president of Lockheed Aircraft Corporation:

Dear Bob,

It is a fine commentary on how I keep track of the real creators at Lockheed when I have to find out about your award for the high temperature insulation material from the Astronautics and Aeronautics magazine.

But I did find out and I'm mighty pleased for your significant contribution—it's an essential part of an important national program and a mighty welcome program for Lockheed.

Please accept my congratulations for a well earned reward and my thanks (shared, I know, by all the Corporation Staff) for an exciting technical contribution toward our present and future business.

Gratefully,

Willis M. Hawkins

Willis Hawkins was a much honored Lockheed engineer who played an early role in the development of a number of historic aircraft including the C-130, the P-80, the air force's first operational jet fighter, adapting the commercial airplane, the Constellation, for military use in WWII and was the principle designer of the submarine-launched Polaris Missile. During the Kennedy era, he was assistant secretary of the Army for Research and Development and oversaw the development of the M1 Abrams Tank. He later returned to Lockheed as senior executive and remained a consultant to the company for many years after his retirement in the eighties.

Bob, of course, knew of Willis Hawkins but had never met him and he felt very honored to receive this friendly letter from such a distinguished man.

More letters and phone calls from friends and well-wishers came from all over congratulating Bob on the award. He was tickled by a letter from a woman he had never heard of before who congratulated him but admonished him to be sure to save the money or at least spend it wisely.

Perhaps what touched Bob the most was a card given to him by his lab partners. On the front is printed. "We knew you could do it!" And inside, "Nobody actually bet cold cash on it, of course . . . but we knew you could do it." It is signed by everyone in the lab.

On September 16, 1976, the other $10,000 was given to Bob with little publicity this time. And much later, with no publicity, he was awarded another $70,000 for which he was very grateful.

It was a big and satisfying surprise for the lab when Bob received this letter:

# VON KARMAN MEMORIAL CONTEST

## *AWARDS LUNCHEON*

For most meaningful contributions to aerospace structural-material technology

May 22, 1974

Mr. R. Beasley

Lockheed Missiles and Space Company

Org. 52-30, Building 201

3251 Hanover Street, Palo Alto, California 94304

Dear Mr. Beasley,

A plaque is being prepared and will be sent to you in recognition of the work of you and your associates in advancing the technology of structural materials. The contest involved a broad base of developmental achievements over the past decade. The Selection Committee carefully considered all submissions including the good work of you and your associates.

Sincerely,

J. B. Montgomery

Theodore von Karman was a renowned Hungarian-American aerodynamist and visionary planner. His ideas made possible innovative aerospace development in the post-WWII era and the award was named after him.

Another surprise for Bob was when he was informed that he had been selected to be in the sixteenth edition of *WHO'S WHO IN THE WEST*. Joyce filled out the biographical data form; Bob signed it and it was sent in. Since the volume, which he had to buy if he wanted one, had 805 pages of closely packed, one-paragraph biographies, he didn't feel too set up about it, but it was an honor of sorts.

One thing Bob yearned for was another sailboat. His first was the one he had as a teenager, a very small secondhand one. He sailed it on the St. Johns River, but it was shipwrecked when a friend borrowed it to take his girl out for a moonlight date. The friend got distracted, ran into something and the boat sank. It was a sad loss, but Bob understood how things like that could happen.

Chuck Dewey, who worked in the lab, had a homemade, bright aqua fiberglass boat he wanted to get rid of, so Bob bought it for

$1,000. It had sails sewn by his wife, Jean, out of a pair of brown and
white striped sheets. By then Bob had bought a Pontiac station wagon
(the second new car he had ever owned), so we would load this seven
footer and go to Lake Vasona, in a little park in Los Gatos. There the
children learned how to tack and bring it around into the wind and
generally enjoyed messing around with boats. The family tried to act
unaware of the titters from other boaters. Eventually we gave it to the
Salvation Army.

After Bob got the second $10,000 award he thought maybe he
could afford to buy a luxury at last. And that luxury he hoped would
be a boat of his dreams. It couldn't be a sailboat, however, because of
the heart condition. It would have to be something not taking too much
strenuous effort.

Family vacations at Lake Shasta and the poker/fishing trips with
the guys on aluminum, flat-bottomed houseboats weren't too bad at
all. They could be handled easily, were practically unable to sink and
were fairly inexpensive to buy. But they weren't luxurious like sleek
cabin cruisers.

Every year we would go to the Cow Palace boat shows in Daly
City looking at dreams we would like to buy someday.

At one show, there was a luxury house boat, a forty-two-foot
Nautaline, with several decks and a fly bridge at the top, which had its
own steering apparatus. It had two inboard engines, a very workable
galley, a head with a shower and enough room to sleep ten. This was it.

The Dixie, as Bob named her, (second choice, Robert E. Lee) was
a true joy. The first time we actually took the Dixie out was on its
maiden voyage, a trip up to the Sacramento River Delta—a network of
dredged-up dikes to make islands, used for farmland. The rest of the
area is filled with waterways and sloughs and is a popular place for all
kinds of boaters.

It was always relaxing for us on the delta. There were sloughs
and islands to explore, sometimes in the little fold-a-boat (Little D)
that opened up to hold the three of us—Bob and me and Bobby, who
was then in his young teens. (The girls were busy doing other things.)

Little D had oars and a little outboard motor about two sizes bigger than an eggbeater. Bob was the captain, Bobby, the crew and I was the admiral. Actually, Bobby and I were both needed when docking, one fore and one aft, to jump on to the pier and make the boat safe with sheepshank knots around mooring cleats. The high superstructure sometimes acted as a sail on the breezy bay and delta and though the twin engines maneuvered very well, it was sometimes a tricky business.

Land around the waterways was usually much higher than the level of the water and it was a common sight to see the top half of a boat sailing through a field. One day, at Mandeville Island, a coast guard-type cruiser carrying a Russian flag passed by. It was scary to see it there. The Cold War was still on. We read later that the Russians had been on some kind of good-will mission in Stockton, up the Sacramento River.

There was a grand camaraderie among the boating community at the delta—friends made, islands to visit and daily adventures. Some of the adventures were exciting, such as the time a fire broke out in Dixie's little engine compartment and another when a snag caught a propeller and broke it. Every day was new and far away from Sunnyvale and Lockheed. There were resorts where we could dock, enjoy a good restaurant meal, wash clothes and watch the boating world go by.

A favorite place was Mandeville Island. Though it had no amenities, it was a favorite spot for other boaters and many friendships were made over the four years we went there. Boaters are a special breed and unless you had a very large cabin cruiser and wore special boating outfits and looked down (in several ways) on surrounding smaller craft, you were instantly part of the fraternity.

Back in the bay area, Dixie was moored at the Blue Dolphin Sales Dock. It was given free dockage for a year in exchange for letting it be shown to perspective Nautaline buyers. Later Dixie, was docked at the Berkeley Marina where we had to pay property taxes on the land under the mooring. It was a great place to entertain guests. Once in awhile, we would run over to Jack London Square, dock and have lunch. Dixie liked all the attention.

Sometimes Bob went up to Alameda and later, to the Berkeley Marina, just to be by himself on the Dixie, to be quiet and do maintenance chores. There was always something to do. He always came home refreshed and at peace.

And, of course, now there was time for more poker/fishing parties closer to home and pleasant times just floating in the bay on lazy Sunday afternoons or entertaining family and friends.

Bob didn't let his health problems keep him from his job. Very small nitro-glycerin pills put under the tongue eased frequent chest pains but always caused a headache. He was always tired and just "threw" himself at work every day, he told me.

Bob was touched deeply by an invitation from Rudy Vasquez to his daughter's wedding reception held in a pavilion in the Rose Garden in San Jose. Rudy was an hourly worker in the lab and rather shy. Bob was delighted that he and I had been asked.

It was a great party, good food, handsome bride and groom, lots of friends and relatives, cute babies for me to hold and a Mariachi Band. It was the first time Bob and I had ever gone to a party as honored guests, but soon we were accepted as regular people and had a great time.

In 1974, a "Cookbook" was written which Ed Law said was the formula for everything from mining sand to bonding the arrays to the shuttle. There were two volumes, one of the processing and the other, of illustrations. They were kept in the Documents Department under the "Proprietary" category. They have since disappeared.

There was also a type of cookbook on the "LI-1500 Process Description" which covered the treatment of fibers and machining of tiles and was written for the group who were to run the pilot plant, D 48-10, under Frank Claus before it closed and after Bob was taken out.

Ed Gzowski and George Hamma discussed the factory approach of taking a list of things to do and doing it that way every day. If the guys made it in five-gallon batches and twenty-five batches were needed, they would make twenty-five, five-gallon batches. Ed remembered that NASA, directed by Rockwell, hired an independent contracting outfit to document the process. Ed said, "They were coming in, watching the laboratory process and diligently writing it down. Well, in order to bond the tile to the substrate, you take a Dixie cup, you pour some RTV-560 and a little bit of hardener in it and stir it around. I envisioned them saying, for making the shuttle tiles, you take a ten-foot-high Dixie cup and a twelve-foot-long tongue depressor . . ."

The *New York Times* on Sunday, September 5, 1976, had two articles about the shuttle. One, titled "A Brick Shield for Spacecraft" by Victor McElheny. In three short columns it gave the outside history of the TPS and its makeup. It even quoted Bob's philosophy—"Nothing's impossible. When you get around to it, the solution is simple, particularly the design." Bob also liked to say that "nothing was impossible, if given time."

The other article by Robert Lindsey, "Here Comes the Space Shuttle" was much more informative about the real challenges the shuttle was having as well as doubts about having one at all.

### Downey, California

After you put men on the moon, what do you do for an encore? Federal decision makers faced this question seven years ago and this month, the nation will get a look at their answer. It's the Space Shuttle, a vehicle that's part airplane, part spacecraft and America's first major undertaking in manned space flight since Project Apollo, the $21 billion adventure that carried the astronauts to and from the moon.

If the Space Shuttle works as planned and its high costs don't doom it politically, space officials say it could virtually end the era of large throwaway rockets because it will be re-usable, like an airplane. Now, every time the Government launches a satellite, it does much the same thing as driving a brand new, multi-million dollar truck off a cliff right after delivering its first load.

The development is a huge undertaking, although not nearly as large as Project Apollo which involved hundreds of companies and tens of thousands of workers across the country.

The $6.9 billion shuttle has had fairly clear sailing through Congress so far, but then it has had a low profile.

As it gains more prominence and its proponents press an effort this fall for White House approval to build three additional shuttles—in addition to the two ordered—at a cost of $500 million apiece, the project appears likely to face increasing challenges, especially if the Democrats are in power after January.

Although the first flights by the Shuttle are not scheduled until mid-1979, Rockwell International Corporation, the $5-billion a-year-conglomerate that is developing the system, will stage the aerospace industry's traditional roll out ritual for the first model Sept. 17.

It will unveil the first of two "orbiters" for the system now authorized by Congress at a desert manufacturing plant in Palmdale, California, about 80 miles northeast of the corporation's space division here. This first craft will be used for landing tests beginning next summer.

"We're ready and we're just about on the schedule we said we'd be on" says George Merrick, the 48-year-old president of the division which produced the command service modules used in Project Apollo for the National Aeronautics and Space Administrations.

The new craft is designed to move men and instrument payloads in and out of orbit in a three-man space freighter that has a huge cargo bay and is slightly larger than a two-engine DC-9 jetliner. It will be rocketed 190 miles or so into space like a conventional satellite with a lift-off heave of 6 million pounds of thrust, remain in orbit for a few days or as long as a month, dropping off new satellites, retrieving old ones and performing other tasks.

Unlike a conventional satellite, the Space Shuttle will have wings and be cocooned in an elaborate sheath of ceramic insulation allowing it to zoom back into the atmosphere, withstand the searing heat of atmospheric friction and then glide down and land like an airplane to be reused, say the engineers working on the craft.

Some critics—including Senator Walter Mondale, Jimmy Carter's Democratic running mate for Vice President—have assailed the shuttle as a kind of make-work project for the aerospace industry designed to keep jobs and bureaucracies after the moon landing program ended.

The critics contend the number of bona fide missions requiring the Shuttle for transportation into space does not justify the high cost of developing it and that economics makes it more sensible to continue using expendable launch rockets.

In effect, they assert the agency is building a machine for which there is doubtful need, so it can later say such a machine exists and therefore must be used because it exists.

Moreover, recent success of Project Viking—the robot spacecraft that allowed exploration of portions of Mars via remote control—has raised anew questions about whether American resources might be more efficiently spent on unmanned rather than manned craft like the shuttle.

The shuttle thus becomes part of the larger debate between those who say man is confined to the Planet Earth and should stay home and pay his taxes and those who say he must seek his destiny among the stars.

Proponents of the Shuttle regard it as an historic turning point for manned space travel, a transition from the sensations and circus-like extravaganzas of flights to the moon, to a routine, workaday utilization of space for productive tasks.

"NASA has identified 570 different missions for the shuttle; there's plenty more to do," said Mr. Merrick.

Besides scientific experimentation, he said, potential tasks range from astronauts' use of instruments to monitor the weather and look for promising mineral fields from space, to experimental manufacturing techniques in the cosmic vacuum, to re-supplying an orbiting space station.

Less is being said publicly, but the Shuttle is also scheduled to be used extensively for military missions in space.

The Air Force Space and Missiles Organization (SAMSO) is spending more than $700 million to adapt and construct launch facilities and extend a runway to 1,500 feet for landing of the Shuttle at Vandenberg Air Force Base on the California Coast north of here.

The Air Force now employs satellites extensively and routinely: with the Central Intelligence Agency to photograph other countries from space; with the National Security Agency to eavesdrop on foreign telecommunications and gather intelligence about foreign radar defenses; for early warning detection of missile launches and nuclear tests, communicating, mapping and other missions.

But all these are robots. Air Force Generals have been trying—without success—to conduct manned operations in space since 1958.

Two days before the first Shuttle Orbiter, the Enterprise (101), used for early non-orbital testing, was rolled out at Palmdale, there was a tour of the new manufacturing facility in Sunnyvale. Kevin Forsberg, Program Manager, said peak production of the tiles (5,000 per month) would be reached early in the next year and would employ about 400 people.

A local newspaper, *The Valley Journal*, interviewed Bob that day:

Lockheed Missiles and Space Company began research on spacecraft insulating materials, including zirconium compounds and alumina and aluminum silicates, in 1957. The development of the all-silica material to be used by the Space Shuttle started in 1961. "It was originally conceived as a radome (RADAR DOME) material for the Apollo at the time the Apollo was just an idea on the back of an envelope" Robert Beasley, Manager of Lockheed's Materials Technology Laboratory in Sunnyvale, said. "We mixed the first batch with a Waring Blender and a spatula. The silica material," Beasley said, "has dielectric properties that allow electricity to pass through as if it wasn't even there. It would in effect, be a space window for radar."

Lockheed may be making the silica tiles into the '80s and Beasley said there may be other applications as well. One possible use is in automobile catalytic converters which get quite hot. Another use would be building huge mirrors in space to gather light for a space telescope so powerful it could look into other galaxies. Silica could be used because it is light and rigid. The Space Shuttle could transport silica mirrors into space for assembly in segments. Silica could also be used to insulate industrial ovens.

"The whole idea of heat conservation is promising," Beasley said. "In most cases," Beasley said, "the new applications would require a downgraded derivation of the silica used in shuttles."

NASA designated shuttles by number. Shuttle 101, *Enterprise*, which didn't have an engine, was flown in the test flight over Edwards Air Force Base in the Mojave Desert and dropped from a Boeing 747. It had just two hundred tiles put there for test purposes.

With the second test flight, 102, *Columbia,* there was not enough time to get all the tiles bonded before the scheduled festivities were to begin and the flight to take place, The empty spaces among the real tiles were filled with low-density foam ones spray-painted black and attached (it was rumored) with double-sided tape.

According to Ed Gzowski, one of the fake tiles was blown loose and took many others with it. Some damage was done to the tiles as a result. It was a portent of things to come later when the tiles were dubbed, "troublesome." Kevin Forsberg's later letter to Bob in 1979 gave a slightly different story.

Down at Rockwell International's Palmdale plant, there, to see the test flight, which would stay within the earth's atmosphere, were over two hundred news people from all over the world plus two thousand guests that included dignitaries from NASA, Lockheed, Congress, the military, industry and members of the Star Trek "flight crew" of the Star Ship Enterprise. At the Open House for the general public the day after the roll-out more than 3,500 people came to see this new-type voyager.

As Rockwell and NASA Ames got more and more into taking over the work of the Material Sciences Lab, Bob knew he would have to start finding new funding for himself and the lab, so it was with some satisfaction when he learned that Ed Burke was proposing a new organization, a "Materials Technology Laboratory."

## Interdepartmental Communication, May 16, 1975

To: R. P. Caren

From: E. C. Burke

Subject: **NEW ORGANIZATION "MATERIALS TECHNOLOGY LABORATORY"**

LMSC has a continuous requirement for an organization with the requisite competent people and skills to undertake out-of-the-ordinary tasks in nonmetallic materials. The requirement demands an extraordinary degree of innovation, ingenuity and resourcefulness in the personnel combined with a deep understanding of the complex interplay of materials development and processing variables. Some examples illustrating the breadth of interest in LMSC in nonmetallic materials are: LI-900 development for Space Shuttle; filament wound Kevlar 49 cryogenic struts; rubber fabrication for Ocean Systems and MSD; 3-D nosetip materials for RESEP; graphite fiber fabrication; slipcast hollow silica electromagnetic windows; composite structural components. Current projects are: technical support and coating; castable inorganic materials to replace cork insulation in missiles; Kevlar 49 composites for ¼ scale model of Trident for electronic signature studies; lightweight mirrors and composite structures for SSD advanced design.

It is in the best interest of LMSC to recognize the importance of nonmetallic materials from a materials development as well as a fabrication/process development viewpoint. Therefore, I strongly recommend the creation of a new Department 52-34—Materials Technology Laboratory—with Mr. R. M. Beasley as manager. The proposed organization will have the following objectives:

- Develop materials from design concepts which lead to fabrication of experimental test components.

- Utilize nonmetallic material developments in process improvements for advanced design applications.

- Provide technical skills and knowledge to major product divisions in areas of nonmetallic materials.

- Facilitate the translation of research results in composite materials to fabricated components in a timely manner.

- Develop unusual processes for fabricating nonmetallic materials.

The unusual capabilities and demonstrated performance of personnel in this Materials Technology Laboratory are a valuable asset to LMSC. This proposed organization will preserve this pool of unique talent and enhance their effectiveness in responding to the demands of the major product divisions.

E. C. Burke,

Director Materials Sciences

cc: R. Capiaux

bcc: R. M. Beasley

After a pleasant business trip to the Kitt Peak National Observatory, Tucson, Arizona, Bob came back enthused about possible work ahead on a new, different project—work on a huge space telescope.

# Interdepartmental Communication, September 4, 1975

To: R. Capiaux

From: W. E. Williamson

Subject: **OUTSTANDING PERFORMANCE OF MR. ROBERT BEASLEY AND DEPT. 52-34**

This letter is to inform you of the outstanding work Bob Beasley and Dept. 52-34 have done in support of SSD efforts to investigate the use of LI-type material for light weight optical substrate applications.

Several future programs will require large reflective optics both in the visible and infrared spectrum regions. Because of these requirements, SSD has funded experiments for light weight optical materials for both polished and replicated surfaces. Mr. Beasley assigned Mr. Harry Nakano to this project and took a personal interest in the project to include some funding of unforeseen problems.

The results of this project to date are very encouraging as an eight-inch spherical mirror has been produced with a surface accuracy of one fringe per inch. Several smaller blanks have also been produced some of which have had replicated surfaces and others have had fused glass which has been polished.

While the project still requires considerable work to completely prove the feasibility of using LI material for large (1 meter to 6 meters) mirrors, the progress to date is due to a large extent by the cooperativeness and interest of all parties involved.

I hope you will pass this commendation on to all parties involved and will continue to provide support for Mr. Beasley in the furtherance of this project.

W. E. Williamson, Manager, Special Systems I

cc: R. M. Beasley

E. C. Burke

However, the laboratory was given no more work for the space telescope's infrastructure or mirrors. Another department was given the contract to build it. So work then consisted in solving problems for other divisions. The lab, now the new Department 52-34, had little responsibility for the tiles. Rockwell and NASA had taken over. Some tiles, now with the designation HTP (high temperature protection), were still being worked on by Bill Wheeler and Jack Creedon in Sunnyvale. Lockheed put out brochures about the improved product, calling it The Third Generation HTP, but NASA Rockwell did not want further changes and the weight savings of the new formulation versus the cost did not add up for them.

On October 17, 1977, after Bob had retired, an Interdepartmental Communication was sent to the Manager of 52-34 (Doug) from Rodger Alleman, Patent Counsel.

Subject: **Disclosure Award Program (NON-CASH)**

**Robert M. Beasley—Disclosure of Invention D-03-6857**

**(Thermochemical Cured Glasses and Ceramics)**

You may be aware that Lockheed Aircraft Corporation has what we believe to be the most generous patent award incentive program in the world insofar as monetary awards are concerned.

The application of corporate guidelines on selecting inventions for the filing of patent applications results in the granting of monetary awards in approximately 5% to 10% of the cases. (Additionally, LMSC usually pays the same awards when the government files patent applications as if the company had filed).

In an effort to further enhance our program and to provide "feedback" by which Lockheed could indicate appreciation to inventors, whether or not a patent application had been filed, a special non-cash award program was instituted a little over a year ago. You may have read of the new program in a recent issue of *"Lockheed Life."*

We are enclosing an award to be presented to personnel in your department, the award constituting a desk pen mounted on a laser engraved oak base with a statement of Robert Gross characterizing an essential element in inventing as well as continued growth for Lockheed.

We ask that you present this award to the persons named, formally or informally, as you feel would be appropriate.

In any event, I would appreciate your extending my personal appreciation and that of Lockheed management to the recipient.

Please call if you have any questions regarding the program.

Thank you,

Rodger N. Alleman

## Patent Counsel

Robert Gross's quote was: "Look ahead where the horizons are absolutely unlimited." (It reminded Bob of his previous employment.) There was an engraved plate that said "Lockheed disclosure of invention award to ROBERT M. BEASLEY." Doug brought it over to Bob from work. Doug usually had an unemotional expression on his face, but this time he gave a little smile and Bob gave a little one back.

It cost several thousand dollars for the company to complete research on the validity of patent claims. Several of the men thought the department could have written a broad patent for techniques developed in the lab during their testing and development of the tile material. However, it was obvious that the company or some part of the management was no longer interested in the future of the material within the company.

It was a general consensus that the patent department did little or nothing to push forward submitted patent proposals. The submitters were usually informally discouraged by the attorneys as to the possibility of any patents being given.

Pat McCormick submitted a patent disclosure for filament winding. He included photographs taken by a Lockheed photographer along with the proposal. The patent lawyers said no. Pat couldn't prove the work was his. Several months later he saw in a NASA magazine article from Wright-Patterson Air Force Base, the very same photos he had submitted to the patent office.

It was time to sell the house in Palo Alto, which had been rented out since the move to Sunnyvale. For some weeks we went up to the house to clean it, take out staples from the wooden walls, paint the rooms and lay some new floor tile. The manual labor seemed to give Bob more energy. It was a hard, but enjoyable, time for all of us, working together.


In December 1976, during an annual review, Bob found out he would not be getting his usual raise. He was getting a very good salary already, he knew, but this was the first time in his career that he had not received some kind of yearly raise. When he asked his boss, Ed Burke, "why not?" Ed asked, "Well, what have you done lately?"

Work no longer seemed worthwhile. He told me that we might have to move to Los Angeles so that he could continue to have a job. He couldn't sleep at night and depression followed him during the day. Life went on, but he was becoming bitter about his whole career and where it had left him.

At the Pilot Plant; a. lightweight inorganic insulation development area,

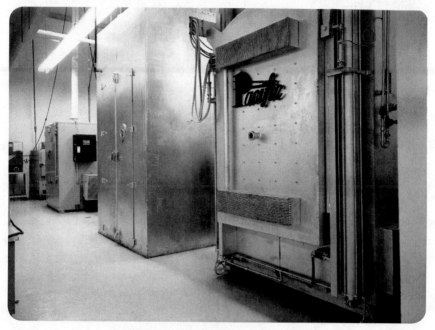

b. high temperature ceramic ovens,

c. industrial washing machines, 1974

Wernher von Braun, Deputy Director at NASA admiring a very hot
block of LI900. Chuck Dewey on the left, 1972

Discussing the status of the LMSC's TPS effort.
Seated, left to right: Bob; seated, Jack
Milton, holding cube of LI900; Kevin Forsberg:
Ray Buttram; H.D. Dargert. Standing: Doug Izu.
S.J.Housten; Bruce Burns.  October, 1972

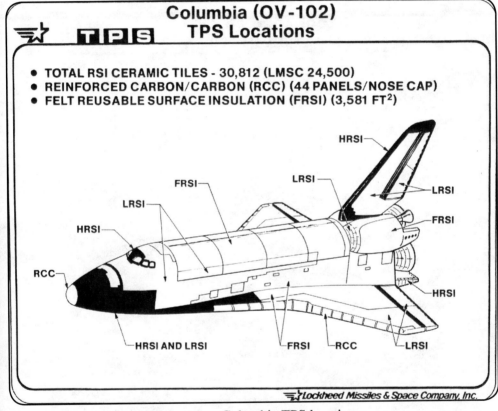

**Columbia (OV-102) TPS Locations**

**TPS**

- TOTAL RSI CERAMIC TILES - 30,812 (LMSC 24,500)
- REINFORCED CARBON/CARBON (RCC) (44 PANELS/NOSE CAP)
- FELT REUSABLE SURFACE INSULATION (FRSI) (3,581 FT$^2$)

HRSI

FRSI

LRSI

LRSI

LRSI

HRSI

FRSI

RCC

HRSI

HRSI AND LRSI

FRSI

RCC

LRSI

*Lockheed Missiles & Space Company, Inc.*

Diagrams: a. Columbia TPS locations;

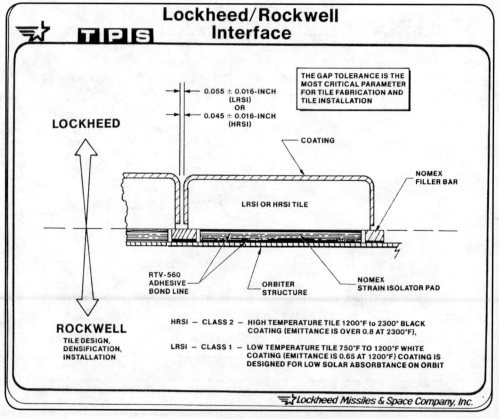

b. Lockheed/Rockwell Interface

# Rigidized Silica Fiberous Insulation

Silica fibers magnified
hundreds of times

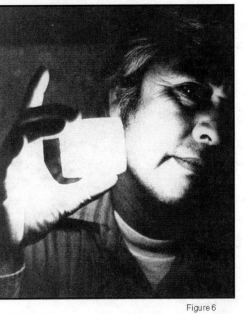

White hot at 2300 ° F (1260 ° C),
the glow from a cube of LI-900
held in bare hand provides the
only light in this photo, taken 10
seconds after removal from the
oven.

© CSM 2000

Figure 6

Rigidized Silica Fibrous Insulation, courtesy of Kevin Forsberg, Center for
System Management, from "If I Could Do That, Then I Could . . ."

# Space Shuttle During Reentry

The tiles prove to be "one of the most successful subsystems on the Orbiter."

-- Aaron Cohen, Orbiter Project Manager

Success of the tiles is a tribute to Robert Beasley, Inventor

Figure 24

Lockheed's concept of the Space Shuttle during reentry, courtesy of Kevin Forsberg. (It was affectionately known as the Red Bird).

# Chapter Seven

# My Journal

### Spring and Summer 1977

In the back of both our thoughts as that Bob was going to need more heart surgery. The first one had only repaired the aorta valve, but it would have to be replaced at some time. It had been five years since the debridement.

I was working at California Nursery School near our home at the time. One day when I was having lunch at home, I got a call from Les Shoff telling me not to worry, but that Bob had been taken to Stanford Hospital with chest pains. He was so calm about it that I wasn't even worried. I had taken Bob to emergency at El Camino Hospital a lot of times when he had chest pains and he had always been released a few hours later with a good report.

We had to laugh a few hours later when Bob told me that when they put him on the ambulance gurney, they didn't know what to do with his briefcase, which he had with him, so they laid it on his chest as they wheeled him out. He liked ridiculous things like that.

He was sent back home with an appointment for the next day. After an extensive exam, they wouldn't let him leave. He was in desperate need of a valve replacement and they would operate in three days.

I called Lou, my parents, who had moved down south and the lab. Mark was visiting in Mississippi. My parents would be coming up to be a support for us. The children and I visited him that night and he seemed very tired but put on a show of good spirits.

Some time after the first operation, Bob had signed on at Kaiser HMO and was assigned to Dr. Henry Lew. Dr. Lew was exactly the right doctor for him. No matter what his inward thoughts were about Bob's situation, he was what you could call enigmatic—never upset, matter-of-fact, always taking his time and even tolerating me when I asked a lot of questions. But he always answered my calls promptly when I had concerns about something that was troubling me about Bob. We both appreciated Dr. Lew and felt comfortable about his care. He, of course, was informed about Bob's upcoming operation. He knew it would be coming in the near future.

The night before the operation, the whole family met with Bob's surgeon and the anesthetist. They were very calm and positive about the outcome for the next day. The surgeon asked if we had any questions. He was a little taken aback when Lou asked if they would put his heart in a dish when they worked on it. That was something the rest of us didn't want to think about and I don't remember the doctor's answer.

I was usually sanguine about things pertaining to Bob's health, though I was careful to follow directions about his care. But this time I felt uneasy.

After the meeting, I was feeling a little better and Bob was showing his courage by acting matter-of-factly about all of it. I knew that that night he would be getting himself ready mentally for what he was going to face. I knew he had done this before the first operation and it brought him peace.

The next morning, Lou came to the house to stay with Mom. Amy and Bobby both had classes and Robin went to work. Dad and I went to Stanford to wait for the operation to be over.

I don't remember how long the operation took, but I remember the surgeon coming out to tell us that the operation was a success and the valve was working perfectly, but unfortunately, Bob had suffered a stroke on his left side while they were working on him and they had no recourse but to continue. They immediately put him on a high dosage of morphine, which was thought to reduce the severity of the stroke. I knew very little about stroke, but I knew that was one of Bob's secret worries. One of his colleagues had had a stroke during a bypass operation the year before and had tried to go back to work, but wasn't able to make it.

I felt no relief that the operation was over. The doctor said there was still danger for a while. I felt a strange reluctance to call the men at work to tell them, but I finally did. I think I just didn't want to admit it even to myself for a few hours.

That evening, the children, Dad and I went to see him. He was groggily glad to see us. He hugged us all with his right arm. We bent over to hug and kiss him.

He was still confused about what was going on. He started to touch his left side with his right hand. He couldn't feel it and wondered if it was still there. It was then we had to try hard to hide our tears.

A few days later, he was put in a room with five or six other men who had had open heart surgery about the same time Bob did. We found out later that heart surgery patients often had many problems: pump fever, disorientation, infection from catheters, to name a few. Besides that, the pain from the incision was often quite severe. I remember one man in the room who seemed to be OK was reading his newspaper upside down. Later, Bob was put in a room with an old woman who was so disoriented; she screamed most of the time. We finally got him out of there. Though he was somewhat confused, Bob was aware of what was going on and was trying to get back to himself.

Dad drove me there for the first few evenings, about a twenty-minute drive from home. Though I knew how to drive, Bob had always driven whenever we were together. After the third day, I drove myself in our old Valiant and stopped for gas near the hospital. I had never used a self-service station before. For the first time, I filled the tank myself, no big deal, really. But just doing this helped me feel I could face whatever we needed to do in the future.

Lou had Mark take her to be with Bob during the day and I went after work in the evening. I didn't know if I would need to keep my job or not.

One evening, I saw Bob's surgeon in the hallway and asked him to tell me about the operation. He was quite surprised that Lou hadn't told me what he told her. I found out that the stroke was considered massive, but fortunately it was on the left side and he still had the power of speech. He thought Bob would get over most of its effects, but there would be short-term memory loss for some time. I told him what Bob had been doing at work and asked if he would be able to retain his hard-earned knowledge and was assured that he would. This was the most welcome news.

The doctor said they didn't know the exact cause of the stroke. It could have been a small blood clot or a piece of calcium or even an air bubble that went to the brain. The operation itself was a success. The pig valve was a little large, but they made a good fit. I told him that I had noticed the night before the operation that Bob's eyeballs were turning upward and I had read that that was sometimes a sign of impending stroke. The doctor said that was a possibility that it had been coming on, but thought not—I couldn't help but remember Bob's upset and unrest during the past few months.

As soon as I could, I went to the library and got all the books I could find about stroke. I learned a lot that would help us cope when he got home. One book I particularly liked said stroke patients always got better. There was always progress in overcoming its debilitating effects. I held on to that and we looked for progress every day, no matter how small and usually found it.

In my reading, I learned that eyesight is sometimes affected and it bothered me that Bob had trouble seeing the new, colorful blouse I was wearing. Unhappily we found he had lost sight in both eyes—large "blind spots" that left him with only peripheral vision and mercifully, a small corridor in the center of each eye that allowed him to read, even if only a few letters at a time.

He was started on therapy right away and responded very well. And every day someone would come in and test his reflexes by scratching the bottom of his left foot with a sharp stick. They were concerned that he had no reaction when they did this. One evening, he told me that every day they scratched his foot and it really hurt, but he was damned if he was going to let them know it. I told one of the nurses and they were pleased to hear it. The test stopped the next day.

The first two weeks at Stanford were hard, but humor kept creeping in. Bob was able to feed himself, but he ate methodically around his plate clockwise. I brought him a little transistor radio to listen to and he kept it on the tray table by his bed. He usually had a little carton of milk with his meal and one evening he picked up his radio and lifted it to his lips. I said, "Oh, honey, you're drinking your radio." It was a lame little joke, but we laughed about it many times.

Most evenings, I would push him around in his wheelchair in the crowded lobby and he would sing, "Fly Me to the Moon" looking up at me with an impish look on his face. Sometimes when he got testy with me, I would tell him I would bite his nose if he didn't behave. Just the picture of that made us laugh.

Kaiser Hospital in Santa Clara had physical therapy classes and after Bob was home from Stanford Hospital, we were signed up for them for several times a week. I remember one of the first days we went. We were walking down the corridor toward the classroom and one of the doctors who monitored Bob along with Dr. Lew saw him walking along with apparently no problem and was amazed at his quick progress. Dr. Schoulos gave him some good advice about use of his left arm. He said it was Bob's tool and to use it as much as he could. Bob followed that advice. He was also determined not to let his handicap show and worked very hard not to let his arm and hand curl up or be limp. And he was successful.

Lou asked if she and Mark could take Bob to the twice-a-week therapy sessions. I, of course, said it would be so helpful. Lou could be with her son and I would have almost two hours to be alone and catch up with myself. However, later, Bob wanted me to take him because the two were not getting along well and he was very sensitive to stress.

After the sessions were over at Kaiser, we took classes for stroke therapy at De Anza College, nearby, working with machines. I was able to use them, too. There were several other wives there whose husbands also had a stroke and we usually sat together out by the swimming pool, having our own little therapy sessions, talking about how we were learning to cope and just listening to each other. Their husbands had had right-side strokes and had a hard time communicating. It was very hard for them. One woman's husband who was fairly young, kept saying over and over "Johnson, Johnson," but couldn't say anything else. She didn't know what to do. I asked her who Johnson was and he was the man's boss. It came to me that her husband wanted to know what was happening at work. At our next session his wife told me that Johnson had come to their house and sat for a long while, letting her husband know what was going on at the office. After that, her husband seemed much calmer. We never kept track of each other after the classes were over, but I'd love to know how they progressed.

At home, Bob and I continued our own brand of therapy. We walked a lot and I bought alphabet cards to see if that would help Bob see better. They didn't. One thing helped Bob keep supple. I would "break" his arm or leg. Calcium deposits are responsible for the freezing of joints. Bob would lie on the floor and I would bend his left arm and shoulder or leg backward and forward at the joints until they were in the same position as the "good" arm or leg. I had a kind of feeling in my own arm or leg, too, that helped me know how far to go. This was painful for Bob, but we even joked about that.

I tried to find activities for Bob to do alone or with me. I even found a place where he could practice golf with one arm and even play with others like him in a course at De Anza, but he didn't want to do anything if he had to look handicapped doing it.

His love for Big Bands came to the rescue and he started to record on tape music from radio stations like KABL that played his kind of music. He began making a kind of anthology. We had all sorts of recording equipment already and even though he couldn't see all the dials and wires very easily, he could handle it all very well. At one time, he got up at 5:30 a.m. on Saturday to record "Vintage Sounds" on KQED radio.

When he became more sure of himself, he walked by himself about a mile down Sunnyvale-Saratoga Road to Peter Pan Restaurant to have breakfast. He loved being out on his own and it was always a positive experience for him. The waitresses loved him and took good care of him. He always had grapefruit juice, oatmeal, an English muffin and coffee. They would butter the muffin and open two little packets of jelly so he could spread it himself. Sometimes I would walk with him so they would know someone else loved him. I decided when he first started this new adventure that I wouldn't put any worry on him about his safety. But I kept an eye on the clock and sometimes drove down to meet him halfway on his way back. He was usually glad to see me.

This new life was a complete readjustment for both of us. I had always been the "wife," the "helpmeet," and Bob, the head of the house, the driver, the bill payer, the protector, the husband. Bob still remained the husband, of course, but it was necessary for me to take up those duties he could no longer perform. It was hard for both of us.

Early on, because he couldn't see and was still confused, he wanted to know where I was all the time even if I was gone for just a few minutes. Amy was still living at home and going to San Jose State. We thought, the first few days at home, she could be with him for a few hours while I went back to work part-time, but it didn't work out. Amy was willing, but I was the one he looked for. I didn't resent this because I loved him and in a way, ever since we became aware of his heart problems, I had tried to do the more strenuous things that needed to be done around the house while he was at work. I wasn't exactly prepared for this huge change but knew already I could cope in little ways at home.

I was so proud of Bob. I had to do many things for him and he was able to let me do them with gratitude and grace. One morning he asked me if his eyesight would ever get better. I told him what the doctors had said, that it was permanent. He took a few turns around the room, straightened his shoulders and said, "I can live with that." He was able to dress himself and take care of all his personal needs after the first few weeks at home. This was important to him and a great help to me.

Les Shoff was such a big help in those early days. Bob was worried about little and big things that had been his responsibility and his memory of those things hadn't come back yet. Les would come and answer all of Bob's questions and mine, too, about things like car care, investments and things like that. He would always leave us both smiling and comforted. Dean Fisher came by to kibitz. Doug Izu was also an angel, visiting often after work, calm and concerned with Bob's well-being. Others called Bob on the phone just to talk. Life would have been dry and dull without these dear friends.

Gradually, I was able to take care of most things to Bob's satisfaction. I had read in one of the books from the library that one of the reactions from stroke was a sense of paranoia and it was hard for him to trust anything or anybody for the first few months. He was also trying to recover his short-term memory. It was interesting that if he made a statement about something, it was usually wrong. I always corrected him because if I didn't, he would hold on to the wrong fact. I'm sure I did the right thing.

I hated what I had to become. Whenever we went anywhere together, Bob would walk a half step behind me. He needed me to guide him, but if I slowed up, he would slow up, too. He was very unsure of himself and I had to be the one to conduct transactions, ask questions and pay bills at restaurants. He looked so normal. Salespeople, mostly men, seemed to take exception to my officiousness. I didn't like it either, but I had to do it.

It was also hard for Bob to let me do the driving. This was always his job. He had taught me to drive and later said it was the best thing he had ever done. I was quite a timid driver and avoided freeways. I had learned to drive in the city, so I didn't mind that. At first, he kept his hand on the dashboard and his foot poised where his brake would have been, but soon he started trusting me and I started trusting myself.

Bob was so happy to learn that I could handle the family finances. From time to time he needed to know about our savings and bank account, so that he could feel safe. Gradually, of course, as time passed, all these things abated and he was again partners with me in all our decisions and activities.

Our children were wonderful through all this. Though Bob was having troubles coming back to himself, the children met him with love, understanding and compassion and best of all, treated him as they always had.

Perhaps it was harder for Bobby than for his sisters, who were both living in their own homes. Still in high school, he was at the age when he had to pit himself against his father as a rite of passage to manhood and even thought he had to become the man of the house and make decisions. I think that he was secretly relieved when he found out I could cope with everything that needed to be done and he could go back to being a teenager.

One day, a few years later, I knew everything between them was back to normal. For some small reason, I don't remember what, they got into a heated argument and were standing toe-to-toe looking for combat. They had been having "discussions" for a few months and I usually tried to be a mediator. This time I was fed up, so I said I was leaving the house and I didn't care whether they killed each other or not. When I got back, instead of blood all over the place, they were watching a football game together and both rooting for the same team.

There were a few "cold blessings" for us. At least Bob had completed everything in connection with the LI material, even into successful IPF production and he no longer had to put up with what the program office or NASA was doing anymore. He no longer had that stress, at last. He and I became a team, closer than we had ever been in our different roles. Friends and colleagues from work called and came around and told him what was going on. I found going through our business papers that Bob has signed up some time ago for GI disability insurance. It paid for his ten-year-term insurance for life and gave him $100 a month. That became his allowance to spend any way he liked and it later rose to $150.

After six months at home, when Bob realized he would be unable to be very effective at work and would be a problem for his coworkers in trying to be his "eyes," it was not too bad for him when Ed Burke wrote and told him that he would have to be terminated from his job.

We were always able to save money, so although we would have to be careful, we would not be poor. Social security would send him a decent amount of disability payments and Lockheed had a very good retirement plan. We had the option to get the full monthly amount, or to have some of it held back for my future if Bob predeceased me. Bob left it up to me to choose. Bob was only fifty-one and I believed he and I would be together for a long time. So I decided we should take the full amount and enjoy every penny of it together. It was a good decision. Our investments would be allowed to grow for my future. And soon we made the final mortgage payment on the house and sold the Palo Alto property for a good price with Mark's help.

The down side was that Bob had no outlet for the creative ideas he still had about the material—he had even thought of a way to make it of lighter weight but still be as strong—by making the fibers hollow. He knew how it could be done, but he had no way to do the work. From time to time some of the men from the lab would come to him with concerns about how some people at NASA were adding little amounts of elements to the basic formula. One of the most important things about the formula was the absolute purity of the silica and they felt this contamination would show up later in cracking or disintegration of the tiles on some future flight. Of course, Bob could only worry too.

It was also sad that very few people from the program office or those he knew at NASA contacted him at all. Perhaps they thought he was in a vegetable state and didn't want to bother him. But the hardest thing for him was in having to shut down his creative thoughts.

The guys at the lab wanted to have a retirement party for him. Bob, almost back to normal except for his eyes and the limited use of his left hand, was pleased with the idea and was looking forward to it. Pat McCormick was the organizer, with the help of the others. He called to ask me if I would mind if they hired a bare young woman to pop out of a hat box during a little presentation. So, I thought, well, OK. It would certainly be different. And I never had been much of a prude.

It was a great party. The large back room at the Bold Knight was filled with well-wishers. Ed Burke was there, too and he and I had a little conversation in which I asked him if Bob could have the von Karman Award plaque that had been given to Bob's group for the invention a few years before. Burke still had it in his office. He was a gentleman and went back about a mile away and brought it back to me. It is hanging in our family room now.

Bob was presented with a beautiful azalea tree, a coffee mug fashioned out of the LI material and signed by the members of the lab, a plaque with an actual tile on it and a card made especially for him by Joe Cappels from Tech Pubs and a big fan of Bob. The card said:

> We'll miss Bob 'cause he's handsome and suave and debonair . . .
>
> The way he pours martinis and how he parts his hair,
>
> And his touch of elegant sophisticated wit . . .
>
> And sartorial splendor (but not too much of it!)

We'll miss Bob as a gentleman and his cordial face,

Miss his skill and his knowledge that made history out in space.

Miss him as a boss who made his staff a family

Through his warmth and leadership (that's how a boss should be!)

But despite his kindness and knowledge on the job,

We'll miss our friend most deeply just because he's Bob.

It was signed inside by all his friends.

Then it was time for the bare lady, Brandi, to leap out of her hat box in front of my unsuspecting husband.

Someone took a picture of Bob's face, bright red, looking very surprised and tickled. I don't know how much he could see, but he had a little dance with her and he had the same expression. I was pleased to see that she had wrinkles on her tummy. Afterward there were a few disapproving comments from some management people, but most thought it made the party one that would be remembered for a long time.

After it was all over, Brandi's husband loaded up the hat box and gave Bob his business card.

The whole evening left Bob feeling much loved. Later on, Pat gave Bob a scrap book of pictures from the party and of others taken on their trips.

So life went on in our marriage and in our lives and life was actually good. We could do what we wished most of the time. Our mixed-up roles returned to nearly normal. We were partners again, but I became surer of my capabilities, which still blesses me. The lemonade we made out of our life might not have been as sweet as it might have been, but it still had a refreshing tang.

Bob being interviewed for television, holding an early square of LI900
made in the lab, 1981

For additional photographs and information go to:
theshirtsleeveinvention.com

# Chapter Eight

# Meanwhile, Back at the Shuttle

With Bob gone, Doug became manager of the new lab, the natural good choice. They were the only ones in the whole company who knew how to help with the problems encountered with the IPF and at the new, much larger plant and they were still sorely needed. Rockwell had begun producing tiles as well. According to Bruce Burns, the two companies worked well together despite the political agendas that perhaps existed at Rockwell and certainly existed at Lockheed. Bud Alne was named manager with Bruce as his assistant. In 1983, Bruce was named program manager. Things went more smoothly after that because Bruce was very well respected, well liked and knew his job.

But, as late as June of 1979, the LI material was being looked upon as not good enough. In an article in the magazine, *Aviation Week and Space Technology*, Lockheed's manager for Refractory Composites, Wilson Schramm told of the need for a new, stronger material because the present one was too fragile. The article went on to say that the new material was being developed at NASA Ames.

The writer of the article, Richard O'Lone wrote, "The new material, invented at NASA's Ames Research Center here, is expected to be considerably tougher than that currently in use. The major change in the new material, which is called fibrous refractory composite insulation (FRCI) is the introduction of boron."

FRCI 12 was pushed as a replacement for LI-2200 in many areas, particularly where LI-2200 was overdesigned because of outer mold line requirements. FRCI 8 was promoted as a replacement for LI-900 but its thermal conductivity was too high and was never used.

What troubled those back in the Lockheed lab was that it had been established that anything added to the pure silica could later cause great problems during reentry. Contamination could cause cracking and eventually the material could turn back into cristobalite. Hi Silversher, who worked as liaison with engineering processing and several others from the lab called Bob when they found out what had been done, but there was nothing he could do about it. He started a letter voicing his concern but never finished it, not knowing where to send it and feeling that his ideas would no longer be taken into consideration, anyhow.

Tiles were being made at Rockwell's production facility at Palmdale and its facility at the Cape (Cape Kennedy), as well as at Lockheed. They were placed in polyurethane arrays to be applied to the orbiter skin. College students were hired to apply the tiles at the Cape.

One of the Stetson students told about her experiences at the Cape in Stetson's *Pro Veritate* magazine:

> Katy Workum spent ten hours a day, six days per week in the summer of 1980 applying tiles during Rockwell's round-the-clock efforts to complete the Columbia for its April launch. "We had to record every procedure," Katy recalled. "We stamped our assigned numbers on each tile and so did the Rockwell quality control person and the NASA inspector. There were incredible details to attend to. We even had to measure the thickness of the bonding material. To make sure the tiles adhered well, vacuum pressure had to be applied continuously, sometimes for seven hours. Tests were run after the tiles were in place to determine if they would resist pressure similar to the forces experienced during travel." Workum said.

A later *Washington Post* article, February 2003: Rob Stein and Guy Gugliotta—reporting on the *Columbia* disaster—found out some little-known history about attaching the tiles. "It took about two man-years of work for every flight. Early on, the glue dried so rapidly the technicians had to mix another batch after every batch of tiles, but they came up with a solution: spit in the glue so it took longer to harden. The trouble was, the saliva weakened the bond between the tiles and the aluminum shell and that would cause the tiles to fall off during flight. When NASA found out about this home remedy they stopped it."

NASA had developed a way to inject a waterproofing solution through the coated tiles but it was dissolving the glue holding the SIP (strain isolation pads) padding on the aluminum skin of the orbiter. One of the people who was there, Paul Fishback, as reported by Matthew Fordahl for the *Associated Press*, was quoted as saying, "Then NASA went out and bought cases of Scotchgard the commercial stuff, right off the shelf. They Scotchgarded the bottom of the orbiter." NASA didn't report this incident but it must have worked.

On the front page of the *Star*, February 13, 1981, it was announced that NASA was delaying the launch of the *Columbia* that was originally slated for March 17 and that it would take place on April 5. The delays were primarily caused by debonding problems with the spray-on polyurethane foam insulation on the external tank. During a fueling test at the Cape, it was discovered that two areas of insulating material on the tank had become loose and NASA was investigating the cause. The insulation was used to maintain fuel temperatures and to protect the surfaces of the tank from heating during liftoff. Despite this setback, major tests would continue with a ten-day dress rehearsal.

But finally, despite delays, waste, politics and rivalries and with genius, patience, faith and determination, the time had finally come. So, on April 12, 1981, *Columbia* took the wings of the morning and lifted up into space. And two days later, instead of having to land, half burned, into the uttermost parts of the sea, it was able to glide into its place, all in one piece, as it was when it left earth, with everyone safe and cool in the shirtsleeve temperature inside.

The first thing Commander John Young did when he exited the *Columbia*, was to check out the tiles. He was quoted later, "We had done it! The whole package. And done it just far better than anyone—including me—imagined. I headed right for the underbelly of the orbiter. There was not one tile missing. Not one! Considering how many human beings worked on that rascal, the complexity of putting those tiles on and the beating they took, that's a wonder. It's the best bricklaying job that's ever been done. American workers can do a heck of a job and the bottom of that vehicle proved it to the world."

Half the world released a collectively held breath and started to celebrate. Bob was quiet but obviously pleased with all the calls and notes from friends and well wishers. The concept of the tiles that he always felt had been given to him as a gift had proved itself. He had never doubted that it would.

In the November 1981 issue of the **American Ceramic Society Bulletin**, on the president's page, Dr. Mueller, then president of the society, wrote:

> The successful landing of Space Shuttle Columbia on April 14th ended almost ten years of worldwide media coverage of the "trials and tribulations" of the Space Shuttle. Seldom, if ever, have ceramic materials had such visibility, albeit often negative. The end result was gratifying not only to those directly involved but also to the ceramic community in general. Although the tile or reusable surface insulation received most of the attention, other ceramic materials contributed to the total system.

> The mid-1960's development of a lightweight material made of silica fibers must be credited to Bob Beasley of Lockheed Missiles and Space Company. At the time, the reusable space vehicle was only a concept and the insulation material had other potential technical applications. By 1970 the initial designs of the shuttle had reached a point where both metallic and ceramic materials were being considered for the outer surface. In the final analysis, the silica-fiber tile was selected. Numerous members of the Society made significant contributions and subsequent refinements to the system.

> My cognizance of the worldwide interest in the shuttle was interesting during a recent visit to Japan. It seems that everyone—engineers and scientists as well as lay persons—were interested in and knowledgeable of the flight of the Columbia. It was estimated that 80% of TV viewing audience witnessed via satellite, the live telecast of launch and landing. This was my first visit to Japan and I was impressed with the rapid developments in high technology ceramics

taking place in that country. It is obvious the result of the recognition of the future requirements of industry and the application of fundamentals to those needs by a large group of knowledgeable and dedicated engineers and scientists. Their work is encouraged by two major factors which long existed in the United States but seem to have diminished in recent years. First is the definitive long-range goals of industrial management. They have plans looking toward the 21st century in a realistic manner. There appear to be clearly defined objectives established for the next five, ten and twenty years, as well as the mental and monetary effort to attain them. The second factor is the cooperative attitude between industry and government—not the adversary attitude that too often seems to prevail in this country.

Much has been said of the work ethic of these people and I do not intend to detract from that, for it is real. But it seems that this may be due to a strong belief in their future—a feeling that once existed here and resulted in the development of an industrial nation which served as a model for the rest of the world. The successes of our space program have been the result of establishing goals, then marshalling the government-industry cooperation to meet them. The "man on the moon before the decade is out" goal pronounced by President Kennedy in 1961 is an example. Walter C. Williams, NASA chief engineer, was quoted in the April issue of the *Indianapolis Star*: " . . . from an engineering standpoint, we've progressed to where we can do about anything we please. What we choose to do—that's beyond the ken of the engineer. That's society's wishes. And we can either be bold society or we can be a timid society. But if we can choose to be a bold society, we can do bold things. The same holds true for our industry, but it must look beyond the quarterly or annual dividend. Many people are still wondering about the boldness of society and industry in our country now that we have nearly reached the 21st century and are wondering if the vision is gone forever."

And, now, some thirty years or so later, some are still wondering.

# Chapter Nine

# New Beginnings

Several days after the successful landing of *Columbia,* Lockheed had a big party honoring those who helped make the tiles. Ed Law, then with the program office, told Bob about it, but Bob felt reluctant to attend it without an "official" invitation. A few days later, Bud Alne, the program manager, had his secretary call Bob and invite us to the celebration.

Almost as soon as Bob entered the large building on the Lockheed campus, he was surrounded by well-wishers. Because of his poor eyesight, he couldn't recognize most of them, but he wished them all well, too. He hadn't realized that so many people knew him, or about him and he was deeply touched. He was the center of attention for the several hours he was there. Alne gave a speech during the celebration in which he said, "From Bob Beasley to the last person who put the last tile on the last array, we all had a major part in the success of the *Columbia.*"

Several days after that, the crew of the *Columbia,* Robert Crippen and John Young were coming to Lockheed to see where the tiles had been invented and made. Bob thought he would like to go to that too, just as a visitor, but someone from the program office called the day before and told him not to come because his being there would lessen the emphasis on the astronauts. He was very much hurt by this.

About a month later, the Commonwealth Club of California, a forum for speakers on important issues, announced that the astronauts were going to be speakers at their May 26 luncheon meeting in San Francisco. Besides the astronauts and their wives, Howard Goldstein, chief of the Thermal Protection Materials Section, NASA Ames; James Plummer, Executive VP, Lockheed Missiles and Space Company; Shirley Temple Black, the past president; and several officers of the club were going to be at the speakers' table in the Grand Ballroom of the Sheraton Palace Hotel.

It must have been a huge surprise when someone from the Commonwealth Club called James Plummer's office and asked him to bring Bob along with him to the luncheon to sit at the head table. Bob was delighted. An hour before the luncheon, a Lincoln Town Car stopped at our house. The uniformed chauffeur came to the door and escorted Bob out to the car. Bob was very much surprised that Vice President Plummer didn't speak more than a few words to him either on the hour's trip up or back from the city, so neither did Bob. Bob had known the VP before he had reached his present position, but they had gone on to their individual goals in the company. Maybe he didn't realize that Bob was over the worst effects of the stroke from four years before. Whatever the reason, Bob was truly amused rather than hurt.

At the speakers' table, Howard Goldstein sat between the two astronaut's wives, James Plummer next to Shirley Temple and Bob sat next to Robert Crippen. He enjoyed himself very much. He met Shirley Temple and remembering her as the little girl he had had a crush on, he felt too shy to talk to her.

Bob continued to be recognized as the inventor of the material, thanks to the exposure he had received from the Channel 5 news segment, which was filmed at our home during the *Columbia* landing. He was interviewed by all the local papers and had phone interviews with a few radio stations. Stetson's **Pro Veritate** magazine ran a two-page article about him and even his home town paper, **The Jacksonville Journal**, called for an interview and talked about his early days as one of their paperboys.

Some of the newspaper articles about him included his photo. One day, soon after, Bob was waiting for a prescription to be filled at the Kaiser Pharmacy in Sunnyvale; a young pharmacist recognized him and asked for his autograph. He signed her piece of paper, "Robert M. Beasley Sr." and then went back and added, "Bob Beasley." He was very surprised and touched.

Several days later, at the Kaiser Facility in Santa Clara, at an appointment with Dr. Lew, there were the newspaper articles up on their bulletin board and the staff treated him like a celebrity. Even Dr. Lew was impressed. He had not been aware of Bob's scientific background and ever after that, treated him more as a scientific equal than as a patient. Bob had always acted modestly when in situations like that, but he was pleased and "pondered them in his heart."

One of the honors Bob most cherished was the one he received shortly after the first success of the shuttle. It was from Stetson, from his Lambda Chi Alpha fraternity brothers. It was handmade with a decal of the Coat of Arms and hand lettered. It said "LXA honors Robert M. Beasley for outstanding service as an alumnus of Stetson University and the Zeta Tau Zeta, awarded October 1981."

The American Society for Metals honored him at a luncheon and gave him a plaque: "This certifies that Robert M Beasley is recognized for special technical achievement by the Santa Clara Valley Chapter of The American Society for Metals for your outstanding technical achievements in the area of materials development—1981."

A few months later, Bob was also invited to a dinner at Stanford University hosted by The American Society of Mechanical Engineers, Region IX and was given another plaque: "In recognition of outstanding accomplishments as Creative Engineer, this citation is awarded to Robert Beasley for Space Shuttle Tile Design whose efforts have contributed greatly to the advancement and have fostered the aims and objectives of the Society as embodied in its constitution."

In 1982, NASA gave framed citations to most of the members of the lab, including Bob, as members of the Thermal Protection System Materials Development Team. Pictures were taken of each honoree with Bud Alne and Bruce Burns to be taken home.

The Northern California Section of the American Ceramic Society invited Bob to the second annual Northern California Section Award meeting, where he was presented with another plaque and $500. This was another honor from his peers that he appreciated.

A sample of LI-900 and an LMSC Star were included in the Santa Clara County century time capsule deposited at the Mountain View Public Library site on January 9, 1977. It will be opened again in 2027, resealed and opened again in 2077.

Sometimes when the "same old same old" got too strong, we would take a trip. The first one was with Doug and Mary Izu who invited us, along with their cousins, on a Love Boat cruise to the Caribbean. Bob was still rather unsure of himself, but being on the water, in luxury surroundings and with good friends, brought him a good way back to himself. We took several more cruises to Mexico and the Panama Canal and one up the St. Lawrence Seaway.

There were trips back east to Maryland and Florida and later to Texas to visit Mark and later, son Bob and his family. We still took trips to Carmel and to San Francisco for weekends. The only problem with trips to Carmel was that we loved to visit the art galleries and went into mild hock to buy paintings by some of our favorite artists.

One memorable trip to the east coast was in 1983. Stetson was having a 100th Anniversary Homecoming, so we planned a long trip to visit Bob's uncle in Jacksonville, Tommy Booth in Orange Park and relatives in Naples while we were there.

The American Ceramic Society always held their annual meetings at Cocoa Beach about that time and Bob thought it would be nice to go to one once more, so we made reservations to attend. These meetings give an opportunity for people to give papers on their latest developments in the ceramic field. The opening meeting was presided over by the president, Dr. James Mueller, who had championed Bob's development of LI-1500 ten years before. The program listed the subjects for the papers that would be read and a lot of them were about new and improved fibers for the Space Shuttle. On the first day, Bob was sitting in the front row, just one of the group listening, when Dr. Mueller said, "No matter what you see and hear this week, the true inventor of the thermal protection system for the shuttle is Robert Beasley who is sitting here in the front row." Bob had not been expecting this and was very touched. Ron Banas from Lockheed was there too and arranged for Bob to go to the Cape and go up into the space shuttle nose, up on its pad. It was a very satisfying trip for Bob.

We were able to take two one-month tours to Europe with a group from De Anza College guided by Jerry Eknoian, Art History Professor and his wife, Karen. There was a special farewell trip up to Victoria with our son, Bob, before his marriage to Anna Guisti.

We enjoyed our five grandchildren: Robin's two, Mike Jr. and Karen and Bob's three, Bob III, Caitlin and Vicki. Amy had become a working musician and we enjoyed going to hear her sing and play in her band. More cats joined the family over the years after Petty: brothers Frank and Ernest, Gatita, Rufus and Tough Guy Beasley.

Sometimes Bob would tell me he felt very happy.

In 1987, it became evident that Bob would need another operation. It would be ten years since the last one. It was thought that, at least, the pig valve would have to be replaced and more bypasses be made. The operation took place at Kaiser Hospital in San Francisco and he almost didn't survive it. The scar tissue from the previous operations caused this one to take nine long hours. After it was over, they weren't sure he would make it, but could be fairly sure after four hours and surer if he lived through twelve more. He was given doses of morphine to sedate him through the ordeal. It was a long recovery. His body had swollen with fluid and at one time there was an infection in one of the incisions.

He told me that once during this time he felt very afraid because he had seemed to be going through a very bright white light. Much later, I came to believe that this had been a near-death experience. He never spoke of it again, but his personality became gentler. There was a complete recovery from the operation and the next year, we took one of our month-long trips to Europe. One good thing—the valve did not have to be replaced. It was as healthy as it had been ten years before.

A front-page article in the March 26, 1982 *Star*, Headlined **NASA says Shuttle tile loss non-critical: Astronauts continue third flight, experiments**

The article went on to say:

The Space Shuttle Columbia—on its third voyage into space—lifted from its Kennedy Space Center, Florida, pad last Monday, March 22 at 11 a.m. EST Astronauts Jack Lousma and Gordon Fullerton were aboard the flight, which was delayed one hour by fueling problems.

NASA has reported that 25 low-temperature (white) tiles were dislodged from the Shuttle's forward fuselage (near the window area) and 12 high-temperature (black) tiles were missing from the base heat shield and body flap. Mission controllers consider these areas non-critical and are confident that reentry of the Shuttle to the Earth's atmosphere will not be adversely affected.

This is the third in a series of four development flight tests. The objectives are to continue engineering evaluation of the reusable spacecraft with particular emphasis on its thermal characteristics.

The April 9, 1982, *Star*, Headlined **"Textbook reentry ends Shuttle's third voyage; tiles do job again during fiery return"**

It went on to say:

"A textbook reentry"—that is how NASA flight director Harold Draughon described the space shuttle Columbia's return to earth's atmosphere Tuesday, March 30. Columbia landed at White Sands Missile Range in New Mexico just after 8 a.m. PST.

And, once again, the LMSC-built thermal protection tiles proved they could withstand the fiery reentry temperatures. A number of tiles in non-critical areas were dislodged from the shuttle during liftoff. "Preliminary observations show the surface of the craft has some 'nicks and dents,'" said Glynn Lunney, manager of the space shuttle program at Johnson Space Center in Houston. "But, overall, the thermal protection system is in better condition following the third flight than after STS-1 and STS-2."

There was no longer any work in the lab at Lockheed for further development and improvement on the material. And it was no longer designated with the LI acronym and was now known as HTTP (high temperature thermal protection).

NASA Ames, as has been noted, had taken over the material and was trying to develop something new to replace LI-2200 in the higher heating areas: FRCI (fibrous refractory composite insulation, twelve pounds per cubic foot). The men at the Lockheed lab called it "fricky." It was made up of 80 percent silica fibers and 20 percent of Nextel fibers and contained a small amount of boron that welded the pure silica fibers and Nextel fibers into a rigid structure during high-temperature sintering in a furnace. The result was a lighter weight than the denser LI-2200. However, those at the Lockheed lab who knew that the integrity of the tiles depended on pure silica fibers were worried about the FRCI tile's life span on future flights, especially because of the added boron.

Lockheed was still producing tiles, LI-900 and the new FRCI. As of June 1982, the company had completed the last of 24,440 tiles for *Challenger,* which was going to be the second space shuttle orbiter to be put into service. LMSC also provided material for Rockwell International's plant in Palmdale, which would go on to make about 5,600 more tiles.

*The Star*, July 1, 1982, Headlined, **"Space Shuttle Columbia launches fourth, final test flight on schedule"**—'*All the things people have said about the Shuttle are true. It's a beautiful machine'*—**Astronaut Thomas (Ken) Mattingly**

It was as though the Columbia Space Shuttle were lifting off for the first time. Observers at Kennedy Space Center, Fla., could not contain their enthusiasm as the picture-perfect blastoff got under way just before 8 a.m. (PST) Sunday. But this was the fourth trip into space for the world's first reusable spacecraft. And when Columbia lands at Edwards AFB at 8:56 a.m. (PST) July 4, the spaceship will have shed its test-flight image and will become fully operational.

"As we move into the operational phase, we are happy to launch on time," said Alfred O'Hara, Shuttle launch director. "We look forward to more like that. It's amazing how far along we've come."

The final test flight of the Space Shuttle was the first to lift off without a single failure in its sophisticated machinery. Astronauts Thomas (Ken) Mattingly and Henry Hartsfield were the first to launch early—a fraction of a second before their planned liftoff time of 8 a.m.

The Lockheed-built tiles sustained numerous "dings" because of hail and rain the day before liftoff. But Rockwell workers were able to repair most of the minor nicks during a planned hold in the countdown. Fixing the tiles, mostly on the Columbia's right wing and stern was accomplished by brushing on an alcohol and bonding agent mix. Unlike previous missions, none of the tiles was lost in ascent.

Columbia's fourth mission is scheduled for seven days and will complete the shakedown of the orbiter and booster systems. Among top priorities for STS-4 are continued studies of the effects of long-term extremes on the orbiter subsystems and a survey of orbiter induced contamination on the payload. Also, a strange, luminous glow that space shuttle astronauts observed on the orbiter during the third mission will be studied with instruments designed by the Lockheed Palo Alto Laboratories.

A number of Department of Defense payloads are also on-board the shuttle. Early this week, the orbiter's solid rocket booster casings had not been recovered, the twin boosters, which give the shuttle its initial power with 48 million horsepower of thrust, sank in the Atlantic about 160 miles east of the Kennedy Space Center. The rockets are designed to be recovered by ship and reused. The incident did not mar the thrill of the first flight for Mattingly and Hartsfield. "You folks gave us a good show," Mattingly told ground control as he and Hartsfield soared to a new shuttle record altitude of 185 miles for the seven-day voyage.

In November 1982, the space shuttle *Columbia,* launched to begin its fifth mission (STS-5) and was now no longer considered to be an experimental vehicle, having been declared "operational" after STS-4.

From *The Star*, November 5, 1982

When the space shuttle Columbia blasts into space at its
scheduled launch time at 4:19 p.m. PST, Thursday, November
11 from the Kennedy Space Center in Florida, NASA will have
embarked upon the first operational use of the nation's Space
Transportation System (STS). And, if all goes as planned,
STS-5 will boast a score of "firsts" upon landing five days later
at Edwards AFB, California.

### Significant Firsts

Significant firsts for Columbia on STS will include:

- First flight to carry and deploy commercial satellites
  into space.

- First flight with a crew of four astronauts.

- First flight of Mission Specialists aboard the space
  shuttle.

- First planned "space walk."

- First use of Extravehicular Mobility Units (space suits)
  in orbit.

The flight crew for STS-5 includes Cmdr. Vance Brand,
USN and Col. Robert Overmyer, USMC, pilot. Mission
Specialists are Dr. William Lenoir and Dr. Joseph Allen.

### First Operational Job

Spaceship Columbia's first operational job will be to haul
two commercial satellites—Satellite Business System (SBS)-C
and Telesat Canada's ANIK-C-3 into orbit.

After the two satellites have been successfully deployed,
the first space walk of the shuttle program will be conducted.
Mission Specialists Allen and Lenoir will don pressure suits
and backpacks with portable life support systems. They will
enter Columbia's cargo bay simultaneously where they will
spend about three hours testing their space suits' cooling and

communications systems. They will also practice procedures that might be used for an actual contingency spacewalk to close bulky cargo bay doors, repair thermal protection tiles or to retrieve a satellite.

## Expanding NASA'S Knowledge

Columbia will operate in several attitudes during the 122-hour flight to expand NASA's knowledge of the thermal characteristics of the spaceship.

In previous flights, Columbia has circled the Earth with its nose, tail bottom and payload bay pointed to the Sun. On this mission, Columbia will spend about 40 hours with its side turned to the Sun and another 20 hours facing the Sun with its nose propped up about 10 degrees. The remaining time will be spent in a payload bay-to-earth attitude for the deployment of the satellites and the last 10-12 hours before deorbiting.

## First Automated Landing

A nominal landing would occur on Tuesday, Nov. 16, at 6:32 a.m. PST. The crew will attempt the first completely automated landing of the orbiter from about 20,000 feet to nosewheel touchdown.

Columbia's next mission, slated for September 1983, will be STS-9 which will be the first flight of the European-developed Spacelab. Columbia will stay at Kennedy Space Center for major modifications to prepare it for that mission.

Challenger—the second orbiter—is scheduled to make Flights 6, 7 and 8. LMSC-developed thermal protection tiles will continue to protect the orbiters and their passengers from fiery reentry heat upon their return to Earth's atmosphere.

As the years passed, there were retirement parties for friends and colleagues. Bob enjoyed going to these and reliving old times. Almost always speeches given by those who had worked with Bob would mention how much they enjoyed the good old days of working in the lab to perfect the tile material. They also mentioned the Christmas

parties, which were really the same every year but were made special
by the good feelings everyone had for each other.

When Doug died—in October 1989—that day, the old lab group,
some who were still working with him, congregated at our house to
mourn and feel a kind of comfort in just being together.

It was decided to have one more Christmas party, just like old times.
There hadn't been one at our house for some years. It was a successful
party but a bittersweet one, remembering old times and those who were
no longer there: Doug and Mary (who had died two weeks after Doug),
Dean, Augie, Bernie's wife, Sherry, Chuck Dewey, Carl Luchetti
and Bob LeBleu. But there was laughter, good food and a sense of
continuing friendship. Santa didn't show up at this one, though.

In February 1991, a retirement party was given for Bruce Burns at
the Moffet Field Officers Club. Delicious hors d'oeuvres were served
and Bob sat with his selection at a small table nearby. I was filling my
plate, when I was approached by a group of five or six young people
who asked me if that was, indeed, Bob Beasley. When I said yes, they
told me he was their hero. They were working on the third generation
of the thermal protection system at Lockheed and had gone through his
logbooks to glean some of his innovative ideas he had written about.
They said they had really been inspired by his career. They asked me
if they could do something for him. I had no idea, so they decided to
surround his table and sing "For He's a Jolly Good Fellow." He was
completely surprised but very honored by this unique tribute.

In the spring of 1994, Bob received a call from Morrie Steinberg.
Morrie wanted to know if Bob would mind being nominated for an
award to be given by the National Association for Science, Technology
and Society. If Bob were chosen, he would be obligated to write an
abstract for *The Journal of Materials Education* to be published by
Penn State University. Bob looked at me and I said if he would dictate
it to me, I would put it down on paper for him to edit. So Bob, very
flattered, said yes and thank you. The call for nominations had been
worldwide and only twelve awards were to be given, so we both thought
there was no chance that Bob and the material would be chosen.

All members of the Materials Section of the National Academy
of Engineering and the presidents of the member societies of the

Federation of Materials Societies were asked to send in nominations. There were certain criteria for nomination: the "advance" or "discovery" or "development" in materials processing, synthesis, characterization and possibly even theory. Nominations would not be restricted to proven major winners in product development; some intriguing innovations not yet developed which would seem to offer real promise (to be judged by the committee) would be very acceptable. Every nomination would comment on: (1) Its novelty or unexpectedness. (2) Its prospects in science and industry. (3) Its possible impact on technology and society.

There were six committee members who would process and choose the award winners: G. Dieter, Dean of Engineering, University of Maryland; J. J. Gilman, Prof. of Materials Sciences, UCLA; A. M. Dines, Inst. for Defense Analysis, Head ONR, London; R. A. Laudise, Director, Materials, AT&T Bell Labs; J. E. Notke, Senior Research Fellow, DuPont; R. Roy Evan Pugh, Professor of the Solid State, Penn State.

A two-page abstract, dictated by Bob and transcribed by me, was vetted by Harry Nakano. It was sent in after Joe Cappel's help in proofreading and printing. Kenneth Benner, who followed Bruce Burns as new program manager, was having a hard time trying to promote a new generation of the HTP both in and out of the company and was very excited about the honor. He helped by faxing the abstract to Dr. Eugene Bazan at Penn State who was heading up the awards program. After that, a few weeks went by without hearing anything back, so we all didn't think too much about it.

On July 18, 1994, a letter of congratulations arrived from Dr. Bazan:

Dear Dr. Beasley,

Our sincerest congratulations. Your research on rigidized structural ceramic insulation has been selected to be honored as one of two dozen exemplars of "real" materials research in the last decade which will or has affected technology and thence society.

The National Association for Science, Technology and Society (NASTS) supported by the Federation of Materials Societies and using the membership of the U.S. National Academy of Engineering materials section as nominators, has launched this new form of recognition as a means of communicating accurately to the press the truly significant research advances.

The centrality of material things in our everyday lives often gets lost amidst the hyperbole which attends the much more abstract activities in Big Science, including such colossi as the SSC and the Hubble Telescope. This has had a corrosive influence on national policy makers' perceptions. This is our experiment to start providing a new class of responsible scientific information.

You will receive an invitation to the event to be held on September 26, 1994, at the National Press Club in Washington, D.C. as soon as the program is finalized.

Sincerely,


Eugene Bazan Ph.D.

Executive Director


The response from nominators all over the world was so great that it was decided to give twenty-four awards instead of the original twelve.

Amy was going to take the trip to Washington, D.C. with us, so we decided to make it a real vacation, visiting relatives in Maryland and exploring Washington environs. Bob put together a display about the tiles and a video was made for the exhibition room that would be there. We stayed in the Washington Hotel and from their top floor restaurant we could see the White House and the armed guards patrolling the roof.

There were several informal parties at the hotel on the evenings before the presentation where the inventors had a chance to "bond." Most of them were down-to-earth people who were delighted with the recognition. What was interesting to Bob was to hear that even those whose work was funded by large companies had as much trouble getting their ideas accepted as the independent inventors. It has long been known that it takes about ten years for any new idea to be accepted and this was true in the experience of most of those we talked to at the NASTS meeting.

On September 26, 1994, at a luncheon at the National Press Club in Washington, D.C., Bob with the rest of the winners received plaques honoring them and their colleagues in recognition of outstanding contributions to science and society.

Back home in Sunnyvale, life continued on a rather low key. There was no publicity at all about the NASTS award, nor did Bob expect any. But the whole time had been satisfying for him, a kind of rounding out of his career—a tribute to the idea.

We still took advantage of the closeness to San Francisco. One weekend, I had a meeting to attend there on a Saturday and we decided to make a long weekend of it. It was also Bay to Breakers weekend and our favorite hotel on Van Ness was filled as were most other motels and hotels in the city. Finally, we were able to get a reservation at an inexpensive motel near Fisherman's Wharf. After the meeting, we decided to walk down to the Wharf for dinner. Bob was beginning to have problems with his left foot, but the walk was downhill and not too hard for him. After dinner, the prospect of walking back up the sloping sidewalks seemed rather daunting, so we hailed a taxi.

I remembered the name of the motel, but not the name of the street it was on. I knew it began with an L and it was only a few blocks away. The driver kept questioning me about what street it was on and finally said, "Lady, there are twenty-three of your motels in this city. Which one do you want?" He was quite shaken when Bob, who had been sitting quietly in his corner of the backseat, spoke up in a loud, authoritative voice, "THAT IS ENOUGH." The cab driver immediately started the car, drove directly to the motel on Larkin Street and even got out and opened the door for us. No words were spoken as we paid our fare. I was so thrilled with my strong, protective hero and I let him know it. For the rest of the evening, he wore a small, satisfied smile on his face.

One of the last parties Bob enjoyed was at Pat McCormick's beautiful home in the eastern foothills of San Jose. It was a surprise for Pat on his sixtieth birthday. All the old crowd was there and it was a warm and happy reunion for everyone.

Starting around the end of 1994, Bob began to have trouble with his left hip and leg, which made it hard to take the walks to Peter Pan Restaurant he enjoyed. Mark and Lou had divorced and Mark was living in San Antonio. Lou's health problems finally brought her to a nearby nursing home and she passed on there in 1993.

In late 1996, he began experiencing frequent chest pains and the thought of a fourth operation loomed, something Bob did not want. As the pains became more severe, a stent was put in the vein leading to his heart but after several weeks, it was apparent it didn't help. However, it allowed us all to be together for the holidays and even celebrate our forty-sixth wedding anniversary.

There were new procedures for bypass surgery, some in the experimental stages such as reaching the heart from the back. It became evident that an operation was the only alternative left. Reluctantly, Bob consented. He told me he was so tired of being hurt and pricked and prodded.

A few days before the scheduled operation, a cardiac catheterization procedure was performed on March 11, 1997. The scene at the hospital was rather upbeat, though I had a very uneasy feeling. I walked beside Bob as they rolled him on a gurney to the procedure room, kissed him on the forehead and said I would see him later. After several long hours, a nurse came to tell me, very gently, that Bob had passed on during the procedure. The attending physician was very distraught, having never lost a patient that way.

I called Robin at home and she was able to come to the hospital right away, but we had to leave a message for Amy at her work only telling her that there had been a problem with the procedure and that she needed to come to the hospital. I called Bob Jr., who was now living in San Antonio, Texas and he was so stunned he could barely speak. He asked me to call his wife Anna because he felt he just couldn't do it.

Robin and I met the physician who was still upset and in tears. He told us that Bob seemed peaceful during the whole time and that they tried heroic means to save him. The doctor was an ardent Catholic and told us he had given Bob last rites. Amy arrived soon after and was escorted downstairs to where we were. We then let her know that her father had passed away and we all tearfully hugged each other, including the doctor, for comfort.

A nurse who had been in the procedure room told me later, that before things started, she said, "Mr. Beasley, are you ready for this?" and he answered, "Yes, I'm ready for this." This was also a comfort, as the nurse knew it would be. Dr. Lew, calling me with his condolences, said the doctor had been too upset to go to work the next day. I had written him a note already, thanking him for being there and for the last rites and for his upbeat attitude that made it bearable for us beforehand. It was now thought that Bob would not have survived the operation, had he even lived through the catheterization.

I remembered Bob's reluctance to have another operation and was grateful, at least, that he would no longer be hurt by prods and pricks and cuts. I thought maybe he had planned it all that way.

Many people called and sent cards and letters of condolence and comfort. One we especially loved was from Bill Redelsheimer who was like a brother to Bob:

Dear Gloria and Kids,

I am very proud of you! It takes courage and poise to face the loss of a man like Bob. I, myself, feel as though I lost a true brother. I've missed Bob's companionship over the years. Try to comfort yourself in the knowledge you've had his presence for so long. He was a merry lad who liked to giggle. I liked that. Not too many men even know how to giggle.

I deeply appreciate your letter and enclosures. They helped Mother and me to understand what that rascal had accomplished. I will try to do as you asked, recording some of our more adventurous escapades. We truly were the terror of all adults in Florida and Georgia—not to mention the Florida East

Coast Railway Company who had the dubious honor of yearly transporting us up and down the length of Florida.

We send all of you our love,

Bill


We held a memorial service several weeks later. Since Bob had always felt a connection, there was a simple Christian Science service. Before the service, an usher brought a man up to the front pew where the family was seated. It was Rudy Vasquez, with tears in his eyes, to see me and we hugged each other. He had always felt proud of his relationship with Bob and knew he had been appreciated by him.

Several people at the service talked about the impact Bob had on their lives. Marlies, Amy's bandmate and longtime friend of the family told how Bob became a father figure for her when she needed it and how she felt part of the family. Ed Law spoke of good times with Bob and told stories that made everyone chuckle.

At the end of the service, Harry Nakano said, "It is apparent that Bob's early training in ceramic research at Corning was the foundation for his vision of space age ceramic materials. It is also apparent that he was a great problem solver, finding simple solutions to seemingly complex problems. These attributes would serve him well in his later development of silica fiber insulation. But most of all, his conviction that a highly purified fibrous silica material could be used as a heat shield or insulation on a spacecraft or missile was what drove him to eventually invent the LI-900 material. Normally, only a Ph.D. type researcher would undertake such a project. It delves into realms of basic material research. Silica fiber, when exposed to high temperatures would transform into a crystalline state from an amorphous state and its thermal expiation coefficient would increase tenfold causing the rigidized silica material to fracture. Bob believed that if he could delay this transformation, the material would withstand more heat exposure.

"In closing, I would like to say that my life was enriched by close association with Bob. Because of his leadership and ingenuity, I was able to participate in the development of the space shuttle tiles. He was not only a good boss, but he was my friend."

This last sentence is the honor Bob would have appreciated most.

# Afterword

The year 2006, was the twenty-fifth anniversary of the first space shuttle flight. New people at NASA concluded that space shuttles were no longer a viable means for space travel. Unmanned space vehicles are proposed as their next focus, much like the *Apollo* in makeup. Private companies are building their own versions of orbiters, one of which is using as their thermal protection shield, a mat version of the LI material. And now the shuttle fleet will stop operation this year. It will be a sad thing for many who remember those early days of the impossible becoming possible.

The invention itself has gone way beyond its original intent. It has been the career for many, many people who helped further its development into what it became. After all the years since its first acceptance as a viable material for the space shuttle heat shield, not many people remember Bob Beasley who had an idea and a vision and pursued it, even in the face of much discouragement.

I've written this book with the help of many others, asked many questions, listened to and accepted much needed criticisms and tried to tell Bob's story as truthfully as I could.

With the fine mentoring I received from Harry Nakano, Bruce Burns and the others who worked with him, and whom he appreciated, I have tried to tell a balanced story and so have left out much of what could have been told, but with the passing of time there is no longer a cause for my zeal. Bob was proud to have worked for Lockheed and honored the people he knew there for who they were and for their accomplishments.

He always knew the idea given to him had led him to Lockheed so that he could fulfill its purpose. And—as I always told him I would—I have written a book about him and I think he would like this one.

Gloria Beasley Lausten

Sunnyvale, California

June 2010

# Appendix A

I asked Bruce Burns, one of my mentors who has done much writing and research on the tile program, especially in its later days, to write up a comprehensive summary with more technical data for those of you who are interested. For this added data, I am most grateful.

## The Tile Program Going Forward
## By Bruce Burns

### General

The terminology used by Rockwell International in its contracts with Lockheed referred to the HRSI (High Temperature Reusable Surface Insulation) Program, while Lockheed's organization to perform the work was called TPS (Thermal Protection Systems) Program. In actual practice the program was usually referred to as "the tile program".

### The DDT&E Contract

The space shuttle Columbia (OV-102) was the end result of a contract known as the DDT&E contract for Design, Development, Test and Engineering. The contract was awarded in 1973 and essentially completed with the first flight of Columbia in April 1981. The contract not only provided for one shipset of tiles for Columbia, but also for replacement tiles as they were needed. The shipset delivery was completed in April, 1979.

One of the first tasks undertaken by Bob's lab was to write a description of the Initial Production Facility (IPF) processing procedures for LI-900 (known as the Cookbook). The document, which consisted of two volumes, one for text and one for illustrations, was released in April, 1974. Lockheed had earlier decided to treat LI-900 technology as proprietary information rather than patent the invention. Thus, the document was released as a Lockheed proprietary data document.

The vision of a shipset of tiles and how they would be produced and installed changed dramatically between the start of the contract and the final tile delivery. The task was something that had not been done before and there were many technical, manufacturing, quality control and installation challenges to overcome. Concerns at the highest levels of NASA led Deputy Administrator Alan Lovelace to appoint a team in 1979, which became known as the Ashley Committee, to ensure the integrity of the Columbia thermal protection system. Dr. Holt Ashley, Professor of Aeronautics and Astronautics at Stanford University, was the chairman of the committee. One of the principle recommendations as a result of this review was to recommend that the tile IML (Inner Mold Line) surfaces be densified with a collodial silica solution in order to distribute the loads from the SIP (Strain Isolator Pad) coming into the tile. The SIP sat between the tile and the aluminum surface of the orbiter, with a layer of high-temperature adhesive (500-600 degree F) on either side.

The DDT&E contract was bid on the premise that most of the tiles on the belly of the orbiters would be flat, square tiles of a constant thickness that could be mass produced. It soon became apparent that all the tiles would be unique and would be defined by Master Dimension data, which numerically located each tile on the orbiter and defined its inner and outer mold lines. Thus, all tiles required a part program based on the Master Dimension data to direct a computerized, numerically controlled machine to cut the tiles individually on all sides.

A system to replace the individual machining of the IML surface of the tiles, individually measuring the tiles for dimensional conformance and individually attaching the tiles to the orbiter surface was developed. Lockheed was directed to design and fabricate a substantial number of "array frames", each of which would contain a group of tiles. The frames were to be used to cut the IML's of the tiles, serve as a shipping container for that group of tiles (restrained in a plywood box) and as an installation tool on the orbiter. They were used for all shipsets. These frames were fabricated from a dense polyurethane foam and consisted of a base with a surface contoured to the outer mold line of the tiles, upon which the coated surfaces of the tiles could be placed and a removable frame that held the tiles in place. The contoured surface was designed to apply a vacuum to the tiles when their IML's were cut. Tiles were loaded into the frame and shimmed to acceptable tolerances. The array frames were then taken to the machine shop where the IML's were cut. After machining and inspection, a vacuum was applied to a plastic bag surrounding the array frame to keep the tiles in place for shipping. The concept became known as "Load and Go". At Rockwell's Palmdale facility, the location of the tiles in an array frame on the orbiter was determined and after the SIP and adhesive layers had been applied to each tile, the array frame was positioned on the orbiter. A vacuum was then applied to a plastic sheet between the coated surfaces of the tiles and the contoured surface of the array frame and the contoured surface of the array frame removed. Curing of the adhesive, at room temperature, took about a day. The removable frame and plastic bag were then removed. Because the removable frame was against the side of the orbiter during curing, these areas were covered subsequently with "closeout" tiles that also accounted for accumulated tolerances.

## The Increment III Contract

A production contract known as the Increment III contract followed. Three shipsets were built under this contract: OV-099 (Challenger), OV-103 (Discovery) and OV-104 (Atlantis). The OV-099 airframe had been the structural test vehicle and had been built before Columbia, so its designation was in the order of manufacture. This contract was initiated in September 1977 and the last tiles for Atlantis were delivered in June 1984. The first tiles for Challenger were shipped in the second quarter of 1980.

The Ames Research Center was assigned the responsibility for research on tiles and tile material by NASA early in the space shuttle program. The research led to changes in the tile shipsets delivered under the Increment III contract. Blankets composed of silica fibers encased or quilted between two silica cover cloths were substituted for about 5,000 Class 1 tiles. The change took place on Discovery, but Columbia and Challenger were retrofitted subsequently. The tile count on Columbia was originally about 23,400 tiles and this change reduced the tile count to about 18,200 tiles. Note, that in addition to the tiles supplied by Lockheed, Rockwell fabricated about 6,300 "closeout" tiles at their Palmdale facility, using tile material (Production Units) supplied by Lockheed. Thus, the total shipset of tiles numbered originally about 30,000 tiles. The blankets were used on the payload bay doors and surrounding areas, called FRSI for Flexible Reusable Surface Insulation and on the OMS pods, called AFRSI for Advanced Flexible Reusable Surface Insulation. Maximum temperatures in these areas were low, so the Class 1 tiles were relatively thin and subject to handling damage. The blankets, which were manufactured at Rockwell solved this problem.

A change in the basic composition of the tiles was also proposed by Ames. While LI-900 was pure silica fiber, the Ames material was composed of silica fiber and 22 percent NEXTEL 312 fiber, manufactured by the 3M Corporation, plus the addition of silicon carbide powder. This material, referred to as FRCI, for Fibrous Refractory Composite Insulation, was proposed in two densities: a 12 pcf density (FRCI-12) to replace LI-2200 tiles (22 pcf) and an 8 pcf density (FRCI-8) to replace LI-900 tiles (9 pcf). Such a change would require requalification of the tiles for flight. Note that silicon carbide powder was already being used in LI-12200, but not in LI-900. LI-2200 was a 22 pcf material that had been developed previously at Ames.

Some thermal response data were provided by Ames to justify the changes which would reduce the all-up weight of the orbiter airframe and based on these data an implementation was scheduled for Discovery, pending the outcome of further tests. Production start of Discovery was scheduled for October 1981.

Lockheed was instructed to proceed with further tests. At the same time, 3M was asked to quote on the production of approximately 90,000 pounds of NEXTEL 312 fiber for the Increment III contract, if the changes proposed by Ames were adopted. At the time, 3M had a single production line that was operating at near capacity. 3M proposed to build a new production line for this order, with the cost to be amortized over the 90,000 pound order.

At the meeting at NASA headquarters in Washington, D.C. in November 1979, Lockheed presented data that showed the thermal conductivity of FRCI-8 to be higher than that for LI-900. Thus, there could not be a size-for-size substitution of FRCI-8 for LI-900. As a result, the technology for FRCI-8 was "put on the shelf" for future consideration. However; the tests for FCRI-12 were encouraging and ultimately about 1,200 tiles were converted from LI-2200 to FRCI-12 on a size-for-size basis. Some LI-900 tiles were also converted to FRCI-12 on a size-for-size basis. Weight savings were estimated at 875 pounds.

The cancellation of FRCI-8 meant that there would be an order for NEXTEL 312 fiber significantly lower than 90,000 pounds. 3M submitted a claim for termination costs for $900,000 which ultimately went to litigation and was settled out of court.

The efficiency with which the tiles were made increased with each shipset. The yield for the Columbia shipset was 44%. Yield increased to 81% for Challenger, to 88% for Discovery and to 93% for Atlantis.

## The Logistics Contract

After the first flight of the Columbia in 1981, there was a requirement for replacement tiles at the Cape. A contract was established to provide tiles and to establish an inventory of Production Units (PU's) and other materials. Over a period of time, equipment for machining and coating tile was installed at the Cape so that replacement tiles could be produced on site. Replacement tile activity gradually declined at Lockheed to what was called "Minimum Tile Capability" of 25 tiles per week upon the completion of the Atlantis shipset. That is, 25 tiles was the minimum number of orders necessary to keep the tile fabrication open. Tiles that were made at Lockheed tended to be more the difficult geometries and those with longer lead time. Initially, with orbiter production on-going, the turn-around on replacement tiles was on the order of 28 days. As production drew to a close, this time was cut to about 5 days. As the Atlantis shipset neared completion, the addition of additional shipsets was being discussed, with projections ranging from 1 to 3 shipsets. It was obvious that at some point production of shipsets would end and in that event, there was concern for sufficient PU's, in particular, to supply the space shuttle program's requirement for replacement tiles for its life span. A number of studies were performed at Lockheed at Rockwell direction, with the end result that about 5,500 PU's were produced per year at Lockheed to supply either inventory or OV-105 production from about 1985 through about 1992.

## The OV-105 Contract

The go-ahead for a shipset of tiles for OV-105 (Endeavour) was received in August 1987. Prior to this date the backshops at Rockwell's facility for orbiter assembly in Palmdale had expanded their capacity for fabricating tiles from just the closeout tiles to include about 13,000 design tiles that had been fabricated by Lockheed for the previous orbiters. Consequently, the number of tiles supplied by Lockheed for Endeavour was reduced to about 7,200 tiles, plus the materials necessary for Rockwell to fabricate the remaining tiles. The Lockheed effort on Endeavour was completed in late 1989. Tile yield was 93%.

## Continuing Tasks Beyond OV-105

The logistics contract continued on through 1992, supplying PU's and materials to the Cape. This work was contracted directly with the Rockwell organization at the Cape which had responsibility for replacement tiles. The contract was negotiated annually. With the loss of Challenger in 1986 and the subsequent stand-down in flight operations, a more focused assessment of PU and material needs could be made. The flight schedule, which had formerly been ambitious, was scaled down, resulting in fewer replacement tile requirements. The more recent loss of Columbia has further reduced the need for inventory, meaning that the forecasts in place at the time the last PU was fabricated have probably provided sufficient PU's and materials to serve the life of the space shuttle program.

## Gearing Up For Other Applications

Articles published in technical magazines on the subject of LI-900 after the award of the DDT&E contract resulted in about 600 requests in 1975-76 for more technical information on the material from other aerospace and commercial companies. Literature was produced and forwarded to these companies and a number of applications were discussed. However, cost of the material was generally a stumbling point with commercial companies. One application was for troughs for molten metals. That company indicated that they would be interested when the price of a PU was reduced to $25. At the time, fiber from Manville was being purchased for $28 per pound and in order to make the product, the purity of that fiber was required. About 7 pounds of fiber were used in each PU. It was clear that commercial applications, if any, would be restricted to a narrow group of applications which would not require any significant quantities of material.

The NASA New Technology office felt there were commercial applications and referred a number of firms to Lockheed with their applications. NASA felt that a cheaper version of the product could be developed to meet the cost expectations. However, this was just not the case. Cost would have to be reduced by an order of magnitude, if not more. One of the more memorable contacts was from a man in Minnesota who wanted to build a house out of LI-900. Sadly, we informed him that LI-900 had an open cell configuration, meaning that a breeze would come through the material if it were not coated to prevent convection. With LI-900 selling for about $1,000 per cubic foot, it would also be an expensive, breezy house. The NASA New Technology office was also interested in selling licenses to firms to produce materials that NASA had patented, including the FRCI materials. Thus, in order to sell FRCI materials commercially, Lockheed would need a NASA license and presumably pay royalties. There were insufficient business prospects to take these steps.

A further problem with other applications was the need for permission from NASA to use government-furnished equipment (GFE) on a non-interference basis for these applications and permission to do stock transfers of raw materials to produce them. Some equipment was owned by Lockheed, but in order to produce products for other applications, GFE was required. Non-interference basis also was not entirely satisfactory because schedules for other applications could not be firmly quoted. In October 1982, Lockheed received an RFQ from Ford Aerospace for LI-900 antenna covers for

ARABSAT. The RFQ was no-bid because of lack of agreement with NASA on the use of GFE and material, as well as a conflict with ITAR regulations. Sandia Corp. requested a ROM quote for similar parts at about the same time, but was no-bid also. The up-side to these two examples was that there was a market, although small, for Lockheed insulation materials for other space applications and later contracts revealed a potential market for military applications. These were applications that put the capabilities of the material to their designed use, where there were few materials that could compete and the need justified the cost.

It should also be pointed out that Lockheed was developing advanced insulation materials beginning in the early 1980's, where the composition of the insulation material differed considerably from the materials being produced for NASA. Thus, use of GFE equipment posed a risk of contamination of NASA products. This could not be tolerated. The end result was a need for in-house funding for dedicated equipment for applications that were not in hand.

In spite of this situation, basic equipment began to be acquired primarily in the old IPF (Initial Production Facility), where a Lockheed-owned drying oven, kilns and spray booths were located. Eventually, a 5-axis numerically controlled mill was purchased and installed in the Building 174 machine shop and a vacuum forming facility was installed in Building 103, along with a new casting tower. A vacuum furnace was also acquired for work on advanced coatings.

## Lockheed Development of Improved Materials

After the development and test phases of the DDT&E contract were completed, Bob Beasley's Materials Lab continued to develop improved materials on limited funds. In addition, the TPS Program had a small budget to work on similar but not identical projects. Some funds from the Lockheed Aeronautical Systems Company based in Burbank were also directed to the TPS Program, under the direction of LASC personnel. All these funds were IR&D (Independent Research and Development) funds.

A new family of high temperature ceramic insulation materials was developed in Bob Beasley's lab, managed by Doug Izu, with

Bill Wheeler being the principal investigator. These materials were named HTP (High Temperature Performance) and were initially disclosed by Bill at the NASA/AIAA Fibrous Ceramic Materials Technology Seminar held at NASA/JSC on March 23, 1983. HTP had significantly improved thermal stability at 2600 degrees F (an increase of 300 degrees F over other materials). Mechanical properties were also significantly higher than other insulation material with the same density. HTP was composed of 3 basic raw materials: high purity silica fibers, high purity aluminum oxide fibers and high purity boron nitride. Production billet sizes were made with 6, 12 and 16 pcf densities. It appeared at the time that these materials could be substituted on a size-for-size basis for tiles on the orbiters that were "slumping" due to over-temperature exposure. A 60 pcf. version of the material was also made for high temperature radome applications. Work was also performed on ways to increase resistance to impact loadings, such as ice falling off the booster tanks, or rain erosion. A process for Integral Multiple Density (IMD) tiles was developed that incorporated a higher density layer of material immediately below the coating. Also, a High Impact Coating (HIC) was developed which consisted of the Class 2 RCG (Reaction Cured Glass) coating reinforced with silicon carbide whiskers. Rain erosion tests were performed on samples provided by Lockheed, showing significant improvement on performance. HTP-50 (50 pcf) material coated with HIC survived with no damage after exposure to rain at 300 mph at a 90-degree angle of attack for 30 seconds. LI-900 coated with class 2 RCG coating was breached at 100 mph under the same conditions. Other developments included sintering silicon carbide fabric onto HTP for leading edge applications, reinforcing Class 2 RCG coating with silicon carbide platelets, reaction bonding silicon nitride onto HTP-12 and densifying HTP with silicon carboxide.

It is well known that the LI-900 tiles which could withstand launch, outer space and reentry environments were essentially transparent to microwave and millimeter energy since the orbiter carried a number of antennas installed in the structure beneath the tiles. The stability of the tiles through all environments was essential to the proper operation of the antennas. In addition, LI-900 had RF properties of low loss and low permittivity that remain constant with increasing temperatures. Work was performed to show that the material could be modified to a specific dielectric constant and loss tangent, by the addition of different fibers. HTP was generally the base material in this work. It was shown that the material could be tailored successfully to the RF requirements desired and a number of test articles were produced, including a vacuum formed spherical antenna.

Another concern with antenna design was protection from laser attack. The tiles act as a shield to laser irradiation. Work was carried out to improve the laser threshold for damage, with a minimum weight penalty. A coating of tungsten deposited on Class 2 RCG coated HTP-12 material increased the laser threshold for damage by a factor of four. Depositing silicon carbide directly on HTP-12 increased the laser threshold for damage by a factor of five, the sample having a 300 w/sq cm threshold for damage when subjected to a carbon dioxide laser for 100 seconds. In addition, should vaporization of the material occur, there would be no organic contamination of mirrors or other surfaces.

The addition of other materials to HTP could serve other purposes. With the proper additions, a silica-based material could become a radar absorbing material (RAM), a material that soaks up radar energy and transforms it into heat instead of reflecting it. Along the same line, these materials could be used to reduce the infrared signature of hot jet engine exhausts. These materials, of course, relate to stealth applications, which were of great interest in the late 1980's and still are. Substantial work was done in this area.

## New Business Contracts

All the improved materials described above were aimed at acquiring new business to keep the TPS program in operation after the shuttle work essentially completed. At the time, there was a potential for Shuttle 2 and other NASA programs. The military also had a number of programs, both approved and proposed, where Lockheed's technology could be utilized.

The primary person on the program who developed new contacts and new contracts was Ron Banas. Ron's box on the organization chart was TPS Acquisition. It was not an indirect position and Ron's classification was Senior Staff Engineer. Ron had been assigned to the program from the beginning, first as a thermodynamics engineer, then as Engineering Manager, before taking over the pursuit of new business. He was the program contact on all the thermal cycle tests at NASA-JSC and was well known to JSC personnel. He had written a number of technical papers about the materials and their performance, usually in cooperation with other members of the program. When these papers were presented at various NASA and AIAA meetings, Ron was always good at searching out people who could help us in our activities, such as firms doing vapor deposition and also in selling our technology to prospective customers. He was well prepared and a natural for the new business function. He was the best. One would think that Lockheed marketing would be involved with this activity, but the job required someone with intimate knowledge of the products and technology, which were outside the mainstream Lockheed line of business. Marketing involvement was primarily to supply the brochures and handouts that were taken to meetings where Ron and other program members manned a table to disseminate information and answer questions. Ron was particularly good at repartee; his replies to negative or vague comments were quick and generally provided a point of view aimed for a positive reaction. New business would not have gotten off the ground without Ron.

New business generally fell into two categories: supply of test articles or parts for test articles and production parts. Some of the test articles and parts for test articles are listed below.

- PU's and tiles for AFE (Aerobrake Flight Experiment) for NASA-JSC

- HTP-6 machined parts for a large, thin-wall titanium tank where the HTP-6 was load-bearing insulation for LASC

- HTP-30-100 laser heat shield tubes for Lawrence-Livermore

- HTP-6 billets for cryogenic ullage control for NASA-Goddard

- HTP-6 coated antenna windows for Raytheon

- HTP-6 vacuum formed parts for an RF transparent oven at NASA-Lewis

- FRCI-20 billets for heat shield development to NASA-Ames

- HTP-12 vacuum-formed parts for the A-12 (the Navy's Advanced Tactical Aircraft-ATA)

The contracts for production parts are listed below. In general, the production contract was preceded by small purchase orders for test articles. Unfortunately, the A-12 noted in the above list never went into production. Also, applications were planned for the YF-22A (the Advanced Tactical Fighter-ATF), but the production of that aircraft was delayed until the mid to late 1990's.

- HTP-16 heat shield parts for the F-117A fighter

- HTP-12 heat shield parts for the B2 bomber

In addition to above, talks were held with the French and Japanese, who expressed interest in the materials for aerospace projects that they were contemplating. No funding resulted from these talks.

## Finis

The cold war ended in the summer of 1991 and most of the new projects that Lockheed was working on or was pursuing were either cancelled, reduced in size, or stretched out. In some cases, these events allowed the customer sufficient time to develop his own material, based on what he had learned from visits to the Lockheed facility. In short, the military business was insufficient to keep the doors open. At the same time, new NASA programs that could use Lockheed materials, of which there were many proposed during the mid-1980's, did not materialize. In October 1991, Ron Banas died and there was no one qualified to take his place. Ron had clearances to several LASC classified programs with possible uses for the Lockheed material. No one else in the program had these clearances, which were essential to pursue the potential with this sister company. As the result of these two factors, the TPS slowly ran down as the final Logistics contract was completed. The business line to continue the Logistics level was about $10 M/yr. This level could have been achieved had the military business continued as planned. Total business from the beginning of 1973 to the end was about $325 M. Building 174, where all of the production tiles were made was eventually cleaned out and turned over to the publications department at Lockheed. The manufacturing area now houses printing equipment.

# Appendix B

# Biographies

I have asked the good friends who have helped me by sharing their experiences and thoughts about Bob and the tile program. Some were reluctant to write very much, but I have done my best to have them write all the pertinent facts about their lives. It is still true that without their help, this book, in all its personal detail, could not have been written. I love them all.

### Bruce Burns

Bruce Burns joined Lockheed at the Palo Alto Research Laboratories in 1959 and began conducting studies on beryllium heat shields in 1968. Between the years 1971 and 1974, he managed four small NASA technology contracts dealing with candidate space shuttle thermal protection systems. In 1976, he was named assistant to the chief engineer for the thermal protection systems (TPS) Program. He was made TPS program manager in 1983 and retired from that position in 1991.

### Jack Creedon

Jack was principal investigator along with Ray Banas in Lockheed's relationship with NAS/ARC. His background is of special value because of his involvement in the RGC effort and also because of the benefits that his exposure to TPS efforts elsewhere in the industry affords. For the RCG effort, he made valuable suggestions for initiating changes to enhance productability and lower cost. He also contributed to resolution of production control problems. Prior to that, he worked for two years on LMSC's 0050 coating of the LI90 insulation. Before that, Mr. Creedon was with Martin Marietta, where he developed a coating to use with the Martin HRSI candidate material.

Mr. Creedon's experience working in this highly specialized development area, his direct and practical approach to a problem and his ability to respond to a tight schedule are consistent with the challenge of developing an improved coating for silica RSI.

Mr. Creedon's preceding nineteen years of experience was with TRW, Aerojet General and Minnesota Mining and Manufacturing—all engaged in research and development of high-tensile-strength glass formulations, composites of glass, graphite and boron and nonmetallic materials.

Mr. Creedon has a BSCE from Northwestern University and he has completed graduate courses at Brooklyn Polytechnic Institute, University of Michigan, Wayne State University, University of Chicago and UCLA.

## Ed Gzowski

Ed was born in Oakfield, New York, a small town in western New York, between Buffalo and Rochester.
His education included Alfred University; graduating with a BS in Ceramic Engineering in 1952 and completing a certificate course in Production Management at UC Berkeley. He was drafted into the U.S. Army and served from August 1952 through August 1954.

Work History:
Acme Brick Company, Malverne, Arkansas, June 1952 to August 1952.
— "After being stationed in Arkansas another year, I decided Arkansas was not for me."

American Standard, San Pablo, California, November 1954 to December 1958.
Ceramic engineer and general foreman.
— Making plumbing fixtures.

Eitel-McCullough, San Carlos, California (now part of Varian) December 1958 to October 1961.
Process engineer and head, Ceramics Department

— Metallized and brazed ceramics to metal components for high power vacuum tubes, developed annealing procedures for glass tubes.

Coors Porcelain Co., Golden, CO, October 1961 to September 1965. Supervisor, Beryllium Oxide Department.
— Manufactured beryllium oxide components for primarily electronic and nuclear applications.

Lockheed Missiles and Space Company, Sunnyvale, California, September 1965 to December 1993.
Manufacturing research engineer, research engineer, program resident representative, quality engineer, materials processes engineer.
— Worked specifically on Missiles Systems Division Programs for four years, Space Shuttle Tile Program for twenty-four years. Was in most aspects of the Tile Program: laboratory, manufacturing support, quality assurance, engineering and supplier interface. Retired after the contract with Rockwell ended.

Ed has been married to Bea for forty-seven years. They have three children: Mike, Carolyn and Suzy and five grandchildren: Brian, Steve, Matt, Ricky and Donovan.

**George Hamma**
I was born in San Francisco on December 22, 1945. My family lived briefly in Oakland, Martinez and Sacramento, settling down in Marysville when I was about five. My father was a civil engineer with the Division of Highways, where he continued until he retired. He died in 2002. My mother, with a degree in art and music, taught all grades K-12 off and on until her retirement. She still lives in Sunnyvale. I also have a sister, Bernita Fuller, living in Southern California.

I went to UC Davis, graduating with a BS in Physics in 1967. I also did some work at San Jose State. At UC Davis, the only way we could complete our physics homework and projects in a human lifetime was to learn the use of computers. This familiarity with programming and systems turned out to be useful later.

Following graduation, after applying to several aerospace companies, I started work at Lockheed Missiles and Space Company in Sunnyvale, in the summer of 1967.

My first assignment a LMSC was an engineer performing hydrodynamic testing at the unique Lockheed Underwater Missile Facility, a towing basin within a vacuum chamber. The testing organization to which I belonged was entering a period of technology purchases and almost everything included a computer. I was the only one in the group with computer familiarity and experience, so I was involved in all systems designs and purchases in the labs. I continued working with environmental testing in Sunnyvale until I moved to the Lockheed Palo Alto Research facility as senior scientist. There I served as an in-house consultant on computer systems and designs for data acquisition and control systems for Lockheed Missiles and Space.

I left Lockheed in 1978 with two colleagues to found Synergistic Technology, Incorporated. There we continued to work with computers and environmental testing to provide systems for data acquisition, analysis and vibration control. I continued with that firm as a principal and vice president until STI was acquired by Spectral Dynamics Incorporated in 1996. I am now working as senior member, technical staff at the Spectral Dynamics factory in San Jose.

I was an executive board member of Digital Computer Users Society. I have presented and published many papers, including with the AIAA, SAVIAC and IEST. I have been honored as a fellow of the Institute of Environmental Services and Technology.

At the laboratory in Palo Alto, my group had the responsibility of performing mechanical testing of samples of the tile material. We received samples machined into fragile cylinders, coupons and bars. These were pushed, pulled, twisted and otherwise broke to find out their mechanical properties. The testing requirements included providing both very hot and very cold environments in which to evaluate the materials. My role was providing systems for the instrumentation and measurement of tests as well as the analysis of the results. We had to make some rather special machines to precisely and accurately test such fragile stuff.

An additional role I had was to support the development of the tile factory at the Sunnyvale plant. There were problems with the systems supposed to measure the tiles once they had been machined to shape. The computers were supposed to communicate together and with the testing instruments and there were difficulties with these connections.

We got around the problems, mostly with HP computers and the final test systems ended up being successful.

I live in Sunnyvale with my wife, Janet and we have two children, a son, Cory and a daughter, Jillian.


**Bernie Francis**
Bernie worked as a support person on Bob's program. His background is in R&D and Ocean Systems Program Planning and Coordination. He retired after serving thirty-seven years at Lockheed.

## Pat McCormick

After my army service, I started with Boeing Company in Seattle, Washington.

Work History:
1957-1960   Plastic toolmaker, Transport Division, Boeing
1960-1964   Leadman Plastic Shop, mock-up and tooling mechanic, LMSC
1964-1965   Production and tooling supervisor, Aquanautics, Inc., Palo Alto
1964-1972   Materials and process engineer, Materials Science Lab, LMSC
1972-1980   Materials and process engineer, member of Research Lab, LMSC
1980-1987   Materials and processes engineering specialist
1987-1990   Staff engineer/laboratory supervisor

After I returned to LMSC in 1965 to work for Bob Beasley and Doug Izu, I started taking night classes at San Jose City College and eventually in 1969 got an AA degree in Electronics. We had many programs going and I think I was kind of Bob's and Doug's gofer. I made whatever setups they requested. I also assisted Chuck Dewey in a lot of machine work.

In the early stages, I developed an identification marking method and also assisted in all the setups such as compaction, firing, densifying, coating, water proofing, bonding and testing.

I retired from LMSC in November of 1999. I still live in San Jose with my wife, Verena. We have three grown children and seven grandchildren.

## Harry Nakano

I was born in 1921 in Santa Clara as the first son of a Japanese immigrant farmer who happened to be a sharecropper of land, which is now the Civic center of California. In 1935, my parents took the whole family on a visit to Japan for about four months. I really liked Japan then, so I decided with my parents' approval, to stay in Japan for a while to learn the language. To put it in better perspective, let me explain. California and the rest of the western states had a strong anti-Oriental political climate at the time. Asian immigrants were not allowed to own real estate and their offspring, who were American citizens, did not have many opportunities in America for employment. Many Japanese felt at that time that there were very few opportunities in America and to realize some gainful occupation they had to be strongly bilingual. Therefore, I thought and my parents also, that learning Japanese was essential to my future. Although Japan at that time was a very a backward and poor country, I felt good living there because I was treated equally as the rest of the Japanese population. This was not so in Santa Clara. I felt discriminated against by parents of my classmates. I was never invited to my friend's houses and I knew their parents didn't want their kids to associate with me. And as I went to high school in Japan, I decided that I should to go to college there because I knew that if I graduated from a Japanese college, I would get good jobs from Japanese firms or government.

I studied hard in high school and was able to pass the entrance exam to enter imperial universities in Japan. In the meantime, on December 7, 1941, Japan attacked Pearl Harbor and we were in WW II. You might think I would be rounded up as an American, but that didn't happen. I also had Japanese citizenship. There is a difference in the way the two countries treat citizenships. Japan believed that if your parents registered their offspring as Japanese citizens, they ignore the fact that they also have American citizenship. Therefore, I was never harassed by the Japanese people or agents of their notorious secret police or military police. I was treated equally with other Japanese. On the other hand, I also had conscription in the Japanese army looming in the near future. Fortunately for me I was taking up science/engineering and was deferred until graduation. The war ended in August 1945 and I was able to graduate in that October. I earned a bachelor of engineering degree with specificy in applied chemistry from Kyushu Imperial University.

In 1947, I was able to return to California as a U.S. citizen. I stayed at my parents' home in Redwood City. And I was so happy and elated to be back in the States where the food and other material goods were plentiful and cheap. I took a long vacation at my parents' home where we concluded that I could never be a farmer, so I went to Chicago with the thousand dollars my parents gave me to start a new life. At that time, California was not very industrialized and there were still remnants of Japanese discrimination. The job opportunities were much better in Chicago. At least, the lower level jobs were open to anyone willing to work. I got my first job as a control chemist in a paint factory in a Kist Orange Company. I was not a good taster and the job gave me a stomach ache, so I quit. My next job was as a control chemist in a paint factory called Bradley-Froman Co. There I learned the rudiments of paint formation for mostly industry applications. I did not like control work and wanted to do more paint formulations. The company would not promote me, so I quit and went to work for a small paint company specializing in custom-formulated paints. I was their solo chemist with much better pay and I enjoyed the work very much. I formulated a low-cost graphite coating that was widely sold as a conductive coating for the television tubes and the little company became very profitable. This little company was known as Stuart Paint Company.

In 1949, Irene and I got married and later moved into an apartment, which was part of a large home owned by her parents. Her parents and her twin sister later moved to California. Both Irene and I had no close relatives in Chicago and we became very lonely and homesick for them. So I placed an ad in the Los Angeles Times for a job as a paint chemist. There were about three responses, but I liked the job offered in Sunnyvale by a start-up, Walter Paint Company. I took a sizable pay cut and had to pay all my expenses, but I thought it was worthwhile to get back to California. Most latex paints used in California then were based on PVA and there were some technical problems with this type of paint, so I then formulated an acrylic emulsion based paint and it became a best seller for the company. After a few years with them, I realized I was getting nowhere, so I changed jobs again. I went to work for Technical Coatings, Inc., which was more to my liking as my work consisted of formulating paints for industrial application. While working there for about three years, the company hired some business analysts and they interviewed all employees. I, like a dumb fool, told them what I did not like about the company's business practices and so forth and I subsequently got fired. This was the first time I was laid off and I was willing to find any job even outside of paint companies.

I applied for a job in Lockheed in Palo Alto. I was offered a position working with inorganic paints, but I didn't have any background for inorganic chemistry, so I refused. Then they offered me a job in adhesives. I was also going to refuse that, but then the interviewer, Dr. De Fano, countered by saying what was the difference? Paint sticks to one side of the substrate while an adhesive sticks on both sides. So I accepted the offer and I was hired into Harvey Crosby's group. There I started to work with Les Shoff and also met Bob. I also remember a year or so later, Doug joined Bob's group.

## Les Shoff

I was born in Amesville, Ohio, the youngest of thirteen children. After five years in the army, I went to Kent State University to study optometry and chemistry and ended up with a job at the Goodrich Chemical Lab.

Later, I moved to Southern California and worked at the Lockheed Chemistry Lab there and then to the new Lockheed Missiles and Space Company in Palo Alto. My work on the thermal protection tiles included my field of expertise in adhesives.

After nine and a half years at Sunnyvale, I retired to travel and enjoy life. Muriel and I celebrated our twenty-fifth wedding anniversary on July 12, 2007.

## Tom Tanabe

Tom was born on December 20, 1932 in Seattle, Washington. He has been married to Joanne since December 18, 1966.They have five children; two are married and they have four grandchildren.

His education includes a BS in Chemical Engineering from the University of Washington. He was employed by Boeing for four and a half years before being hired by Lockheed.

Programs he was involved in:
Poseidon Program (four years)
Space Shuttle Tiles
Hubble Space Telescope
Various Secret Programs
Space Station
During employment in the tile program, Tom developed the coating for the gray tiles (1200 degrees F or less area).

# Appendix C

# Acknowledgments

Bob included this note at the end of his article for *The Journal of Materials Education,* which was published at Penn State:

Many people, each of whom I consider expert in their respective fields, helped from time to time in laboratory development and testing, pilot plant and production facilities and a variety of support functions. I would like to acknowledge them here: Herb Allen, Ed Bahnsen, Ron Banas, Bruce Burns, Bob Griffith, Joe Cappels, Jack Creedon, George Cunningham, Chuck Dewey, Paul Ferguson, Bernie Francis, Bill Gennoe, Joe Gentes, Warren Greenway, Ed Gzowski, Mike Homna, Doug Izu, Ed Law, Carl Luchetti, Bob LeBleu, Pat McCormick, Harry Nakano, Doug Oeser, Augie Ozelin, Tom Patton, Bill Ravenell, John Robinson, Hi Silversher, Les Shoff, Bill Short, TomTanabe, Rudy Vasquez and Joyce Waltham. I would especially like to mention those who worked most closely with me in the development of the LI material and left their "fingerprints" on it: Bill Wheeler, Dean Fisher, Al Pechman and Steve Garofalini.

Dr. Morris Steinberg is responsible for giving me the opportunity to work in the exciting field of aerospace and I am most grateful for it.

# Appendix D—Logbook

## Logbook—August 18, 1960

This logbook, the property of Robert M Beasley, was begun on this date, August 18, 1960. The contents are the sole property of Robert M. Beasley and his heirs.

Patty J. Dalton
Notary Public
In and for the County of Santa Clara
State of California
18th day of August 1960

### New Method for Preparing Inorganic Fibrous Materials

It has occurred to me that there are other possible methods for preparing inorganic fibers than those presented in patent applications, while in the employ of Horizons, Inc. (12/9/57 to 7/31/60). Since making this trip and having an opportunity to collect my thoughts without the influence of surrounding activities, based on pursuing the problem from the approaches based on my earlier inventions—then thought to be the only possible methods—I now believe that there are workable and possibly superior methods for achieving inorganic fibrous materials. These methods would definitely represent entirely new approaches to the problem. Even though they now seem obvious, simple and straightforward, it must be that they did not occur to me previously since my thoughts and those at Horizons were limited to the drying of dilute solutions—either on surfaces or in dehydrating solutions—to achieve the end product. (These previous thoughts are substantiated by the earlier applications.)

The new methods visualized at this time might be those or rather include those as outlined and described on the following pages.

Where indicated, some crude experiments have been performed
to establish the reality and feasibility of the methods envisioned.
These experiments, conducted during the past three days, were of the
simplest nature since they were performed in the kitchen unit of the
Flamingo Motor Lodge, Palo Alto, California, in the presence of my
wife, Gloria Marie Beasley.

1.  The preparation of fibers from inorganic chemical setting
    materials. In this classification would fall such materials as:

    A.  Inorganic cements
    B.  Phosphates
    C.  Mixtures of phosphates and cement
    D.  Phosphates mixed with oxide materials
    E.  Colloids
    F.  Colloids mixed with gelling agents
    G.  Colloids in combination with coagulating gelling or
        dehydrating or precipitating materials
    H.  Any or all of the above, mixed or in combination with
        materials such as gums, resins, binders, sugars, etc.,
        which might aid in achieving the proper conditions for
        fiber extruding, pulling or slinging or throwing as will be
        outlined in the method for achieving fibrous dimensions

2.  The preparation of fibers from inorganic or metal organic salts or
    combinations of these.

    A.  Unaided except by conditions designed to render the materials
        of proper viscosity and setting properties to make the forming
        methods visualized practical.
    B.  As above, except aided by admixtures, additions or
        combinations designed to achieve the necessary conditions for
        forming.

    The methods visualized for forming these materials into fibrous
dimensions involve the arts of extruding, pulling, or slinging materials
of adjusted viscosities. This might be clarified by examples.

1.  Extruding

    The materials so treated or combined to display the desirable viscosity and accompanying conditions necessary so that they may be extruded or forced through small orifices or holes in a die or cavity. Common examples of this forming method in use would be as toothpaste in tubes, ceramic extruded ware, man-made organic fibers, extruded metals, extruded glasses and extruded plastics, candy, etc.

2.  Pulling

    The pulling of viscous materials into filaments, films, or sheets. Common examples of this method would be found in the glass forming industry, metal industry, plastics, candy, etc.

3.  Slinging

    The slinging of viscous materials into a medium—say, such as air—in which they "set up" before combining or in some cases—collected. Slinging is interpreted to also include blowing. Glass and candy fibers are common examples of this method.

4.  Combinations of the above.

    It is believed that in many cases an orifice would be extremely helpful in controlling the dimensions of the fibers.

Using these methods it should be possible to control the dimensions of the fibers as to shape (cross section) and length. Fibers or rods should be possible in the cross section range of 1 micron (or 1 less) up to any size desired. Film or sheets should equally be possible being influenced by orifice, viscosity, type and rate of pull and other accompanying variables.

Additional treatments might be considered in the forming methods:

An example might be that of an after treatment in a controlled humidity to either (and or) aid drying, setting, flaw healing, surface resolution, etc.

Fibers thus formed might then either be ready for use or might be fired, decomposed, impregnated, coated, etc. Depending on treatments and compositions fibers might be organic, inorganic, metal oxides, carbides, metallic, ferrite, ferroelectric, piezoelectric, magnetic, resistors, conductors, nuclear fuel, nuclear shielding, etc. This is considered of little matter being primarily a choice of treatment and composition and this disclosure considered to be that of methods of achieving fibrous, film or sheet substances.

More specific examples using chemical specie might clarify what is in mind in this disclosure.

1. Chemical setting materials—

Wollastonite in combination with Alkophos CE (a product of the Monsanto Chemical Co). Mixtures of this powder (Wollastonite) with the viscous liquid or the phosphate (Alkophos CE) yield a highly viscous fast setting solid inorganic material which possesses high strength upon setting and also may be fired to vitrification by methods known and common in the ceramics industry. A mixture of these materials designed to yield the proper viscosity for the methods of forming cited can easily be prepared. It may then be formed by these methods into filaments or sheets depending on the conditions utilized. The materials could then be used in the "set up" on vitrified forms.

2. Extremely fine grained powders of inorganic metal oxides might be mixed with viscosity aids to enable them to be formed with the methods cited. In the case of extrusion—a plasticizer might be added.

In the cases of pulling or slinging, sugar, resins, etc., might be added so that when slight heat is applied the suitable viscosity for forming might be achieved. After forming the cooled material would retain its shape and then could be sintered.

3. Zirconium acetate solution could be concentrated by vacuum drying, heating in a double boiler, etc. to form a concentrated gummy material. In doing this a large quantity of HCL might be added during the concentrating process to prevent gelling—this is considered to be important! Then the zirconium acetate-HCL residue can be heated gently to achieve the proper viscosity or just dried down to the desired viscosity. This type of material can

be easily pulled or slung. It sets rapidly when in extremely fine cross-sectional dimensions. The so formed fibers or film may then be sintered to increase strength and/or when a stabilizing material for example as a calcium specie or chrome salt specie has been included—sintered to achieve a stabilizing zirconia specie.

By actual experimentation it has been noted that a zirconium acetate-HCL residue does exist as a gum. Now it is visualized that this gum might be "pulled" into fibers exactly in the manner of forming fiber glass except that very low temperature might be used or when the gum and exhibits the proper viscosity and exhibits the proper coherence as achieved in the original concentrating process (which also might include drying as exposed to air), no heat at all would be necessary.

This gum can also be formed into fibers of extremely small cross-section by utilizing the slinging out of small orifices or blown from such apertures—extrusion might also be possible.

A superior zirconia product can be achieved by utilizing small admixtures of stabilizers and/or grain growth inhibitors. Chromium acetate is believed to be an excellent addition to achieve conditions of stabilization against polymorphic inversions and grain growth or crystal development. Fibers of extremely small size will be transparent and seemingly amorphous to microscopic examinations. When formed in extremely small diameters, round fibers formed in the manner described will be quite flexible and should exhibit the desirable properties of glass fibers in addition to the ultra high temperature properties associated with stabilized zirconia.

This example using zirconium acetate should demonstrate the possibilities of using metal oxide salts which after firing can be converted to metal oxide species.

When using organic salts the possibility of using reducing atmospheric firing conditions to produce carbides are always present. This possibility is of extreme interest when forming tungsten salts by this method.

By observation of material properties made during my research efforts during the last 9 years I know beyond a shadow of a doubt that these methods described are both workable and feasible. I have watched viscous materials formed in the glass industry and "models" of these materials using resins, gums, glycols, sugars, etc. in the study of these forming methods and find the visualized methods to be analogous. Of course, an important difference is that the formed materials visualized here are usually after treated—say, by firing or sintering—to offer a useful product. Sugar in fibrous form—say as cotton candy—is useful only as a candy; however this same product carbonized in a reducing atmospheric firing might be highly useful in the missile or resistor industries. The pulling of sugar fibers from a slightly heated mass has been demonstrated by me. This same sugar could have been easily combined with an inorganic or organic substance, which after firing to remove the sugar would have remained as a coherent fiber or film of a useful product.

RMB

## New Method of Preparing Foams

The same material described in the past section might be prepared by the inclusion of foaming agents into the viscous materials—then drying—and then firing or sintering

The foaming agent might be chemical or blown air, entrapped air, expelled gases from a chemical reaction, etc.

*Drawing of fine continuous fibers from the Zirconium Aacetate + Chromium Acetate-HCL gum as previously described—*

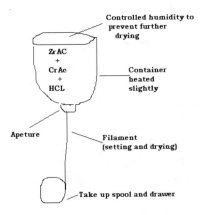

The "set" filament might be taken directly to a "take-up" spool removed and then sintered or it might pass through this spool through a firing tube or chamber and then taken up on another spool on a continuous basis. Using the fiber glass experience, many filaments may be "drawn" from a single chamber.

### Car Mufflers—Inorganic or Ceramic

Inorganic cements or chemical setting inorganics might be utilized in the preparation of ceramic mufflers.

An example of the latter would be the use of Wollastonite and Alkophos CE. What is visualized here is that a mixture of these materials might be used to coat a metal muffler for longer life—or an entirely new muffler might be made as follows.

This inorganic material could be used to coat or impregnate paper or other combustible or inexpensive materials as follows—

Paper

A paper liner for a metal container could be impregnated with this mixture and placed in the container before setting. This would form a ceramic inner shell, which would be resistant to the destructive forces and conditions present in a muffler. Then paper muffling configurations properly impregnated could be placed in the container to finish the muffler.

An example would be to merely coat the inside of a metal can or tube with the viscous ceramic chemical setting material and then insert an impregnated corrugated paper roll into the container as the muffling device. The corrugated roll would provide a multiplicity of ceramic channels for the gases to pass through and be muffled in. Since the ceramic muffler would be resistant to heat, it could be placed near the manifold so as to run hot for more complete combustion of the gases to minimize exhaust fumes and reduce smog inducing expellants.

Instead of paper sheet or corrugated material, excelsior or even grass or straw could be coated and utilized as a muffler charge in a coated container.

Time has not permitted fuller description of these inventions as I want to get this book notarized to establish the conception dates. After this is done a more specific description will be added along with evidence of reduction to practice. These concepts have been thought of since my separation from Horizons, Inc. and before starting to work for Lockheed Missiles; therefore, it seems expedient that I not delay in establishing this fact for my protection and that of my heirs.

Robert M Beasley
1026 Amarillo Ave
Palo Alto, California

Patty J. Dalton
Notary Public
In and for the County of Santa Clara
State of California
20th day of August 1960

## 21 August, 1960. *Viscosity—Fibers*

Everything I look at seems to produce fibers! Tonight at dinner, I had pancakes and I noticed the following while talking after the meal. Some of the coffee (coffee, cream and sugar) spilled into the saucer and partially dried—as it dried down to the right viscosity conditions, fibers could be pulled from the deposits by merely "baiting" with the tip of a spoon. To be sure the fibers were short at best, probably ¼" in length, but nevertheless, fibers. The same sort of thing could be obtained by "working" (drying) the syrup.

These observations make me certain—or more certain than ever—that all that really needs to be done is to obtain the right viscosity of material to pull fibers. No doubt heat will not be needed even—it should be possible to merely dissolve a salt in water and dry down to the proper conditions of viscosity. If heat is used, it is possible that some of the materials will become decomposed or granular. I'm sure that most any material, which will result in a tacky, viscous type of solution or deposit will work. Probably metallic acetates, sulfate, chlorides, etc., would be ideal. The main requirement would be nongranular, viscous material.

If all this is true, it should be possible to simply dry such materials down to make a supply of such viscous liquids and then handle them similar to glass—i.e., bate and pull them from an orifice or reservoir pool onto a rotating mandrel or take up wheel—the thought being that the attenuated filimentized fluids would set up (dry) rapidly enough when the large cross-sectioned area is exposed—sort of like glass filaments "setting" due to loss of heat when attenuated. Of course, if this is possible, then one wonders if other glass forming operations—pulling, drawing and blowing, wouldn't also work. Even slinging the material through orifices should cause attenuation for bulk staple fibers.

I have a little chromium acetate powder in my belongings and will try this as soon as they are delivered. I am certain that these things will all work.

RMB

23 August, 1960

I am really fascinated with my observations. I can hardly wait for my material to arrive. I heated some sugar to melting and found that fibers can easily be pulled at great length. However, I found that putting a minimum amount of water with sugar yields a mostly granular material—somewhat as expected. But if the sugar is completely dissolved in water and then the solution is slowly and gently dehydrated then the resulting tacky material can be attenuated to short fibers just as I did with the coffee the other night. This didn't work ideally under the conditions tried, but did serve to establish the feasibility and reproductibility of the concept.

R M Beasley

23 August, 1960

I will try the experiment outlined above for sugar with my chrome acetate when it arrives. I believe the thing to do will be to make a thin water solution of this material and let it dry down until it is the right viscosity for attenuation.

R M Beasley

September 3, 1960

I have found the CrAc (chromium acetate) and made about a 30 percent mixture with water. I will now have to let this dry down (loss of water) to the fiber producing viscosity. It will work—

I dried down small amounts of solution on the stirring rod and a piece of glass (the bottom of a glass jar) by blowing air over the solution. When the right viscosity was obtained, beautiful long filaments could be pulled. They are so fine that they float in the air like spider webs and are hard to capture. However, a "baited" stirring rod can be rotated while pulling and the fiber wound right up on it. Though on such a small diameter it is hard to get the material off in any degree of length, pulling straight out, it is possible to pull fiber a foot and a half before breaking. Also, when the solution becomes too dry, it can be restored by blowing moist breath over it—a drop of water seems to always be too much for such a small amount of deposit.

I will just have to let the solution dry down to get enough material to wind or pull great lengths.

RMB


September 5, 1960

I fired a small amount of the fibers I pulled the other day the sample was introduced at 500°F and then the temperature was increased to 650°F and held for 1/2 hour before raising to 1,500°F for 1/2 hour. The sample was removed right into the room from that temperature.

The material was existent as fibers—both black opaque and clear as glass. However, there was some indication that they, the longer ones, may have broken during firing—particularly the heavier or thicker ones. This is not for sure though—just an impression. The fine fibers were round, clear and similar in size to "E" glass.

RMB

September 10, 1960

The solution mixed the other day to where fibers could be pulled readily last night. In fact, I pulled the whole time I watched a late movie on TV. Pulling single fiber is quite slow—particularly when trying to catch the floating ends in a jar.

I'm certain this material could be pulled continuously and taken up on a large wheel. When I unpack the small record player my children have, I am going to try to use the turntable as a take-up wheel—the machine will probably work standing on its side.

Also, when I find my 1/4" drill, I am going to use it to sling fibers. I think I can make some kind of container to fit on it and the container can have holes in the side and the solution slung out of it.

RMB

September 12, 1960

My stock solution dried down too far, so I put wet cotton on top of the closed bottle.

September 13, 1960

The dried solution (CrAc) was restored to fibering consistency by the humid atmosphere. Fiber could again be pulled.

I'm satisfied that chrome oxide fibers can practically be produced by these methods from salt solutions. I'm going to try some other salt.

RMB

September 17, 1960

I found some magnesium acetate and made a dilute solution—to be dried—as I've done with the chrome.

Small droplets of this material seemed to give fibers. Fiber was aided by heating the solution gently over a light bulb.

I tried the CrAc solution—pulling and slinging—with drill and turntable. The setup was as follows—

Diagram for drill slinging

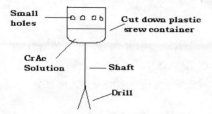

This was tried out by holding the form inside a three-gallon pail and running the drill. Fibers were thrown out, but the pail is really too small and also the solution seemed a little too wet or not viscous enough. However, fibers were obtained in a real quantity compared to the amount I've been able to pull by hand.

Diagram of turntable

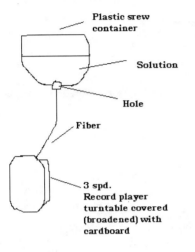

This gave indications of working—long fibers could be pulled, but they broke every time I tried to feed them onto the turntable. The speed seemed too fast and the solution either too wet or too dry. With proper control and conditions this would work well without doubt. I could get about a ½ turn around the cardboard once in awhile, but then a joint would come up and snap the filament.

I have also found a very small amount of zirconium acetate solution and am going to dry it down. As a check, fibers—beautiful ones were pulled from a mixture of ZrAc and CrAc dried on a piece of glass and stirring rod. Chrome would probably be a good addition to the Zr to prevent grain development during fibering.

RMB

September 24, 1960

I tried the ZrAc (zirconium acetate) solution in the drill and turntable setup. The material, a small amount dried separately, worked wonderfully well in the drill and the pail. The fiber clung to the sides of the pail at first, but as the solution evidently dried further, the fibers actually floated around in the air in the pail and could be caught and collected. They were a little coarser than the ones pulled by hand, but this is probably a function of the hole size, drill speed, viscosity, etc. The results were really thrilling. There was a problem of the rotating part containing solution and orifices becoming clogged by the solution drying in the holes and a buildup of fibers wound around it.

As for the turntable—the solution was not viscous enough to control.

RMB

September 25, 1960

I left the bottle of ZrAc open last night and today and it has dried down to a stiffer material. I found that it could be baited with a stirring rod and long fibers could be pulled. My wife could pull fiber about 8-10 feet long by backing slowly across the room while I held the supply of solution.

Fibers could be taken up on the turntable for about five turns (about five feet) if I could turn the table without jerking by hand and if the joints in cardboard didn't snap them. I met these conditions at ½ dozen times out of many trials in which lesser lengths were obtained. In doing this work, I found that the solution tended to become too dry at the orifice in time and had to be cleaned away—putting wet cotton around the hole aided enough to indicate that a moist atmosphere at the orifice to keep the solution fluid there would probably be ideal. All of the fibers were about the size of "E" glass. I am going to fire some of these fibers. My solution is just about used up. A little bit has gone a long way—primarily because too dried material can be put back into the solution. More solution has been ordered.

RMB

September 29, 1960

I fired the ZrAc fibers with great success. They were fired slowly at 600°F for one hour and then raised to 1200°F for one hour. I fired them the beginning of the week and have shown the fired product to a number of people at work—Dean Fisher, M. Steinberg, Roy Nevell, Bob Lamaroux, etc.

The fibers were not contained, so they are in the form of "E"-glass-size wool and are transparent, fully flexible and so light that the mass can be blown across a table top. Really beautiful! $ZrO_2$! They look just like glass fibers.

I now know that all the methods of making fibers visualized are a reality. The material could probably even be blown into fine tubes. I say fine because thick sections of the material tend to crack when dried in the room. However, this might be overcome by using controlled optimum drying conditions. In doing this, I'm sure that hooks like on natural fibers could be developed on the surface of the continuous fibers if they were subjected to a humid atmosphere. These would result from very slight resolution. Additional salts such as urea could be added to aid this tendency—or even chlorides!

RMB

October 12, 1960

I tried the last of the ZrAc solution in the drill and must have hit the viscosity just right for the fiber floated in the air in the pail. They had to be collected every minute or so or they would float right out into the room. This would be a high-speed method for making staple fibers.

RMB

November 26, 1960

I showed Dean Fisher my setup when he was over at the house on Thanksgiving. He saw the turntable, drill and some long formed fibers still on the turntable.

RMB

W. D. Curtis
Notary Public
In and for the County of Santa Clara
State of California
22nd day of April 1961

## NOTE

Bob had brought with him a few samples of various solutions in small vials given to him by salesmen at Horizons and in November, in Palo Alto, as he requested, the Titanium Alloy Manufacturing Division, National Lead Company, sent to the house a gallon sample of TAM 22 percent zirconium acetate solution and a 2 lb sample of TAM—high-purity zirconium oxychloride and included his study data sheets on those products. They also offered any additional assistance he might need.

# Appendix E—Patents

# Horizons, Inc.
## United States Patent Office
**3,110,545**
**INORGANIC FIBERS AND PREPARATION THEREOF**
**Robert M. Beasley, Shaker Heights and Herbert L. Johns,
Cleveland, Ohio, assignors to Horizons Incorporated, a
corporation of New Jersey**
**Filed Dec. 1, 1958**
Ser. no. 777,193 20 Claims. (CI. 18-54)

## United States Patent Office
3,082,051
**FIBER FORMING PROCESS**
Eugene Wainer, Cleveland Heights and Robert M. Beasley,
Shaker Heights, Ohio, assignors to Horizons Incorporated, a
corporation of New Jersey
Filed July 24, 1959
Ser. No. 829,220 12 Claims. (CI. 18-48)

# Lockheed
## United States Patent Office
3,953,646
**Two-component ceramic coating for silica insulation**
Fletcher, et al. (April 27, 1976)
Inventors: James C. Fletcher, Administrator of the National
Aeronautics and Space Administration, with respect to an
invention of; Alexander Pechman, (Mountain View, CA);
Robert M. Beasley (Sunnyvale, CA)
Filed: June 24, 1974
Appl. no.: 05/482,104

# United States Patent Office

3,955,034

## THREE-COMPONENT CERAMIC COATING FOR SILICA INSULATION

Fletcher, et al. May 4, 1976

THREE-COMPONENT CERAMIC COATING FOR SILICA INSULATION

Inventors: James C. Fletcher, Administrator of the National Aeronautics and Space Administration, with respect to an invention of; Alexander Pechman, Mountain View; Robert M. Beasley, all of Sunnyvale, California.

Filed: June 24, 1974

Appl. no.: 482,105